If I Had
Only One
Sermon to Preach

If I Had
Only One Sermon
to Preach

*Nineteen Preachers Reveal
What Motivates Them*

Edited by Richard Allen Bodey

A Division of Baker Book House Co
Grand Rapids, Michigan 49516

© 1994 by Richard Allen Bodey

Published by Baker Books
a division of Baker Book House Company
P.O. Box 6287, Grand Rapids, Michigan 49516-6287

Printed in the United States of America

Library of Congress Cataloging-in-Publication Data
If I had only one sermon to preach : nineteen preachers reveal what motivates them /
    Richard Allen Bodey, editor.
        p.   cm.
    ISBN 0-8010-1080-2
    1. Sermons, American. 2. Evangelicalism—United States.
I. Bodey, Richard Allen.
BV4241.I54   1994
252—dc20   94-17260

Contents

Preface

I f you are a preacher and you knew when you would preach for the last time, what sermon would you preach? Very likely—unless you know that your pulpit ministry is fast drawing to a close—you have never thought about the matter. There's nothing necessarily wrong in that.

One thing is certain, however. All of us who preach will someday preach for the last time. We can't be sure when that time will come, soon or late. I know of one man who had barely finished his sermon, when he fell to the floor dead. Happily, only a few of us will terminate our preaching ministry on such an unanticipated dramatic note. But we, too, must someday exit the pulpit for the last time. And we shall get no opportunity for a sermonic postscript.

"What would you preach, if you knew you would be preaching for the last time?" An intriguing question! One worth pondering, too, from time to time. It should lend a *healthy,* not gloomy, solemnity to all of our sermonizing from week to week. It should force us to reflect—more often and more intently, perhaps—on the essential verities of the "faith that was once for all entrusted to the saints." It should encourage us to make sure that we sound all of these grand themes at frequent intervals. It should restrain us from peddling peripheral pronouncements and chasing theological rabbits down remote and obscure paths. It should make us more intentional and systematic in our preaching, if we are inclined to be whimsical or haphazard.

In this book, a group of seasoned, well-known evangelical preachers present the sermons they would very likely preach, if they knew they were preaching for the last time. The sermon by Jill Briscoe is an exception. It is designed specifically for pastors, seminary students, and their wives, although much of it is equally applicable to other Christians as well. All of the sermons are Christ-centered and focus on essential evangelical truth. Yet they are not wearisomely repetitious. On the contrary, they display a pleasing breadth and variety. Even the two sermons by Sinclair Ferguson and Warren

9

Wiersbe on Psalm 23 are strikingly different. Wiersbe's sermon is a delicious slice of the homiletical imagination he stoutly encourages in a volume he has recently prepared for publication.

The contributors were drawn from a variety of traditions and denominations: Baptist, Episcopal, Mennonite, Presbyterian, Reformed, and United Methodist; several serve unaffiliated churches. A unique feature of the collection is that it includes sermons by a husband and wife team: Stuart and Jill Briscoe.

All of the contributors explain why they chose their particular sermon. Each sermon should be read in the light of the accompanying explanation.

Contributors had freedom to choose the Scripture version of their preference. Unless otherwise noted, Scripture quotations throughout each sermon are taken from the version indicated after the sermon text.

The editor and contributors alike send forth these sermons with the prayer that they will strengthen the resolve of their partners in the pulpit who read them to steady the focus of their preaching on the grand particularities of the gospel through which alone their hearers can be saved. They also pray that others who read them will see with sharper vision or fresh insight the truth of the gospel and its importance for their daily lives.

Editors incur debts to many, and I am no exception. I am, obviously, deeply indebted to the contributors, who, without exception, accepted the challenge of this project promptly and cheerfully. Their knowledge of God's Word and their homiletical skill need no comment from me; they speak for themselves.

Since I edited my first volume several years ago I have forged valuable friendships with a number of people at Baker Book House. Once again, I have found them an unfailing source of professional excellence, judicious counsel, generous encouragement, and hearty support. I am especially grateful to Paul E. Engle, Editor of Professional Books for many helpful suggestions, and to Mary L. Suggs, Managing Editor of Trade Books, and her staff for meticulous and painstaking work with the original material of the book.

To my wife Ruth I am indebted for the many hours she spent in the tedious labor of typing and proofreading.

May the living Lord Christ who is the supreme subject of all of these sermons be pleased to use them for his glory.

I

Myron S. Augsburger

———⇒•◇•⇐———

An alumnus of Eastern Mennonite College and Seminary, Harrisonburg, Virginia, Myron S. Augsburger returned to become professor of theology at the seminary and president of both institutions. He served three pastorates in Florida and Virginia, one of them in Harrisonburg. Since 1951 he has been an evangelist for InterChurch Crusades, and now also serves the Christian College Coalition in Washington, D.C.

Augsburger earned the M.Div. degree at Goshen Biblical Seminary, the Th.D. at Union Theological Seminary (Virginia), holds six honorary doctorates, and has done postdoctoral study at Princeton Theological Seminary, George Washington University, Mansfield College, Oxford, England, and the University of Basel, Switzerland. In 1980 he was named Educator of the Year by James Madison University in Harrisonburg.

He has written more than twenty books, including *Pilgrim Aflame, Quench Not the Spirit,* and the *Commentary on Matthew* in the Communicator's Commentary series, and is a contributor to *The Mennonite Encyclopedia.*

———⇒•◇•⇐———

I chose this text and theme because it is the heart of the gospel. Some of us work from the core of faith and extend that out as far as we can in its implications for life. Others work more at setting boundaries to "preserve" the faith in their social and cultural context. It is my conviction that clarity on the foundations of the faith will in turn take care of so-called boundaries, because of the uniqueness of

Christ. Consequently, this message is needed to help the church achieve more clarity on its essential message and to remind us how dramatically we can influence the world when we truly live the gospel of reconciliation.

We have separated the sacred from the secular in our society, the personal from the public in too many of our churches, the word of the gospel from the deeds of the gospel in our lives. This theme calls us back to Christ and to his reconciling life and work in the world. I cannot believe that he, as our Lord, would expect anything else from us than what he himself did when he was here on earth.

The Cross Is Timeless

But now in Christ Jesus you who once were far off have been brought near by the blood of Christ. For he is our peace; in his flesh he has made both groups into one and has broken down the dividing wall, that is, the hostility between us. He has abolished the law with its commandments and ordinances, that he might create in himself one new humanity in place of the two, thus making peace, and might reconcile both groups to God in one body through the cross, thus putting to death that hostility through it. So he came and proclaimed peace to you who were far off and peace to those who were near; for through him both of us have access in one Spirit to the Father. So then you are no longer strangers and aliens, but you are citizens with the saints and also members of the household of God, built upon the foundation of the apostles and prophets, with Christ Jesus himself as the cornerstone. In him the whole structure is joined together and grows into a holy temple in the Lord; in whom you also are built together *in the Spirit* into a dwelling place for God.

Ephesians 2:13–22 NRSV

The cross is the expression of God's love, of God's grace, of God's character. God's supreme act of grace is his self-giving love on the cross. Here we are confronted with the plan and pattern of the ages. God has chosen to overcome evil by expressing his superior holiness and love. This is the grand exposé of all time: God overcoming evil, exposing its perversion by expressing the quality of his love. The cross is God's timeless word to the world. It is the word that I want to emphasize in this message.

God is a God of grace:
taking the initiative to come to us,
bridging the gaps,
accepting us with our sins,
saying to us, "Your problem is now my problem."

God expresses forgiving grace:
   resolving his own wrath at our sin,
     absolving it in love,
       freeing us from the guilt of estrangement,
         bringing us into his family as his children.

God also works in transforming grace:
   making us new persons,
     transforming us from self-centered to God-centered beings,
       creating a redeemed community,
         enriching society by the presence of his Spirit in his people.

We must recognize that God's grace is available to us through Christ. "He is our peace." When we respond to Christ in personal faith, we enjoy his peace. He is also the great reconciler, the only full reconciler, our reconciler. In the cross he reconciles us with God and with one another. In the cross he makes of two, Jew and Gentile, one new humanity, one family, thereby making peace. This reconciliation of humankind to its God and to itself is the greatest social change conceivable, and it is a change grounded in grace. This powerful love and grace changes persons and corrects the social and spiritual alienation within the human family. It is God's answer to sin, self-centeredness, hostilities, racism, individualism, and selfishness.

There is an old Jewish story that long before King Solomon built a temple on Mount Moriah, long before King David bought that mountain as a place for sacrifice to God, long before Abraham brought his son Isaac there to offer him to the Lord, two brothers had established a place of business on the mountaintop. Their business was threshing grain for their neighbors. Each day the brothers would thresh the grain brought to them, deduct a share for their wages, and the neighbor would take his finished grain away. At the close of the day the brothers would divide their own grain into equal parts. Each filled his bags and carried them to his own granary. One of the brothers was married and the father of twelve children. The other was single. One night the single brother awoke and, thinking about the business, said to himself, "This isn't fair. My brother has fourteen mouths to feed, and I have only one. He certainly needs more grain than I do." He got up, filled a bag with grain, and carried it over to his brother's granary. In the early morning, the married brother awoke and, thinking about the business, said to himself, "I have twelve children who will take care of me when I get old. My poor brother is all alone, with no one to care for him when he is old. He needs more grain than I do." He got up, filled a bag with grain, and carried it to his brother's granary. This went on night after night, until one night the single brother overslept. Awakening, he hurriedly carried his grain to his brother's granary. But the married brother had gotten up earlier than usual. On his way to take a bag of grain to his brother, he collided with his brother in the darkness of early morning. When they realized what was happening, they fell into each other's arms and wept. And God looked down from heaven and said, "That is where I'll build my temple—where two men love each other so much that they both will sacrifice for the good of the other."

God moved first in sacrificing himself for us, in reaching out to us and offering us a chance at reconciliation. God, in Christ on the cross, made the ultimate sacrifice out of love for us. This is what Dietrich Bonhoeffer calls "costly grace." Being aware of what it cost God to redeem us means that when we fully engage in this sacrifice, we ourselves are changed. To act as though we can benefit from the cross without entering into the meaning of the reconciling sacrifice is what Bonhoeffer terms "cheap grace." When God reconciles us to himself in Christ, we become a people of grace, a witness and a picture of reconciliation to society.

This good news of reconciliation is God's wonder for today, for ours is a day of competitive selfishness, of violence and racism, of the affluent isolated from the needy, of parochial nationalism indifferent to the global village, of urbanization with extensive slums, of illiteracy and limited education for many, of an increasing gap between the "haves" and the "have-nots," of satisfaction with thought-claims rather than deeds, of a narrow secularism that omits the spiritual, of a postmodernity that seeks individual gratification.

This is a word of hope to a dysfunctional society. The grace of reconciliation has never been more relevant to personal and social problems than it is today. Reconciliation is God's special word today: God's word of hope as we race toward 2001, God's word of transformation for people in a fallen world, and God's word of power to create a new people in an alienated society.

Reconciliation Is Grounded in the Cross

At Calvary God expressed—yes, actualized—the depth of his love, the character of his caring. He said, in essence, "Your problem is now my problem," and he carried it to the death. In the cross of Christ, God's unconditional love is revealed in its fullness. This is the larger meaning of love, of engaging another in the intimacy of full identification and solidarity. Love means suffering with another: sharing identification that humiliates, a participation that wounds, but also heals! This is the cost of the incarnation, of God's identifying fully with us; of Jesus' crucifixion, humbly suffering for us; of his resurrection, overcoming the problem for us. Paul writes, "[He] was handed over to death for our trespasses and was raised for our justification" (Rom. 4:25).

In the same act of crucifixion and sacrifice human perversity is accentuated in its rejection of God. But there is good news, the gospel of grace. Standing before the cross, we find ourselves in the one place where we can meet God in honesty. Here we truly face the character and depth of our sin of rebellion. In stark contrast, we see the full character and depth of God's love. Here we meet One with his arms outstretched—to us! As we respond to him in faith, we enter into a new relationship and are made members of the family of God.

A number of years ago, when my wife and I moved to Washington, D.C., and planted a church on Capitol Hill, I had a significant encounter with a man on the street. He was sitting on a bench, and I stopped to chat. Suddenly he asked, "Are you a preacher?" When I replied that I was, he almost sneered, asking, "What difference does it make in my life that Jesus died on a cross two thousand years ago?" I looked at him, thinking of theories of the atonement that I had studied in theology, but then asked, "Do you have friends?" "Of course I have friends," he replied. "If one of them is in trouble, what do you do?" "Why, I help him out." "But what if it gets difficult?" I pressed him. "You hang in there!" he responded. "But what if it gets *really* difficult? When can you cop out?" "Man," he said, "if he's your friend, you never cop out!" I smiled and said, "God came in Jesus to be our friend. We were in deep trouble, but he hung in there with us. When could he cop out?" The man looked at me in silence. Then it was as though lights went on in his eyes. He smiled and asked, "Is that why Jesus had to die?" I said, "That is one reason." He got up, squared his shoulders, looked at me with a smile, nodded, and walked off down the sidewalk. I watched him go, and said to myself, "Man, you don't know it, but you've just been evangelized. You'll never get away from the impact of hearing that God is One who says, 'Your problem is my problem!'"

The reconciliation Christ performs is at the heart of the gospel. It is grounded in the cross, and it is the extension of the cross. God acts in Jesus:

- to express the wonder of his grace
- to extend his forgiveness
- to overcome our rebellion
- to bring us into fellowship
- to reconcile us into the family

Our text says, "[We] who once were far off have been brought near by the blood of Christ." Christ has reconciled us by his blood at the ultimate cost to himself. There is nothing shoddy or shallow about the nature of salvation or forgiveness. This sacrifice is so sublime and so stupendous that we can never fully comprehend it. In fact, forgiveness—the most costly and difficult thing in the universe—is not understood in our society. Many professing Christians do not understand it adequately. Limited understanding means limited appropriation, limited release from our burden, limited joy.

Forgiveness is not simply a pronouncement of release. Forgiveness is not something we receive and then run away with. Nor is it something we can process and package. Forgiveness is always found in the context of relationships. Forgiveness is an innocent person accepting his or her own wrath at the sin of another and smothering that indignation in love! Forgiveness reconciles and releases people, and creates a new identity, a new relationship, a new lifestyle. Forgiveness renounces any quest to control another's life, standing with the other, offering itself at personal cost to help the other. This is what God does in his forgiving spirit, opening himself fully, personally, intimately to us! In turn, we must open our lives intimately to him.

Now we are participants in the commonwealth of God's people. We belong to God, to one another, to the redeemed community, to God's kingdom in the world.

Reconciliation Is the Power for Social Change

By his cross Christ made of Jew and Gentile one new people, the people of God. This is the greatest social change in history. The cross is God's way of changing people, of overcoming the problem of estrangement, of correcting evil, for there is no correction without suffering. God suffers the pain of our rebellion and the pain of reconciliation. We suffer slightly in the surrender of our rebellious self, being as Paul says, "crucified with Christ" (Gal. 2:19) and being liberated, as Peter says, because we have "suffered in the flesh" (1 Peter 4:1).

And the cross is timeless. For thousands of years God has worked in this way, overcoming evil with good, exposing evil for what it is by expressing his love as the character of what he is! For two thousand years the risen, sovereign Christ, at God's right hand, has continued to extend the same love. Having demonstrated divine love on the cross, he continues to overcome evil, not by exercising his superior power, but by expressing his superior love—overcoming evil by calling persons from evil into love and reconciling persons to himself! Hallelujah!

As we enter into this reconciliation by responding to Christ in faith, we are changed into new people with a new relationship, a new freedom, a new Master, a new purpose, a new spirit, a new lifestyle! We now have a new calling as "ministers of reconciliation" (2 Cor. 5:18 KJV). We are to be extensions of the cross by demonstrating its power to overcome evil with good (Rom. 12:21). We are the people of God, the people of his kingly rule. We become a visual language to society, showing that there is a new community, a "Christian Counter-Culture," as John Stott labels it in the title of one of his books.

As believers and disciples we are now the body of Christ. As one's body gives visibility to one's personality, so as the body of Christ we give visibility to Christ in the world. This body comprised of alienated people now reconciled and made one in Christ—Jew and

Gentile, black and white, Easterner and Westerner—is the global evidence of the universality of Christ's work. The Christian faith is not to be identified with any one people, race, or nationality. It calls into being a new people to live by a new covenant. We are the people of God's kingdom: transnational, transcultural, transracial, trans-anything! We are citizens of heaven here on earth (Phil. 3:20).

Our identity and our character come from our being "in Christ," from our solidarity with him. Our text says, "He is our peace." In Christ there is love, not hostility; forgiveness, not revenge; peace, not violence; submission, not resistance; service, not dominance. Here is a radically new order of life. We remember Christ's words, "Blessed are the meek, for they will inherit the earth" (Matt. 5:5). That is to say, the meek are the ones who engage and enter into the larger meaning of our present life on earth.

This spirit of life creates a new social order and turns people from usury to support, from competition to partnership, from defensiveness to love, from violence to compassion, from war to peace. In Christ we become a people who express his heart, his caring, his mission.

I once heard Canon Michael Green of Oxford make a striking statement about this new community, the church, at the Lausanne Congress on Evangelism in 1974. He said, "We must rediscover that the church itself is a part of the kerygma," that is, of the gospel. It is good news to announce and demonstrate this new caring community in a world of lonely, fragmented, shattered people. It is good news that there is a community of faith, of love, of caring, of accountability and support, of purpose and hope.

Reconciliation Is a Fellowship in the Spirit

Our text says that we are built into a dwelling place for God in or through the Spirit. God is not far removed from us. He has come to us. Our risen Lord is not absent but present in his Spirit. When two or three of us gather in his name he is among us! He is with us now. We are not left to try to live the new life by our own striving, but we are given new life by and in his Spirit. "If anyone is in Christ, he is a new creation" (2 Cor. 5:17 NIV). There is a mystery in this relationship, much like the mystery of love, an awareness that relationships consist of more than simply the cognitive aspects of life.

19

Discipleship is, first of all, a matter of the spirit; it is living by the Spirit of God. Obedience to the "orders" or commandments of the Christian walk are not first, as though the Christian life is a new legalism. Rather, the spirit of faith and the aspiration for a different walk must always be primary. We must first open our own spirit to the Holy Spirit. It is the Spirit within us who makes us new. It is the Spirit among us who makes us one. It is the Spirit upon us who enables us to live in newness.

We like to celebrate our being justified, but we too often overlook the fact that we are justified "in him," made righteous in Christ. This righteousness is a new right-relatedness to God. We stand justified in God's presence only because of Christ. We are now "in Christ." The rebellion has ended. The estrangement is over. The perversions are being corrected. Paul wrote the Philippians that he once labored to establish his own righteousness, a mere "rightness" with the law, but when he surrendered to Christ and identified with him he found that he had entered a "rightness" with God himself through his faith in Christ (Phil. 3:9). This new relationship with God is transforming, for the indwelling Spirit is changing us as surely as light overcomes darkness. We may be at different stages in the dawning, but as the light breaks over us, the darkness flees. This change happens in relationship: we are changed step by step, but our new relationship to God is complete, final, and secure.

The community of the Spirit is created by his presence and by his work through a common core of faith. When we are Christ's disciples, we are joined together in his body. We experience our oneness by our common identification with him. Some of us work primarily at clarifying this core, at interpreting the meaning of our faith in Jesus Christ, the Son of God. Others work more at establishing boundaries, at drawing lines that rule persons in or out. We need to focus on the core of faith and then push its implications out as far as we can, with all of its applications. Guiding us in this endeavor is one of the functions of the Spirit among us.

- What does it mean to know Christ truly?
- What are the implications of taking Christ in his wholeness seriously?
- What does it mean to see Christ's example itself as the Word of God?

20

- What are Christ's claims on every aspect of my life?
- What is Christ's mission for me?

When we come to Christ, we do not come to an experience that can be owned, possessed, or guided by us. We come to the sovereign Lord who becomes our Master, and we become his servants. Christian faith is not just a perception, but a fidelity. It is not mere intellectual acceptance of certain beliefs, but valuing those beliefs by putting them into practice. This valuing is what the New Testament calls "walking in the Spirit," for the Spirit is the Spirit of Jesus. The community of the Spirit is centered in Jesus, and it lives in Jesus. We are called to "walk just as he walked" (1 John 2:6).

Ours is the joy of fellowship, of belonging, of purpose, and of meaning. Ours is the satisfaction of investing our lives in something of eternal value and timeless meaning. We are the body of Christ. We are called to be extensions of his redemptive mission. We are to be expressions of what it means to participate in divine grace. He is our peace. We are now his peacemakers. We are living proof that he has brought us to peace!

Bishop Festo Kivengere of Uganda was one of God's choice servants in this century. He stood beside Archbishop Luwam and saw him killed by Idi Amin. He and his wife fled through the hills by night into a neighboring country and were then flown to London to save their lives. He sat in All Soul's Church, wrestling with the implications of his Christian principles for his attitude toward Idi Amin. Finally, engaging the grace of forgiveness, he wrote a little book entitled, *I Love Idi Amin!* But this did not happen in isolation. It happened in relation to his total experience of God's grace. In another context, Bishop Kivengere relates his conversion when he was in his late teens and how he went around telling people about his new life in Jesus. One day he rode his bicycle fifty miles to find a white man whom he hated, to tell him of his new life in Jesus and that he forgave him and now loved him. Englishman though he was, the man stood there weeping, tears running down his cheeks, as he and Kivengere clasped each other in their arms.

This is reconciliation at work. This is new life in Christ. This is the new creation by God's grace.

2

Richard Allen Bodey

—❖—

Richard Allen Bodey is professor of practical theology at Trinity Evangelical Divinity School, Deerfield, Illinois. He previously served six Presbyterian pastorates, and was chairman of the department of practical theology at Reformed Theological Seminary, Jackson, Mississippi.

Bodey earned the M.Div. degree at Princeton Theological Seminary, the Th.M. at Westminster Theological Seminary, the D.Min. at Trinity Evangelical Divinity School, and did graduate study at the University of Toronto.

Author of numerous articles and published sermons, he also contributed to *The Encyclopedia of Christianity,* the *Zondervan Pictorial Bible Encyclopedia,* and the *Handbook of Contemporary Preaching;* he is also contributing editor of *Good News for All Seasons: 26 Sermons for Special Days, Inside the Sermon: Thirteen Preachers Discuss Their Method of Preparing Messages,* and *The Voice from the Cross.* He has conducted workshops at the National Conference on Preaching for five years.

—❖—

I believe it is the sacred duty of Christian preachers every time they climb the pulpit stairs to expound biblical truth—more precisely, biblical truth as directly related to Jesus Christ and his gospel. I would be especially careful to do so, if I knew that I was preaching for the final time.

I would also be careful to preach a sermon that would at once make plain to my hearers its importance for their lives for both time and eternity. With these considerations in view, I would focus primarily on the good news of eternal salvation in Christ.

I prepared this sermon twenty-eight years ago. Since then, for more than two decades I have enjoyed—along with my seminary teaching—the privilege of an itinerant preaching ministry. This ministry has taken me into many churches in nearly twenty different denominations in various parts of the nation. During these years I have preached this sermon 125 times. On every occasion, at the close of the service some—often many—people, including young people, have told me that they found fresh comfort and courage in it, as they faced the prospect of that final frontier. I pray that this sermon may do the same for you who read it in this book.

Soli Deo Gloria!

———◆———

Are You Afraid to Die?

———⊰•◇•⊱———

Since, therefore, the children share flesh and blood, he himself likewise shared the same things, so that through death he might destroy
the one who has the power of death, that is, the devil, and free those
who all their lives were held in slavery by the fear of death.

Hebrews 2:14–15 NRSV

Are you afraid to die?

"What man," asks R. W. Gilder in his book *Love and Death*,
"can look on death unterrified?" The French philosopher Rousseau
declared more bluntly, "He who pretends to face death without fear
is a liar." And the famous Swiss psychoanalyst Carl Jung said that
he found fear of death at the bottom of every soul, even those who
professed to be indifferent toward dying.

We are all enslaved by the fear of death. Our fear is chiseled into
the very names with which people have labeled death: the Dark
Angel, the Grim Reaper, the King of Terrors. Even in our sophisti-
cated age of instant TV replay and interactive computers, genetic
engineering and organ transplants, electronic superhighways and
space shuttles, we are unable still to free ourselves from bondage to
this fear that has haunted and tormented the human heart ever since
our first parents sinned. According to Elisabeth Kübler-Ross, well-
known writer on death and dying, "The more we are making
advancements in science, the more we seem to fear and deny the
reality of death." Indeed, many professing Christians seem to fear
death almost as much as modern pagans do.

But the fetters can be broken. The shackles can be loosed. Christ
can set us free from the fear of death. He can liberate us from its
bondage. The author of Hebrews tells us that this is one reason Jesus
took our flesh and underwent death himself. "Since, therefore, the
children share flesh and blood, he himself likewise shared the same

things, so that through death he might destroy the one who has the power of death, that is, the devil, and free those who all their lives were held in slavery by the fear of death."

I want us to take a close look at the fear of death. I want us to examine some of the chains with which death binds our hearts in terror. Then I want us to see how Christ shatters them when we put our full trust in him.

The Fear of Loneliness

One of these chains is the fear of loneliness.

After God had created Adam and placed him in Eden, he said, "It is not good that the man should be alone; I will make him a helper as his partner" (Gen. 2:18). Not even the perfect charm and beauty of his earthly paradise were enough to make Adam's life complete. He needed one thing more. He needed someone with whom he could share the wonder and adventure of life. So God made Eve and joined her to Adam in the sacred bonds of love.

God has created us with a built-in need for love and companionship. We are complete only in relationship. One writer captured this truth in the striking title of her book, *You Can't Be Human Alone*. What normal person wants to be a hermit? Solitary confinement, long regarded as the most severe punishment in our penal system short of death, has driven people stark, raving mad. A famous doctor, when asked what he thought is our most devastating disease, replied, "Loneliness—just plain loneliness." A moment later he added, "Doctors can't cure it."

Especially do we feel this need for companionship in our moments of great crisis. In our weakness we cry out for the comfort of another's voice, the bracing grip of another's hand. Even the strong Son of God when he went to wrestle in the agony of the garden took his closest disciples along with him.

What could be more lonely than death?

A pastor was talking with his little boy who was dying. The little fellow looked up into his father's face and asked, "Daddy, am I going to die?" With broken heart and trembling lips the father replied, "Yes, Sonny, the doctor says so. Are you afraid?" "No," answered the little boy, "I am not afraid. But I wish somebody could go along with me."

No small part of death's terror for us lies right here. A lecturer at a seminar on dying explained that one of the greatest fears of dying patients is that people are going to desert them, and that they will be left to die alone.

The fact is we must all do our dying alone. There are no companionships in death. When we breathe our last, when we close our eyes for the last time on earth's familiar scenes, we slip out into the darkness alone. Loved ones may stand vigil by us to the end, but they cannot go with us beyond the veil. Bereft of all human comfort and support, defenseless before this savage and insatiable foe, we enter the gates of death alone. Well may we shudder at the thought.

But Jesus Christ smashes the chain and sets us free.

The loneliness of death is not what it seems. We are alone, yet not alone. Christ is with us. He who on the cross cried out in bitter anguish, "My God, my God, why have you forsaken me?" (Matt. 27:46), has promised never to leave or forsake us. Though the cruel hand of death severs us from all human companionship, it cannot sever us from him. "Even though I walk through the valley of the shadow of death," said the psalmist, "I will fear no evil, for you are with me" (Ps. 23:4 NIV). When we come to that valley, we shall find that the Good Shepherd, who has been our constant guide and protector, is with us still. In his keeping we can go on unafraid.

When he was a young man John McNeil, the Scottish evangelist, worked as a ticket clerk in a community seven miles from his village home. Every Saturday night he walked the distance home to spend the Lord's Day with his family. One Saturday it was past midnight when he set out. The road wound through a dreary glen. Two miles from his home, high wooded hills on both the right and the left made the darkness denser still. He had heard tales of travelers who had been ambushed and robbed on the road. As he neared this most forbidding stretch, he ran so fast his feet barely skimmed the ground. Suddenly, out of the darkness boomed a strong masculine voice. "Is that you, Johnnie?" It nearly bolted him to the ground. Then he realized that it was his father, who had come to meet him at the worst place in the road. "The rest of the way home," said Dr. McNeil, "I feared no evil, for my father was with me."

Never will our Savior let us walk through death's dark valley or cross its deep, chill river alone. The gospel song is true:

> I won't have to cross Jordan alone;
> Jesus died for my sins to atone:
> When the darkness I see,
> He'll be waiting for me;
> I won't have to cross Jordan alone.

The loneliness of death frightens us. But we hear the voice of Jesus, "Fear not, for I will be with you; do not be dismayed." And our fear melts before his promise.

The Fear of the Unknown

A second and stronger chain with which death binds our hearts in terror is the fear of the unknown.

To our human view, the realm of the dead remains forever shrouded in uncertainty. We can make no contact with it. We know nothing at all about it. No one ever returns to unlock for us its secret. Sensational reports by people who allegedly have "come back" after having been pronounced clinically dead raise more questions than they answer. Neither science, nor philosophy, nor even religion can tear away death's veil of mystery. "A fearful leap into the dark!" That is how the atheistic philosopher, Thomas Hobbes, summed it up as he stood on the threshold of eternity. At best, the human mind can only speculate on what awaits us beyond the veil. But our anxious hearts cry out for something more solid than flimsy guesses in the dark.

Think how much is at stake here. For all we can tell, the dead are as nonexistent as the unconceived. What, then, if death is the end of everything? What if when our hearts stop beating, we are blown out like a match in the wind? What if death plunges us into a voiceless abyss of extinction? Destroys forever the loving ties between husband and wife, parent and child, friend and friend? Before unanswerable questions like these, the bravest heart grows numb with fear.

But, once again, Christ smashes the chain and puts our fears to flight.

Death is not the end. In Christ we are not destined for an eternal void, a bleak and silent wasteland of destruction. He died and was

28

buried, and on the third day he rose again in the power of an endless life. By his resurrection he has brought life and immortality to light. And he shares with us his triumph. "Because I live," he says, "you also will live" (John 14:19). "I am the resurrection and the life. Those who believe in me, even though they die, will live, and everyone who lives and believes in me will never die" (John 11:25–26). Death is not the end, not the final curtain falling on the senseless drama of human life. It is the grand beginning. It is a passage to another, larger life, a gateway on the skyline. In Christ, the final word is not death. The final word is life—eternal, imperishable, radiant, glorious life!

But this is not all. To silence our anxieties, Jesus gives us some hints and suggestions of what the life beyond is like. What does he tell us about it?

First, he says that we shall be with him. "I go to prepare a place for you[.] And if I go and prepare a place for you, I will come again and will take you to myself, so that where I am, there you may be also" (John 14:2–3).

Have you ever noticed that when Paul anticipates death, he never talks about going to heaven? "My desire is to depart and be with Christ" (Phil. 1:23), he writes. "Away from the body," he says again, "we [are] at home with the Lord" (2 Cor. 5:8). In the Book of Revelation, whenever we see the saints in heaven, they are always with Jesus.

"What is heaven to a reasonable soul?" asked Martin Luther. Answering his own question, he replied, "Nothing else but Jesus."

To be with Jesus, to see him face-to-face, to dwell in the sunlight of his love forever with never a shadow between us, if we know him at all—yes, if we know him at all—we know that nothing could be half so wonderful as that. It is enough. If we shall be with him, all will be well.

Again, Jesus indicates that in heaven we shall have fellowship with God's people from all ages. "Many will come from east and west," he said, "and will eat with Abraham and Isaac and Jacob in the kingdom of heaven" (Matt. 8:11). Won't it be thrilling to meet all those heroes and heroines of faith of whom we read in the Bible and in the history of the church and come to know them as our brothers and sisters in the family of God?

29

But there is something even more wonderful in this thought. For it includes reunion with our own dear ones in the Lord. Do you remember these words of Jesus: "In my Father's house are many rooms" (John 14:2 NIV)? The Father's house! When Christians die, they go home. And what is home? A true home is the place where love dwells, where heart embraces heart in closest union, where the richest joys, the tenderest memories, and the fondest dreams are shared. And where those who love each other share a common love for Christ, heart will find heart again in deeper union and fuller joy in God's eternal home.

Death will not mock our hearts forever. Death cannot separate God's children forever. In heaven our bitter tears of farewell will turn sweet in the gladness of reunion.

On his wife's tomb a man inscribed these words: "Till death us unite." For Christians that is no idle dream. Love's broken cords will be reknit. In his eternal home our heavenly Father will at last restore to us all whom we have loved in Christ and lost a while. Nor shall we ever part again.

And then, Christ assures us that in the world to come we shall enjoy a life of perfect happiness. In the Book of Revelation John recorded the visions of this heavenly glory Christ revealed to him. In contrast with this present world, there will be no sorrow, grief, or tears. We shall be set free from all cares and burdens, all trials and temptations, all frustrations, failures, wants, and fears. Pain and suffering will cease. There will be no more cancer, no more cardiac arrests, no more strokes, no more Alzheimer's disease, no more AIDS. There will be no tornados, hurricanes, earthquakes, fires, floods, or famine. Nothing that displeases God, nor any trace of his curse will be found there.

There will be no funeral chapels or cemeteries, for death itself will be swallowed up in an ever-flowing floodtide of life. Every barrier to life, every fetter of the soul, every cloud of unhappiness will vanish, because sin will be forever gone.

Crowning this happiness will be our new relationship to God. We shall see him face-to-face in all his splendor. We shall be holy as he is holy. We shall dwell in his presence in unbroken fellowship with him. In the strength of new and enlarged powers we shall serve him with untiring devotion. With the angels we shall join in adoring worship around his throne. Secure in his love and favor, and possessing every possible good, we shall reign with God and with our Savior in an ecstasy of joy forever.

The British Bible scholar G. T. Manley told of a little Muslim girl who had been looking at some gospel pictures. The next day she greeted her teacher with a beaming face. "Oh, Sitt!" she exclaimed. "Last night I saw Jesus in a dream and he is a hundred times better than the pictures!" Just so we shall find that heaven, too, is a hundred times better than the pictures.

Endless life with Christ; fellowship with the whole family of God's children, including reunion with our own loved ones in the Lord; and happiness beyond imagination in the very presence of God himself—by this revelation Christ liberates us from the dread of the unknown.

The Fear of Judgment

But by far the heaviest chain with which death binds our hearts in terror is the fear of judgment.

On every hand voices warn us of a reckoning up ahead. With deafening insistence conscience thunders it. Reason proclaims that if life has any meaning at all we must render account of it to God. History in some of its most dramatic moments foreshadows it. In solemn tones Holy Scripture again and again confirms these lesser witnesses. "Man is destined to die once," we read elsewhere in this same Letter to the Hebrews, "and after that to face judgment" (9:27 NIV). God "commands all people everywhere to repent," Paul told the Athenians, "because he has fixed a day on which he will have the world judged in righteousness by a man whom he has appointed, and of this he has given assurance to all by raising him from the dead" (Acts 17:30–31).

Someday God will summon us all before his judgment throne. How momentous are the issues of that judgment! How final and far-reaching! From the lips of One who knows the most secret secrets of our hearts, and whose judgment is unerring, we shall hear the verdict that proclaims and seals our eternal destiny. From that verdict there is no appeal. Never!

Judgment! A terrifying thought, indeed! How shall we escape God's wrath and condemnation? How many of us, even before the court of our own conscience, would care to defend our innocence of all moral fault and blame? How many would dare to claim that our life has always and in all things been pleasing to God?

No, we are dyed indelibly with our guilt. Nothing we do can ever rub it out. We have revolted against God and throned self over the empire of our hearts. We have smeared the tablets of his law with our protests and obscenities. We have mocked his vengeance by our disobedience. With our lusts and passions, our envy and worldliness, our pride, our hatefulness, our ingratitude and unbelief, we have defiled the temples of our souls in which he longs to dwell. We have even despised his love. If he has a scrap of self-respect—I say it reverently—if he has a scrap of self-respect, he cannot let us off, as if our sins were nothing worse than the pranks and capers of a mischievous boy. If he really is just and holy, if he loves righteousness and hates sin, as again and again he says he does, then he must surely cast us off. That man was a fool who said, "When I get to the judgment seat of God all that I will ask for is justice." If justice is all we get, every last one of us—the best as surely as the worst—will be banished from the presence of God and severed from his love in hell forever.

When in death's hands we read that summons to judgment, who does not pale with horror? But, blessed be God, Christ comes again and shatters this chain, too, driving our very worst fear away on the tides of his everlasting mercy.

What is the heart of the gospel? Just this: at Calvary, the sinless Son of God bore God's judgment on the sins of all of us who put our trust in him. In his own soul he absorbed and exhausted God's wrath against us. With his own blood he paid our penalty and purchased our peace with God. By his self-sacrifice he so perfectly satisfied all the claims of divine justice against us, that God can remain righteous, yet cancel our sins, set us free from the punishment our sins deserve, and clothing us with the righteousness of Christ, accept us as his own.

"There is therefore now no condemnation for those who are in Christ Jesus" (Rom. 8:1), cried the apostle. The very moment we come in faith to the cross God gives us our pardon and welcomes us into his family. Then and there we pass forever out of death into life in Jesus Christ our Lord. No longer do we dread the day of judgment. We face it instead with confidence and expectancy. The verdict is not in doubt. Our acquittal is secure. In a very real sense, as far as our acceptance by God is concerned, there is no judgment for us at all.

Upon a life I have not lived,
   Upon a death I did not die;
Another's life—Another's death—
   I've staked my whole eternity.

* * * *

Bold shall I stand in that great day,
   For who aught to my charge can lay?
Fully absolved by Christ I am
   From sin's tremendous curse and blame.

At the cross of Christ—and only there—the fear of judgment is banished from our hearts. The chain falls off, and we go our way in peace.

The fear of loneliness, the fear of the unknown, the fear of judgment—wonderful, wonderful Savior, he liberates us from them all.

Are *you* afraid to die?

If you are not trusting Jesus Christ as your Savior, you have every reason to be afraid. "It is a fearful thing," the author of our text warns us elsewhere, "to fall into the hands of the living God" (Heb. 10:31). Yet, this very minute you can find peace with God. Christ invites you to leave with him the whole burden of your sin. As the mighty Conqueror of death, he pleads with you to commit your eternal destiny to him and trust him completely. Then he will put your fear to flight.

If you are already a Christian, there is nothing in death for you to be afraid of. Nothing at all. You may still naturally shrink from it and wish you could avoid it, since death is, after all, an enemy, not a friend. But never again do you need to tremble before it in dread and terror.

Death cannot harm you. Christ has drawn its sting. He has broken its power over you, and in his keeping you are safe forever. Fix your eyes steadily on him and your fear will vanish. Free from the torment of its bondage, you can travel home in peace, singing as you go faith's triumph song, "'Where, O death, is your victory? Where, O death, is your sting?' . . . Thanks be to God who gives us the victory through our Lord Jesus Christ" (1 Cor. 15:55, 57).

3

D. Stuart Briscoe

—⊳◆⊲—

A native of England, D. Stuart Briscoe embarked on a career in banking after graduation from high school and became personal assistant to the chief inspector of the bank. He began to preach at the age of seventeen. After twelve years he left the business world for ministry with the Torchbearers, a youth organization with a global outreach. Since 1970 he has been senior pastor of Elmbrook Church in suburban Milwaukee, Wisconsin.

An internationally noted preacher, Briscoe conducts a television and radio ministry and has written more than twenty-five books. Among them are *Discovering God, Tough Truths for Today's Living: A Study of the Sermon on the Mount,* and *Spiritual Life.* He also wrote the volumes on Genesis and Romans in the Communicator's Commentary series.

—⊳◆⊲—

Having over forty-four years preached hundreds of sermons—good, bad, and indifferent—I cannot imagine what I would do "if I had only one sermon to preach." But at the time I was invited to contribute to this collection of sermons I was preaching from the parables of Luke under the general title, "What to Do While Your Life Is Happening." The parable of the rich fool (immediately) seemed to be appropriate because of its emphases on greed, which is a fundamental problem, on death's certainty, and on eternal considerations that need to be continually brought to our remembrance.

—⊳◆⊲—

Life on Loan

———⬦———

Someone in the crowd said to him, "Teacher, tell my brother to divide the inheritance with me."

Jesus replied, "Man, who appointed me a judge or an arbiter between you?" Then he said to them, "Watch out! Be on your guard against all kinds of greed; a man's life does not consist in the abundance of his possessions."

And he told them this parable: "The ground of a certain rich man produced a good crop. He thought to himself, 'What shall I do? I have no place to store my crops.'

"Then he said, 'This is what I'll do. I will tear down my barns and build bigger ones, and there I will store all my grain and my goods. And I'll say to myself, "You have plenty of good things laid up for many years. Take life easy; eat, drink and be merry."'

"But God said to him, 'You fool! This very night your life will be demanded from you. Then who will get what you have prepared for yourself?'

"This is how it will be with anyone who stores up things for himself but is not rich toward God."

Luke 12:13–21 NIV

Life goes on, and many things that happen are directly related to actions we have taken and decisions we have made. But, obviously, many things are totally outside our control. Sometimes we feel that life is just happening to us, that life is getting away on us. The question we have to ask ourselves is, "What am I supposed to do while my life is happening?" The answer, in a nutshell, is that we should live in dependence on what God has said in his Word and in obedience to it. There is no clearer enunciation of this than in the teaching of the Lord Jesus in his parables.

Take the parable in our text, for example. In order that we might get the full impact of this incident let me sketch the background.

The Lord Jesus was teaching his disciples in the middle of a crowd of thousands of people. He always taught with the crowd in mind, however inconvenient. He began his public ministry by gathering a group of disciples together with the express purpose that after he had died and risen again, they might then take the good news of the gospel to the uttermost parts of the earth. He was already training them for that task, not only by giving them information, but by letting them see firsthand the needs and condition of the multitudes to whom they would be sent.

He pointed out to them that there was a great deal of religious hypocrisy. He warned them to be on their guard against hypocrisy in their own lives. The reason for this warning, of course, was that they were to be witnesses, and if there is one thing that destroys an effective witness more quickly than anything else, it is hypocrisy. Credibility disintegrates once profession and performance contradict each other. Not only do people not listen to the witnesses anymore; they disregard them as persons and despise what they are saying. After David sinned Nathan came to him and said that he had not only totally messed up, but that he had also given the enemies of God opportunity to blaspheme God's name. So Jesus said, "Beware of hypocrisy."

He then went on to explain that witnesses should expect opposition. He constantly told his disciples that he was going to be given a hard time by those who resisted his message, and that they should not expect better treatment. He warned them that they would often find themselves in tremendous difficulty and under duress. But he reminded them that the Spirit of God would be available to them, and that he would empower them. He would give them the words to say and help them remember the things that were important, and he would wing their words to the hearts of many people. So when they found themselves encountering opposition they should respond with fortitude, great certainty, and considerable equanimity, because the Holy Spirit would be at work within them.

Jesus also warned the disciples that anybody speaking against what they were saying in the power of the Spirit would be guilty of blasphemy against the Holy Spirit. This was pretty heavy stuff! The interesting thing, however, is that while this heavy teaching on discipleship was going on there was at least one person in the crowd who was not listening. The reason he was not interested in discipleship was because he had a personal problem and could not think past it. Everything else was irrelevant. He was totally unconcerned about hypocrisy, about being a witness to Christ, about being equipped by the Spirit of God to speak powerfully and to stand up against all opposition, and the fact that some people might be guilty of blaspheming the Holy Spirit, a sin for which there is no forgiveness. All this was of no interest to him at all. Do you know why? He was thinking about money. His mind was totally captured by his finances.

Have you ever found yourself in church, confronted with tremendous spiritual truths? Where you were spoken to about eternal issues and you discovered, somewhat to your amazement, that it was all like water off a duck's back? All because your mind was absorbed by some personal priority that had nothing to do with what God was trying to say to you? I imagine that all of us at one time or another have experienced this.

This is what happened on the occasion Luke describes. In the midst of all this heavy-duty teaching a man in the crowd shouted out, "Teacher, tell my brother to divide the inheritance with me." I imagine that was quite a shock to the people who were listening to Jesus. To have their attention diverted from this crucial teaching about the kingdom and the fact that they were going to play a role in it must have been shocking, to say the least! Particularly as the man started shouting about a gripe and a grumble and a fight and a quarrel he was having with his own brother over money! I have observed that so often when money gets into a situation, you have a problem. It is amazing how sensitive people become when the subject of money crops up. This is even more the case when you're dealing with an inheritance. You've heard the old saying, "Where there's a will, there's a way." But when you're dealing with an inheritance, you often discover that where there's a will, there's a quarrel. When it comes to getting our fair share it is amazing how dramatically perceptions of what is a fair share differ. Many families have foundered on the rocks of inheritance.

This problem was particularly significant in the days of Jesus. The children of Israel had settled in the promised land that God had given to them. The land had been systematically divided into sections for each of the tribes, then clans, then families. All the Israelites had their own piece of real estate. Over the years as people died their land was divided into ever narrower strips.

Suppose that a man had six sons. When the man died there were two possibilities as far as his property, his inheritance, was concerned. His strip of land could be divided into seven narrower strips, each brother getting one piece and the oldest brother receiving a double share because of his particular responsibilities. Or the land could be kept in one piece and hopefully the six brothers would work it together. But getting six brothers to work together is a problem. If they were all married it would be practically impossible! The potential for trouble is high. Do you know why? Because everybody is looking out for himself!

So Jesus found himself interrupted by a man who wanted his strip of land. "Tell my brother to give me my share of the inheritance," he said. Notice Jesus' response. "Man," he said, "who appointed me a judge or an arbiter between you?" He point-blank refused to get involved. In fairness to the aggrieved gentleman, I should explain that the rabbis were often involved in situations of this kind. That's why it was very difficult for them to get life insurance! They were often in no-win situations. So Jesus refused to get involved, not only because he did not want to have his time consumed by such matters, but also because he saw an underlying problem that needed to be addressed. The underlying problem? Greed! "Watch out," Jesus said. "Be on your guard against all kinds of greed. A man's life does not consist in the abundance of his possessions." That's a solid piece of teaching straight from Jesus. Here is one thing to do while our life is happening: watch out and be on guard against all kinds of greed!

Let's make absolutely certain we know what we are talking about. "Be on your guard" is a military term. Jesus is saying, in effect, that like soldiers on alert, we must be constantly aware of the human capacity for greed and its inherent dangers. If not, there is a very high probability we will be suckered into activities and attitudes far removed from what the Lord has in mind for us. It is, therefore, imperative for us to be constantly aware of our own capacity for greed.

For one thing, we need to be on our guard against cultural norms. Tony Campolo in his book, *The Seven Deadly Sins,* writes, "Our society has built its economy on the production of things that people are conditioned to want but do not really need." Now let that sink in. He adds: "Many of the consumer goods we spend so much to buy did not even exist a generation ago. We buy these things because we have been manipulated into wanting them through advertising and peer pressure."

He is absolutely right. It is obvious that people need jobs in order to feed their families. But to have jobs that pay, they must be producing something. Therefore, as populations increase and expectations escalate, production must keep pace. But you can't continue to produce if people aren't buying, so you've got to persuade them to buy. That can mean convincing them they need what they have been encouraged simply to want.

The problem in all this is that we have a tremendous capacity for greed, and the whole system tends to manipulate and exacerbate this inherent problem. That's why we need to heed what Jesus said to the people in his day: "Be on your guard constantly against all kinds of greed." If he said it then, what would he say to a culture that has developed incredibly skillful ways of manipulating people's inherent capacity for greed? The word "greed" means literally, "having or wanting to have more." The basic idea behind *pleonexia*, the Greek word for greed, is "more, still more, wanting more." A secondary meaning suggests not only having or wanting to have more, but having more than my fair share, with particular reference to what everybody else has.

Years ago a friend of mine who worked for a major league baseball club told me that the day after it signed a superstar another star on the club came storming into the manager's office and shouted, "I don't know how much you're paying that [expletive deleted], but I want one dollar more." He couldn't possibly spend all he was already earning, but he had to have more, and he had to have more at the expense of somebody else. That is raw greed.

The Lord Jesus reminds us that humankind has an inherent capacity for "all kinds of greed." Notice, "all kinds." Greed will come at us from all directions. It has all kinds of causes. This desire for more has all kinds of characteristics and produces all kinds of consequences.

On one occasion the Lord Jesus was talking to the Pharisees, who were very much concerned about the effect of external things on people's lives. Jesus pointed out to them that externals are not the

41

problem. It is what goes on inside us that's the problem. He then listed all kinds of things that come out of our hearts. High on the list was greed. He called it, along with all these other things, an evil thing. This inherent desire for more and more is fundamentally evil (Mark 7:22–23).

Paul reminded the Romans that people know God to a certain extent, yet without exception they have turned away from what they know of him. Therefore, God has allowed them to live with the consequences of their rebellion. One of these consequences is that their minds are depraved. So they can't see things straight, including seeing when enough is enough. As a result of our rebellion against God and our resistance to what we know of God, our minds are depraved, our hearts have become evil, and, among other things, we are enslaved by greed (Rom. 1:29).

Another thing the Bible says about greed is that if we live estranged from God, not in tune with God, we lose our sensitivity. This leads to sensuality, including the desire to indulge in every kind of impurity with a continual "lust for more" (again, the word is *pleonexia*) (Eph. 4:19). It's not a pretty picture. Jesus was not so much concerned about being interrupted as he was about the condition of the interrupter's heart. Jesus understood what was the matter with him. He had a depraved mind and an evil heart. He had given himself over to sensuality and had lost all spiritual sensitivity. He was wallowing in impurity with a continual lust for more. All this was going on in the heart of the man.

As we have noted, greed has all kinds of characteristics. It manifests itself in a variety of ways. The tenth commandment says, "You shall not covet [that's this same word, "be greedy for"] your neighbor's house. You shall not covet your neighbor's wife, or his manservant or maidservant, his ox or donkey, or anything that belongs to your neighbor" (Exod. 20:17). This list reminds us that greed, or covetousness, comes in a variety of forms. One of the most common is the desire for more possessions. The more we get of something, the more we want. There is something about human nature that works this way. One of the richest men in the world was asked on one occasion if he had enough money. "No," he said. "I really want more." His questioner then inquired, "Well, how much is enough?" "A little bit more than you've got at any one time," he replied. That is, to a large extent, the feeling that we get. Enough is just a little bit more than we have at any one time.

It's not only possessions that we're greedy for. Very often we're greedy for power. We want to control our lives, to make people and situations fit into our plans. Coupled with that is the desire for more prestige. It's amazing what we will do to get more possessions, more prestige, and more power. The desire for more can lead to actions which, under other circumstances, we would never contemplate. This is why we must be on our guard against all kinds of things that will push us to want more, more, and still more.

There are all kinds of consequences as well. There is a parallel word to the Greek word *pleonexia*. It is *philarguria,* meaning, "the love of money." The love of money is one aspect of greed or covetousness. Paul says a very striking thing in 1 Timothy 6:10: "The love of money is a root of all kinds of evil."

Many years ago there was a popular song that said, "Money is the root of all evil." That is a misquotation of Scripture. Money is not *the* root of *all* evil. The *love* of money is *a* root of *all kinds* of evil. There are all kinds of evil coming from all kinds of sources, and the love of money is a major source. It is very interesting to observe how greed and the love of possessions and the desire for more pervade all aspects of human experience.

On the international scale this was obvious at the ecological summit held in Rio de Janeiro in 1992. When the summit was first conceived, the conveners had tremendous plans. They were going to address many of the terrible problems confronting the human race, and look at some possible solutions. But do you know what they discovered? Many of the proposals to deal with the problems were headed off by various interest groups. Practically everything that was suggested was so watered down that the documents signed had no teeth in them and could not in any way be implemented. Why? Because everybody was looking out for their own best interests. No one suggested declaring internationally, "This fragile little globe of ours, over which God made us stewards, has been totally fouled up by us because of our greed. Let's confess it, let's come together, and let's cooperate in managing the earth God's way." No one thought of that. There were too many special interest groups on the international scene. The industrialized nations were concerned about the depletion of natural resources in the underdeveloped nations. "Stop raping the land," they said. "You're destroying the ecological balance of our world!" The underdeveloped nations replied, "We have to use our natural resources to catch up with you. If you don't want us to deplete our resources, share your wealth with us." The one group said, "No," so the other group said, "No." International special interest won another round, and we all lost.

On the national level the story is the same. The United States has only 5 percent of the world's population. Yet we use up 25 percent of the world's energy and are responsible for 22 percent of the carbon dioxide that poisons the atmosphere. Why do we keep on doing it? Because we don't want to change our standard of living. The world can go to hell in a handbasket just so long as we've got what we've got. We want our gadgets. We don't care how much energy we burn up. We don't care what happens to the environment or the atmosphere, so long as our lifestyle is not touched. It's a crucial problem. It's something we have to address.

On the personal level we see the same thing. What we want is what we want and we want it now, but we don't want to pay for it! So Jesus' admonition to be on our guard is most appropriate.

Notice that Jesus amplified his point by telling one of his famous stories. This one is about a man who had been farming and had produced a bumper crop. He was very excited about it because it gave him great security. His only problem was that he didn't have anywhere to store his crops. But he was astute and realized that the one thing to do was to pull down his barns and build bigger ones. Then he could put everything in his barns and take early retirement. In our culture he would be regarded as a model of success. He said to himself (it's interesting how people talk to themselves), "You have plenty of good things laid up for many years. Take life easy; eat, drink, and be merry." He was certainly an outstanding success as an egotist. If you look at his words, everything was "I," "me," "my," and all of his conversation was addressed to himself. He was utterly self-absorbed. There was only one pebble on the beach as far as he was concerned. What he's got, he's got, and what he's got, he's going to keep, and what he's keeping, he'll do with exactly as he wishes. He was a quintessential, successful egotist.

Recently I was talking with Dr. Peter Toon, an Anglican theologian. He said that he thinks one of the fundamental problems in our society is individualism. He noted that the word "individual" was first coined in the seventeenth century. Prior to that the common word was "personal." The difference between that which is "personal" and that which is "individual" is profound. That which is personal has to do with me as a person among persons. I recognize that I am personal, but I also recognize that my life cannot be lived independently of other persons. But the word "individual" means that that which is related to me is independent of everybody else. The fundamental flaw in the society we are living in today is rampant individualism. We have decided that it doesn't matter what happens to everybody else, so long as *I*, the individual, am all right. That is quintessential egotism. And the man in Jesus' story was totally successful at it. The word "individual" hadn't even been invented in his day, but he was a perfect illustration of it.

He was also a very successful materialist—so much so that he didn't understand that you can't satisfy a soul with material things. He was the sort of person who assumed that the answer to the inner needs of the human being lies entirely in material things. So he said to himself, "You have plenty of good things laid up for many years. You've got lots of things, so be satisfied with these." But only materialists think that we can satisfy ourselves with material things.

Then, too, he was a very successful hedonist. "Eat, drink, and be merry" summed up his philosophy. This, of course, is hedonism. Hedonism grew out of Greek paganism. The Greek hedonists reasoned that you must at all costs embrace pleasure and at all costs avoid pain. You are free to do whatever it takes to achieve these objectives. It doesn't matter what happens to everybody else, because in the end you are the only person who rates.

Jesus introduced a man who was totally enraptured with himself, interested (exclusively) in himself. He thought he could be satisfied with material things, and assumed that his eating, drinking, and being merry could go on forever. His only problem was that just because he was a successful egotist, materialist, and hedonist, he was a total failure as a human being. How do we know? God said so, and that is an evaluation worth noting. God summed him up with one monosyllable: "fool!" That doesn't mean he was stupid, and it doesn't mean he was a clown. It means that he was the sort of person who says, "There is no God" (Ps. 14:1). Or, to put it more accurately, the fool says "No!" to God.

It is quite possible that this man was a philosophical atheist. But he was, for all intents and purposes, a practical atheist. There is a difference between the two. Our world is full of people who would never for a moment adopt philosophical atheism. They would never dare to say, "There is no God." Nevertheless, they go about the business of living day by day as if God did not exist. To what do these people say "Yes"? They say yes to themselves, yes to materialism, yes to hedonism, yes to sensuality, yes to impurity, yes to a continual lust for more. If you live your life that way, not only will you be a practical atheist, but when your time is up, you'll be totally unprepared for what lies ahead.

"You fool!" God said to this man, "this very night your life will be demanded from you." The word for "demanded" is an economic word. A banker would use it if he said to a borrower, "It's time for you to repay your loan. I demand repayment. If you don't pay me, I will foreclose." God told this materialistic, egocentric hedonist, this successful failure, "You fool! You have lived independently of me. You have been interested only in possessions, power, prestige, and position. These have been your gods. These have been your idols. You fool! Don't you realize that your life was on loan and I'm going to foreclose? And when I foreclose I'll evaluate your life, and all you will have to offer me is a wasted life. You fool!"

It's a sobering thought to realize that our life is on loan. God will foreclose when he's ready, and we can't prevent him. It's a sobering thought to realize that life does not consist in the abundance or the excess of the things for which we are living. And it's a sobering thought to realize that the only thing that really counts in life is what Jesus calls being rich toward God.

How do you get to be rich toward God? By recognizing that you are basically egocentric, basically materialistic, basically hedonistic. Confessing it, repenting of it, seeking forgiveness for it. Asking God by his Spirit to touch your heart and renew your mind, to give you a new perspective and a new set of priorities. And beginning to think in terms of eternal issues and to recognize that what really counts is what counts with God.

Here are some questions to ponder. Is our culture in agreement with Christ on this point? Do you see any conflict between the teaching of Christ and the teaching of our culture? Ivan Boesky used to wear a T-shirt bearing the slogan, "Greed is good." Before he went to prison he bragged, "He who has the most things at the end of the game wins." John Paul Getty said, "The best things in life are things." But the Lord Jesus said, "Be on your guard against all kinds of greed; a man's life does not consist in the abundance of his possessions." With whom do you agree: Christ or our culture? How does your view show? Are you solely a creature of our culture? Or are you a child of the King?

4

Jill P. Briscoe

———◆———

Jill P. Briscoe, a graduate of Homerton College, Cambridge, taught in the British school system. She later was superintendent of a nursery school and youth director with Capernwray Missionary Fellowship. In 1970 she moved to the United States with her husband, Stuart, when he became pastor of Elmbrook Church, Waukesha, Wisconsin.

Jill is lay advisor to the women's ministries at Elmbrook Church. She and her daughter Judy work together as a mother-daughter team in an active speaking and writing ministry. Jill has spoken in many countries and is the author of more than forty books, including children's books, study guides, poetry, and devotional material. She has three grown children and six grandchildren.

———◆———

Satan reserves his sharpest attacks for the most effective servants of the Lord. If he can cause a leader to fall, great harm is done to the Lord's name, work, and glory. The ministry offers the Spirit-filled Christian the opportunity to do great things for God. Those great things will not go unnoticed by our enemy, the accuser of our souls.

I have a heart for ministry couples and ministry wives in particular, having been one myself for over thirty years. I believe that ministry is a privilege rather than a punishment. It is my greatest joy to encourage shepherds as they have encouraged me. I have the conviction that we must support one another, pray for one another, encourage one another, and hold one another accountable. Above all, we need to keep the privilege of serving Jesus uppermost in our minds as the punishments come along. It was with this conviction, seeking to forewarn and therefore forearm, that I preached this message at the commencement service at Gordon-Conwell Seminary in 1992.

Because many—probably most—readers of this book will be pastors and seminary students (I hope their wives will read it, too), I chose this sermon as my contribution to this book.

Losing Heart: Temptations in the Ministry

⟫·◇·⟪

Jesus, full of the Holy Spirit, returned from the Jordan and was led by the Spirit in the desert, where for forty days he was tempted by the devil. He ate nothing during those days, and at the end of them he was hungry.

The devil said to him, "If you are the Son of God, tell this stone to become bread."

Jesus answered, "It is written: 'Man does not live on bread alone.'"

The devil led him up to a high place and showed him in an instant all the kingdoms of the world. And he said to him, "I will give you all their authority and splendor, for it has been given to me, and I can give it to anyone I want to. So if you worship me, it will all be yours."

Jesus answered, "It is written: 'Worship the Lord your God and serve him only.'"

The devil led him to Jerusalem and had him stand on the highest point of the temple. "If you are the Son of God," he said, "throw yourself down from here. For it is written:

> 'He will command his angels concerning you
>   to guard you carefully;
> and they will lift you up in their hands,
>   so that you will not strike your foot against a stone.'"

Jesus answered, "It says: 'Do not put the Lord your God to the test.'"

When the devil had finished all this tempting, he left him until an opportune time.

Luke 4:1–13 NIV

Paul was able to say that he didn't lose heart in the ministry. Yet today all over the world God's leaders are doing just that—losing heart. This concerns me greatly, for if God's leaders "lag" and "flag," how can their followers follow? How will inroads be made into the devil's territory? How will Christ's kingdom come?

51

We need to be alert and aware of Satan's methods. I have been involved in ministry for over thirty years now, and it has been my experience that Satan can tempt me in the good times as he can in the bad times, in the rich times as thoroughly as in the poor times, in the healthy times as diabolically as in the sick times; he can cause me to lose heart in such a way that I can lose my ministry altogether. The devil doesn't really care what our circumstances are. He rides the back of any of them, and, like some evil jockey, whips the horse along at a frantic pace, turning it whither he wills. Looking at the way Jesus handled our evil adversary may help us.

> Jesus, God in embryo, growing to man-size
> a baby boy became.
> He lived in Nazareth—God in Galilean cloth—
> eating our food, sleeping in our beds,
> attending the village church
> where he listened with great attention
> to the village preachers.
>
> At the age of thirty he went into the
> ministry—perfectly and supremely
> obeying the first commandment to
> love the Lord his God with all his heart,
> mind, soul, and strength.
>
> Baptized by John, he was led by the Spirit
> into the desert—to find Satan, drag him out
> from behind his rock, and force him to attack
> in order that he could overcome him.

Satan was not stalking Jesus; Jesus was stalking Satan! Jesus—the source of this account in the Gospels—apparently wanted us to know that he did win the battle for us that day.

There will be days in our ministry, however, when it will be extremely difficult for us to believe that. It will appear as if Satan, not Jesus, has won the war. Satan's devices have not changed. He is "fixed" evil and has no possibility for any change whatsoever. His avowed intent is to prevent us—as he tried to prevent Jesus—from being willing, obedient, suffering (if need be) servants of the

Lord. The more we try to focus on the Father, to fix our heart in his Word, and to make sure we are living in the fullness of the Holy Spirit, the more Satan will focus on us.

Reading the Book of Job, I am struck by the Lord God's conversation with Satan. He asked him, "Have you considered my servant Job?" We are not told if Satan had considered God's servant Job before the Lord drew his attention to him. Quite honestly, this incident gives me little encouragement to be godly. After all, if I seek (in any measure) to be as righteous and pleasing to God as Job was, then maybe I risk having the Lord God draw that wretched evildoer's attention to me! I want to say, "Lord, don't do that!" Be that as it may, I am convinced that the more holy and useful you are, the more you love God, the more you develop a heart for his world and his people, the more you can expect Satan's close attention.

It is my observation that our Lord Jesus was tempted in three main areas during his sojourn among us: the area of his legitimate needs; the area of his spiritual gifts; and the area of his personal worship.

The Area of Our Legitimate Needs

Satan first attacked Jesus in the area of his legitimate needs. After a long fast, Jesus was very hungry. "If you are the Son of God, tell this stone to become bread," Satan suggested (v. 3). Someone has suggested that God had not seen fit to satisfy his Son's legitimate need for food in his particular circumstance at this time. So the question now arose: Was Jesus willing to accept this difficult period of privation as his Father's express will for him, designed for his spiritual good? Jesus was being tempted to use his powers to take matters into his own hands concerning his very legitimate personal needs. But he decided to live by "every word that comes from the mouth of God." He apparently asked his Father about it, and having heard him, duly decided to do the will of God and stay hungry. Jesus chose to live by his Father's Ten Commandments rather than by the devil's three suggestions! We must do the same.

On some occasions in his ministry, Jesus faced a period of privation when the will of God meant he literally had no roof over his head. "Foxes have holes and birds of the air have nests, but the Son of Man has no place to lay his head," he said (Matt. 8:20). I believe he meant "The Son of Man doesn't even have a branch to perch on—never mind a nest!" Probably most of us in ministry will never find ourselves homeless, but many of us will undoubtedly find that our homes are not our own. A parsonage or mission house may be our earthly lot until the day we retire; then the senior citizens' residence designated by the body we have served may be our only option. Those of us who are women may find this can get to us and cause us to lose heart. In a very real sense, Satan takes full advantage of our "nesting instincts" and rides this particular horse for all it's worth.

I remember struggling over this as a young wife and mother living in mission housing. I was tempted to take matters into my own hands, to get a job and provide for some legitimate needs that could not be met on our meagre missionary budget. I had both the ability and opportunity to satisfy some of these needs. But after waiting on the Lord, I discerned his specific directive to turn my energies in another direction altogether: to start a nursery school for the mission and work for free! This I did, having determined years before to live "by every word that comes from the mouth of God." The secret, I have discovered, is to live by his dictates, not by my desires or Satan's devices.

Another legitimate need Jesus denied himself at that particular time in that particular place was that of a companion. I'm sure he would have been very glad to have had John's company out there in the desert, but he went out there all alone. Sometimes that's how it has to be. It can be very lonely in leadership. Sometimes, for his own sovereign purposes, God calls us to suffer the loss of personal relationships for a period.

For ten years, my husband was asked to travel for the ministry we served. Sometimes we were separated for months. It was hard on all of us—especially Stuart. The children and I had one another. This was the only way, however, this job could get done. God had not seen fit to provide us with the means of meeting our personal needs in that particular place at that particular time. The hard thing, I discovered, once I had discerned that "this" was the particular privation the Father had designed for my spiritual profit, was not to lose heart.

I remember how tempted we were to take matters into our own hands and leave the mission organization altogether, get back into secular work, and use our own trained skill-power to provide for our family. Having become convinced that we must wait for his permission to make such a move, we decided that until God led us out as thoroughly and surely as he had led us in, we would stay put. It helps at such times to look back on your guidance and "encourage yourself in the Lord."

One of the most common ways Satan gets us to lose heart is through money—or, to be more exact, the *lack* of it. We used to have a saying in England: "If you're in full-time Christian work, the Lord keeps you humble and the brethren keep you poor!" When we get inside the ministry door all too often we find ourselves saying, "Oh, I never expected *this!*" All too often "this" has to do with the stress and strain that arise because we find ourselves in a severe money crunch. Do we know how to be poor? Maybe we think we do, or maybe we really do. But do we know how to go on being poor all the way through our lives—and not lose heart? It seems to me that the more qualified we become theologically, the poorer we may end up! A seminary professor seems to make less and less, not more and more. Yet if that is the way God leads us, are we willing to accept that lifelong privation as God's will for our spiritual good?

For the pastor's wife, the tests can come when the family lives on food stamps. You can't send your children to the "good" fee-charging preschools members of your congregation are able to afford or get everyone's teeth fixed. Your husband—especially if the ministry is his second career—will be tempted to think of all the things he "could" have provided if he had stayed where he was and served the Lord in the marketplace. Satan will use our legitimate needs to get our attention, capture our thoughts, and fill our souls with self-pity, bitterness, and resentment. We may then lose heart.

The Area of Our Spiritual Gifts

If Satan is not tempting us in the area of our legitimate personal needs, he will very likely hurl temptations at us in the area of our gifts and talents. He gave Jesus a mind-trip to the pinnacle of the temple and tempted him to consider the possibility of using his own gifts for his own benefit. He suggested that Jesus do something *mega!* Satan tempts us all in this area. There is "mega mania" out there.

I am not suggesting that Jesus never did anything mega. Feeding five thousand people with a small lunch, healing lepers with a touch, walking on water, and raising dead people is pretty mega! But these displays of Jesus' giftedness were never intended for his own self-aggrandizement. In fact, he was always warning people not to advertise his miracles. Paul addresses this aspect of Christian ministry when he says, "We do not peddle the word of God for profit" (2 Cor. 2:17).

I serve a megachurch. But if I do not ask God to help me maintain a minimind-set, I am going to be in big trouble and end up a meganuisance to God and the work of his kingdom. Success can at times be a lot more dangerous than failure. If our hearts are focused on God, fixed in his Word, and full of the Spirit, we will hear the Spirit's voice above the loud suggestions of the devil.

Satan uses the frustrations that inevitably come our way in ministry when we find ourselves overqualified for the job. To be overqualified for the service we are asked to engage in and to be underequipped for that same task as well provides a perfect opportunity for the devil to move in and cause us to lose heart.

When my husband, who had been working on the inspection team of a large bank, gave up his career to run the finances of a mission, he became really frustrated. Trying to upgrade and change equipment, methods, and systems became a bone of contention among some of the established staff who "had 'always' done it this way before."

It's hard, when attitudes are wrong or when resources are meagre, to work at half-throttle, or to lay aside some of our training or gifts, until God makes a way for us to use them again.

I laughed when I saw a poster above the desk of a secretary in a missionary office in a third world country. It read:

> We the unwilling
> Led by the unknowing
> Are doing the impossible
> For the ungrateful.
> We have done so much
> For so long with so little
> We are now qualified
> To do anything
> With nothing!

Jesus must have known the frustrations of being overqualified for the job God sent him to do. Yet he managed without many of the resources we are in danger of believing are indispensable for viable ministry today: video equipment, microphones, computers. He refused, however, to let Satan determine what he did with his gifts! He knew that people were his best resource. It is still the same today. If God provides modern means and gives us permission to use them to enhance our ministry, we would be out of order not to do so. But if he does not do this, we must say as Jesus did, "Don't push me, Satan. I will not be pressured into using my gifts unless at God's command or for any reason other than 'God aggrandizement.'"

We must grasp this important principle. Otherwise, we will begin to view our spiritual self-worth through the numbers grid. "If 'so few' people come to church when 'so many more' could have come," we reason, "there must be something wrong with me." If the Old Testament prophets had gauged the worth of their ministries by the size of their congregations, some of them would have been in real trouble! When Jesus had a very small "church" of twelve people, we could say he had a "miniministry." But he ended up doing megathings with that minigroup by focusing his heart on the Father, fixing his mind on God's Word, and making sure that he was full of the Holy Spirit. He let God determine which of his gifts and abilities were used when and where. Needless to say, he didn't lose heart! Aren't you glad? Where would the human race be if he had!

So the devil will be hanging around the pulpits of our churches until the end of the world when we won't need them anymore. I once heard John Stott say, "The pulpit is a dangerous place for any son of Adam!" (Or daughter of Eve, I might add!)

If we are tempted to focus on our gifts rather than on the Giver, we may fall easy prey to the second temptation of Christ. We may find, as G. Campbell Morgan testified he found, that it is very easy for us to be concerned about homiletical ability and fluency, theological profundity, and biblical accuracy, while God says, "Preach on, great preacher, without me."

The Area of Our Personal Worship

The third area of temptation that Christ faced had to do with his personal worship. Having failed to accomplish his goals thus far, the devil came out into the open and shouted at the Lord, "*Wor-*

ship me! Just once, just for a moment, let me be God! Ask me for anything in the world, and I will give it to you."

Christ didn't argue with Satan's audacious claim to have the ability to come up with the goods. He is after all the prince of this world. But Jesus is the King, and he simply answered, "Worship the Lord your God and serve him only" (Luke 4:8). If the devil had persuaded Christ to ask him for even one little thing, it would all have been over for you and me! Fortunately, his heart was focused enough to resist the temptation to link up with any power on earth other than the Holy Spirit to accomplish anything other than the powerful purposes of God as God himself had determined them.

The Christian world today offers us great opportunity to become power-hungry. All too often we want to build our own empire rather than seeking first the kingdom of God. We fall into the greed trap. We charge for preaching the gospel (something the apostle Paul told us not to do), and we abuse the stewardship of God's resources that he has entrusted to us.

The tender area of our sexuality is another danger zone. How often the devil blatantly draws our attention to our sensual senses! He is the author of the spirit of the age, which is characterized by Money, Sex, and Power. He lights a candle, puts on soft music, and whispers, "Be king for a day. Be queen for a day. I'll give you the world, if you'll only ask!"

"I'll *never* commit adultery!" a young pastor's wife told me vehemently. "Never say 'never,'" I cautioned. How many of us "really" know ourselves well enough to be on red alert in this area of our lives and relationships? The devil will move in a King David (or a Bathsheba) next door, just when your spouse is busy traveling or not meeting your needs.

At such times we must "worship God and serve him *only*." We must resist the very understandable human desire to respond to flattery, understanding, and interest shown at a close personal level by any man other than our husband, or any woman other than our wife, no matter how high the spiritual position they may hold.

Worship keeps us honest. In God's presence we are forced to confess, "I liked that man's attention, Lord," or "I sensed as she spoke to me a 'connection' that is off-limits to both of us." A

David or a Bathsheba may listen with a far more sympathetic ear than our own partner. One or the other may affirm our self-worth in a way our spouse has long since stopped trying to do. Maybe you are working together on a church project and find, with a thrill of pleasure, that your gifts are complementary; in contrast, your mate and you always seem to clash or conflict when you try to work together. All these shenanigans fall into the same category: the third temptation. Can't you see that the devil is offering you the world in ways like these? Watch out! To follow your base instincts can lead to worshiping Satan and what he offers you of this world.

It is in worship that we can be honest enough to confess our reaction to another person's presence that we know is off-limits. It is in worship that we can tell God we secretly enjoyed the eye contact, the opportunity to flirt a bit. "Haven't done that for a long time!" says the flesh, licking its lips. "It felt so good! It can't be all that dangerous," Satan encourages. It is in worship that God will share with us his abhorrence of evil, until we hate what we have been doing enough to take measures to resist that temptation. Our warfare must come out of our worship. Our walk must come out of our worship. Our work must come out of our worship. And our words must come out of our worship as well!

Years ago I learned a salutary lesson. I came to understand that if my words were ever going to make a definitive difference in the hearts and lives of people, they must first worship. This discovery led me to pen the poem "Wings" for the daily devotional that bears the same title:

> Give my words wings, Lord.
> May they alight gently on the branches of men's minds,
> bending them to the winds of Your will.
> May they fly high enough to touch the lofty,
> low enough to breathe the breath
> of sweet encouragement upon the downcast soul.
>
> Give my words wings, Lord.
> May they fly swift and far,
> Winning the race with the words of the worldly wise
> to the hearts of men.

Give my words wings, Lord.
See them now
nesting—
down at Thy feet—
Silenced into ecstasy,
home at last.

As I began to receive worldwide opportunities to increase my speaking gifts, I reconfirmed my conviction that if my words had not first worshiped, they would never win the race with the words of the worldly wise for the hearts of people.

But there has been another lesson for me in all of this. I have found that only after worship do I know the words with which to answer Satan as he comes at me with all barrels blazing. He is always more than a match for my own feeble efforts to resist his clever arguments, persuasive suggestions, and honeyed words. But he is no match for *the Word*. My personal worship gives me words not only for the hearts of the worldly wise, but also words for the war—the real war between good and evil for the hearts and minds of all, a war that is going on all around us every day of our ministry.

Maybe all that you have just heard is after the fact. Perhaps somewhere along the road you did lose heart, and along with it, an opportunity, a reputation, a ministry, maybe even a marriage partner or family.

I have a final word of encouragement for you. If you've lost heart, Jesus knows where you lost it. He loves to find lost things, like lambs, coins, sons—anything precious that has been lost in the heat of battle.

He is a God of pardon as well as power, a Sovereign who is merciful and full of compassion. He has been here: hay in his hair, dust on his feet, splinters in his fingers, pain in his eyes. In all points he was tempted as we are—yet without sin. He overcame that we might overcome, too—even our failures. So let us not lose heart. This is my prayer.

5

William C. Brownson

President and broadcast minister of "Words of Hope," William C. Brownson has conducted this radio program of the Reformed Church in America since 1972. He earned his M.Div. degree at Columbia Theological Seminary, and his Th.D. in New Testament at Princeton Theological Seminary. He has served Reformed churches in New Jersey and in Chicago, Illinois, and was professor of preaching at Western Theological Seminary, Holland, Michigan, for ten years.

His widespread speaking ministry has taken him to many churches, colleges, universities, and conferences. A frequent contributor to the *Church Herald* and other Christian periodicals, Brownson has written *The God of Surprises, What Christ Is Doing Now, How to Live Happily, The Glory of the Cross, When We Question God, How It All Began, Courage to Pray,* and several other books.

Paul asked his friends in Colossae to pray for his preaching of Christ, "that I may make it clear" (Col. 4:4). That's my prayer and aim also as a herald of the gospel. If I had only one sermon to preach, I would want to make the message of salvation luminously *plain.*

In repenting and believing we see not only how to make an initial response to the gospel, but also how to go on appropriating the good news at deepening levels for a lifetime. And, in finding salvation completely in our relationship to the crucified and risen Jesus, we grasp the heart of the New Testament message.

The Gospel Made Plain

Two others also, who were criminals, were led away to be put to death with him. And when they came to the place which is called The Skull, there they crucified him, and the criminals, one on the right and one on the left. And Jesus said, "Father, forgive them; for they know not what they do." And they cast lots to divide his garments. And the people stood by, watching; but the rulers scoffed at him, saying, "He saved others; let him save himself, if he is the Christ of God, his Chosen One!" The soldiers also mocked him, coming up and offering him vinegar, and saying, "If you are the King of the Jews, save yourself!" There was also an inscription over him, "This is the King of the Jews."

One of the criminals who were hanged railed at him, saying, "Are you not the Christ? Save yourself and us!" But the other rebuked him, saying, "Do you not fear God, since you are under the same sentence of condemnation? And we indeed justly; for we are receiving the due reward of our deeds; but this man has done nothing wrong." And he said, "Jesus, remember me when you come *in your kingly power.*" And he said to him, "Truly, I say to you, today you will be with me in Paradise."

Luke 23:32–43 RSV

The meaning of the gospel, the essence of the evangel—in twenty minutes! That's a welcome assignment for anyone who loves to preach, but an almost overwhelming one, too. How to focus attention on the center, how to capture anew, to be captured by, the heart of the Christian message—that's what we're about. Who is sufficient for that? None of us, surely, to tell it as we ought. But all of us can tell it as God gives us grace to see—his story become ours.

I've pondered how to go about it. We can herald the *facts* of the gospel and what they mean, as Paul did: "For I delivered to you as of first importance what I also received, that Christ died for our sins in accordance with the scriptures, that he was buried, that he was raised on the third day in accordance with the scriptures, and that he appeared" (1 Cor. 15:3–4).

We can celebrate the *grace* behind the gospel, announcing with John that "God so loved the world that he gave his only Son, that whoever believes in him should not perish but have eternal life" (John 3:16).

We can tell of the gospel's *transforming effects,* confessing with the apostles that "the love of Christ controls us, because we are convinced that one has died for all; therefore all have died. And he died for all, that those who live might live no longer for themselves but for him" (2 Cor. 5:14–15). To do any of those would be to express "the meaning of the gospel."

But I want to lift up before you a vignette from Luke's Gospel, a moment on that hill outside Jerusalem called "the place of the skull," a brief interchange between Jesus and the men who died beside him. This is what I call "the gospel made plain."

Here is the central *figure* of the gospel—Jesus, the only begotten of the Father, the Son of Mary, the Word made flesh. Here is the central *event* of the gospel—his crucifixion. For this he came from his glory. From this he rose, exalted to be Lord over all. Here shines forth the central *theme* of the gospel—God's saving mercy toward a guilty, perishing human race.

Here I see the gospel in person, the gospel in action, the gospel meeting us in our final extremity, the gospel in its full pathos and power. Here is hope in the darkest of times. Here is a word for weak, struggling, guilt-ridden human beings who want desperately to live, yet must die. It is good news for everyone, luminous and compelling—the gospel made plain.

Do you remember the call with which Jesus began his ministry? It summarized his message and mission. "The time is fulfilled, and the kingdom of God is at hand; repent, and believe in the gospel" (Mark 1:15). Jesus called for repentance and faith, in response to the saving gospel of the kingdom. In this scene on Golgotha, we see those great realities placarded before us. Here they are, as we say, in "living color."

Repentance

Think first of repentance. Luke uses the term more frequently than any other biblical writer, but never offers a definition of it.

What he gives us is something far better. He shows us through persons with whom Jesus dealt and through parables that Jesus told, how repentance works. Here is the reality itself: repentance in action.

There's the unforgettable younger son who had demanded a share of his father's estate and had gone far away to squander it. There, debauched, impoverished, wretched, and lonely, he came to himself and remembered his father's house. "I will arise and go to my father, and I will say to him, 'Father, I have sinned against heaven and before you; I am no longer worthy to be called your son; treat me as one of your hired servants'" (Luke 15:18–19). So he trudged back, humbled, brokenhearted, yet daring to hope that he would be received. Repentance before our eyes!

Or what of the tax collector in that moving temple scene? He stood afar off. He could not even lift his gaze. Overcome with contrition, he beat his breast and cried, "God, be merciful to me a sinner" (Luke 18:13).

But those are stories Jesus told. There were also real people like that who met him and were forever changed. Look, for example, at the woman who washed Jesus' feet with her tears and wiped them with her hair. That was repentance—deep, self-humbling brokenness of heart. And what an extravagant outpouring of love and gratitude!

Then there was the crucified malefactor, a common criminal. All around Jesus swirled a tempest of hate and reviling. Priests wagged their heads in scorn. Soldiers tossed off their coarse jests. Even the thieves on either side of him jeered bitterly. How foreign to that hellish scene was his word: "Father, forgive them; for they know not what they do."

The crowd was accustomed, on these occasions, to hearing shrieks, threats, and curses. They knew also the murderer's grim vow: "May my death expiate all my sins." How strange to hear a tormented victim cry, "Forgive them!" One of the thieves beside him grew silent. He seemed profoundly affected by what he had just heard. Who wouldn't be?

But the man on the other side of Jesus' cross was unimpressed. Again he challenged the sufferer beside him, "Are you not the Christ? Save yourself and us!" This time an answer came back quickly, not from the center cross but from beyond it. For the first and only time,

65

a voice on Golgotha spoke in Jesus' defense. Who would have expected it from a condemned man? What had happened to this other thief?

Here is repentance made plain. The man's whole outlook was changed. Until this time, like the raging man on the other cross, he had never really faced what he was. Someone has said that the path we are most loath to take is the one that leads to ourselves. This man had never admitted to himself and to others his guilt, his ill-deserving. Now it seemed that he saw in the one beside him the man he should have been, and that broke him down. "We are receiving the due reward of our deeds; but this man has done nothing wrong."

What about us? Have we known repentance like this? We say, "Well, here we're dealing with a criminal, a lawbreaker." Yes, but the first and greatest of the laws of God, of his commands, is that we are to love him with all our heart, with all our soul, with all our strength, with all our mind, and that we are to love our neighbors as ourselves. That standard exposes each of us; we are malefactors all. And when we see the blameless one suffer for the guilty—the mystery of crucified love—when we hear him pray, "Forgive them," we know that he prays for us.

The man who repented heard God's whisper in those moving words, "Father, forgive them." And that's what leads us to true penitence—the sight of our guilt and ugliness against the background of his suffering love.

Faith

Real repentance is never far away from faith. We see this embodied here also—faith made plain. We turn from our sins only when we find a gracious God to turn to. We have no heart to repent until his mercy dawns on our lives. How it dawned on this man! Unbelief was all around him. Most of the onlookers had never trusted Jesus. Those who had, had almost lost hope. Others were jeering, "*If* you are the Christ, *if* you are the king of the Jews . . ."

But for this convict, there were no "ifs." "Jesus, remember me when you come in your kingly power." The man was hardly a theologian. He understood little of the vast meaning of Jesus' death. Yet his simple prayer fairly throbbed with genuine faith. For one thing, he saw and believed that Christ was a king. He could see majesty where others only mocked. He dared to believe what was more astounding: The one dying in weakness beside him would come one day with royal power! More than that, he called on Jesus as his hope beyond the reach of death.

There's a touching, refreshing simplicity about this kind of faith. How it sweeps away a host of nonessentials! How it exposes our cluttered notions about what it is to believe! Can baptism be essential for salvation? Surely it was not for this man. Are good works required for acceptance? This man had few to offer and little time to make amends. What about membership in a religious institution? He wouldn't have had the faintest notion of what that means.

Had he lived longer, had he survived the ordeal of the cross, things would doubtless have been different. Surely then he would have been baptized, would have joined other Christians, would have adorned his faith with good works. But the fact is that he didn't. It's the thing he *did* that is so significant. He hoped in God's mercy. He called on Jesus out of a penitent heart. That is the faith of the gospel, simple and grand.

The question for us is: Does that faith live in our hearts? Have we heard, whispered in our inner ears, what came once to young Pascal: "I thought of thee in my agony"? Have we ever called on Jesus Christ out of a sense of our own sin and need? Have we relied on him entirely for forgiveness, hoped in him for life eternal? Have we seen in him the saving rule of God come to earth and submitted gladly to his lordship? That's what it means to believe.

Salvation

Repentance, faith, salvation. The best news here is in the promise of Jesus: "Truly, I say to you, today you will be with me in Paradise." He gave that penitent seeker more than he asked. The man prayed, "When you come." Jesus promised, "Today." He asked wistfully, "Remember me." But Jesus pledged, "You will be with me."

One thing is luminously clear: death for this man was to be an entrance into the unveiled presence of the Lord. We don't know much about heaven. In fact, we know precious little. But we do know this, and this is enough: Tell believers that one day they will be with Christ forever and that is all the heaven they need. "To depart and be with Christ," as the apostle Paul put it, "is far better" (Phil. 1:23).

From the dawning of the Book of Genesis to the final vision of the Revelation, *God with his people* is the grandest theme of all. Made for God, to dwell in his presence and enjoy his fellowship, we disobeyed and turned to our own way. Forfeiting our true life, we became exiles and wanderers. But God came seeking for us. He called a people to himself, and chose to dwell among them.

But the veil before the inner sanctuary in tabernacle and temple testified that the way into the holiest, the way of approach to God, was not fully opened yet. In the death of Jesus a new and living way has been prepared for us into the very presence of God. The veil of the temple has been torn in two. All the barriers have been broken down. We are reconciled, forgiven children. We look forward to a day when God himself will be with us and we shall be his people and he shall be our God. All the wealth of that hope belonged to a nameless lawbreaker when Jesus said, "Today you will be with me in Paradise."

There's one more thing to notice here about the gospel made plain. Whenever Luke pictures someone who repents, believes the gospel, and experiences salvation in Jesus, he also describes another person whose reaction is quite different. With the prodigal son is the elder brother who cannot rejoice in his father's goodness, cannot welcome his brother home, but remains outside the feast and sulks. Along with the publican in the temple is the Pharisee who advertises his virtues, thankful to be more upright than the rest. He asks nothing, needs nothing, and gets it.

In marked contrast to the weeping woman at Jesus' feet is Simon the Pharisee. He shows no warmth of welcome to Jesus, no enthusiasm of gratitude, and thinks ill of the Master because he was willing to receive attention from such a wretched woman. Finally, there is the thief on the other side of Jesus' cross, the one who hurled out mockery and scorn to his final breath.

Do you see how the two in each case, and supremely these two on Golgotha, stand for all humankind? There is one of the two with whom you and I must surely identify. Sinners all—no difference there. "All we like sheep have gone astray; we have turned every one to his own way; and the LORD has laid on him the iniquity of us all" (Isa. 53:6). Pascal remarked that there are two classes of people in the world: the righteous who believe themselves sinners, and the sinners who believe that they are righteous. Mercy is offered freely to all. It is not our sin that condemns us at the last, but our refusal to acknowledge it. Misdeeds will not doom us, unless we have scorned the mercy that could blot them out. Our hope is simply and only this: to embrace the gospel made plain, to be among the sinners whom Jesus saves. All our life and service, worship and witness, strength and comfort, begin with this: "Jesus, remember me!"

6

Robert E. Coleman

―――⊷◆⊶―――

R obert E. Coleman is director of the School of World Mission and Evangelism and professor of evangelism at Trinity Evangelical Divinity School in Deerfield, Illinois. He also serves as director of the Billy Graham Institute in Wheaton, Illinois, and is dean of the Billy Graham International Schools of Evangelism. He was a United Methodist pastor for six years and taught at Asbury Theological Seminary prior to his appointment at Trinity in 1983. He received his B.D. degree from Asbury, his Th.M. from Princeton Theological Seminary, and his Ph.D. from the University of Iowa.

Coleman is a frequent speaker at colleges, seminaries, and conferences around the world. He is a founding member of the Lausanne Committee for World Evangelism, and president of the Academy for Evangelism in Theological Education. He has written twenty books, including *The Master Plan of Evangelism, The Great Commission Lifestyle,* and *The Spark That Ignites.* Translations of his books have been published in eighty-five languages. English editions alone have a combined circulation of more than 4.5 million copies.

―――⊷◆⊶―――

I pondered a long time when asked what I would say if I only had one sermon to preach. If I knew the nature of the audience, a response would not be quite so difficult. But even then a number of options come to mind.

I selected this sermon because of its wide coverage; it appeals to unbelievers as well as believers. In the case of seekers, the message lifts up the atoning work of Jesus and tells how one can be saved.

For Christians, the emphasis on evangelism and commitment comes to grips with some areas where the church certainly needs to be challenged.

Though focusing on the warfare of Satan, the sermon is cast in a positive light. It stresses how we can overcome the powers of darkness and become more than conquerors. This is a theme, I think, that persons living under pressure constantly need to hear—one that brings assurance and joy to my own soul.

Living in Triumph

━━➤◆◅━━

Now have come the salvation and the power and the kingdom of our God, and the authority of his Christ. For the accuser of our brothers, who accuses them before our God day and night, has been hurled down. They overcame him by the blood of the Lamb and by the word of their testimony; they did not love their lives so much as to shrink from death.

Revelation 12:10–11 NIV

Some of you may remember the gospel song entitled "Victory in Jesus," especially the rousing chorus. The words and music of this song may not reflect every person's worship style, but however expressed, that joyous assurance of victory resounds through the witness of the church universal. Christians live in triumph. We know that whatever comes in this world, however difficult our circumstances, we are more than conquerors through Jesus Christ.

That is why I like to meditate on the throne scenes recorded in "the revelation of Jesus Christ" (Rev. 1:1). Though much of the narrative in this final book of Holy Scripture concerns the judgments that will come on the earth in the last days, intermittently the scene shifts to heaven, and we get a brief glimpse of that worshiping host in the presence of God. They come "from every nation, tribe, people and language," an assembly so vast that it cannot be counted (7:9; cf. 19:1, 6). The Great Commission is fulfilled; in the councils of eternity the celebration has begun. Listening to what the multitude says can help us measure our lives now by that destiny to which the church is moving. One of those loud voices in heaven is recorded in our text.

There are various ways that Revelation 12:10–11 can be placed in the chronology of the endtime. But whatever your view of the millennium and the events surrounding the return of our Lord, the victory announced by the heavenly voice always rings true. That is the reality celebrated by the people of God—in this world and in the world to come. The One in whom we triumph is "the same yesterday and today and forever" (Heb. 13:8).

In this present age, of course, the church faces continual opposition. No hint here of an easy life. We have an adversary who seeks to destroy those who "hold to the testimony of Jesus" (Rev. 12:17). He is "that ancient serpent called the devil, or Satan, who leads the whole world astray" (v. 9). The fury of his attacks will increase in intensity as the end of the world approaches, "because he knows that his time is short" (v. 12). To be unmindful of his designs and the demons at his command would be naive indeed.

The Bible teaches that this embodiment of evil is the instigator of sin and betrayal (Gen. 3:4–5; John 13:2). He tempts and slanders the righteous (Job 1:9–11; Matt. 4:1–11). He inflicts suffering on the innocent (Job 2:7). He sows discord (Matt. 13:38–39); he removes the good seed of the gospel (Matt. 13:19); he blinds the eyes of unbelievers (2 Cor. 4:4); he prowls about like a roaring lion, seeking whom he may devour (1 Peter 5:8); he will try to deceive the very elect (Matt. 16:23; 24:24). Let's face it. As long as we live on planet earth, we are engaged in mortal conflict with satanic principalities, rulers of darkness, and forces of evil in the spirit world (Eph. 6:12).

But we need have no fear. Did you not hear the voice from heaven? Satan is a defeated foe. "Now have come the salvation and the power and the kingdom of our God, and the authority of his Christ. For the accuser of our brothers . . . has been hurled down." Christ has brought deliverance; his reign has been established.

The devil now has no way to condemn the "brothers." The blameless One, whom Satan could never lay a charge against, has taken away the guilt of humankind, and thereby removed any grounds for an accusation to be made. Moreover, the accuser no longer can even enter the courtroom to bring a charge against the redeemed, for he has been disbarred from practice—cast out from the presence of the Judge.

Evangelist Amanda Smith used to tell about a confrontation with the devil in one of her journeys, when she was reminded of all her past sins. "Now what do you say?" the accuser sneered. Without even bothering to look around, Amanda said, "Drive on, Gabriel; drive on!"

74

That is the response of the redeemed to the accusations of the devil. We do not have to listen to his recriminations, for "there is now no condemnation for those who are in Christ Jesus" (Rom. 8:1). We are set free.

Our Victorious Gospel

How the church experiences Christ's defeat of Satan is indicated in our text, as the voice from heaven goes on to say: "They overcame him by the blood of the Lamb and by the word of their testimony; they did not love their lives so much as to shrink from death."

That first phrase—the blood of the Lamb—stresses the essential message of the victorious gospel. It is literally true as we sometimes sing, "Our hope is built on nothing less than Jesus' blood and righteousness."

Blood—the substance of life that flows through our veins, continually nourishing and cleansing our bodies and when poured out becomes a symbol of death—is a term used 460 times in Scripture. If related concepts implying the shedding of blood are considered, such as sacrifice, altar, atonement, covenant, priesthood, and many others, I doubt if there is a page in the Bible that does not have some allusion to the blood. Like a scarlet thread, it weaves the whole of God's written Word into one harmonious witness to the cross on which the Prince of Glory died.

The text underscores this fact by joining the blood with the figure of the Lamb. For thousands of years the slain Lamb had been foreshadowed in Jewish sacrifices whereby an innocent and unblemished victim was offered to God in the place of the person who presented it. When in true repentance and faith the worshiper identified with the shed blood, as if it were in fact his or her own, the offering expressed more eloquently than words a heart in full conformity to the will of God. Equally precious, the blood on the altar displayed God's reception of the sacrificer, and was therefore a graphic witness of divine grace. Though his holy nature demanded death for sin, the blood proclaimed that God so loved the world that he was willing to bear the judgment of his own law by taking its consequences on himself.

The Old Testament sacrifices, of course, were but a promise of the perfect One to come. They all pointed to the day when God in the person of the Son would die for his beloved. Recall that it was during the Passover feast, at the very time when paschal lambs were being slain in the temple, that Jesus was led outside the city gate and nailed to the cross. There for hours he hung in anguish, his blood draining from his pierced hands and feet. As his breathing grew harder, his body convulsing in pain, he at last lifted his voice, and cried, "It is finished!" (John 19:30). Everything typified for thousands of years in the Jewish blood sacrifices had now fulfilled their purpose. Atonement was at last complete. The work was finished. Once and for all, Jesus—in our stead—offered his precious blood to God, "a lamb without blemish or defect" (1 Peter 1:19; cf. 3:18).

Through the voluntary giving of himself to death, Jesus has rendered powerless "him who holds the power of death—that is, the devil" (Heb. 2:14; cf. 1 John 3:8). And "having disarmed the powers and authorities" of evil, "he made a public spectacle of them, triumphing over them by the cross" (Col. 2:15). The shackles of sin have been broken; the grave has lost its prey.

The late Robert G. Lee liked to tell of his trip to the Holy Land, when the guide of the touring party pointed in the distance and said, "There is Calvary." Seeing the sacred place for the first time, such a sensation came over Lee that he began walking faster, and soon was running up the hill. When the others caught up with him, they found him standing on the Mount, his head bowed, still panting for breath. Breaking the throbbing silence, the guide asked, "Sir, have you been here before?" There was a long pause. Then in a whispered tone, the preacher replied, "Yes, I was here nearly two thousand years ago."

All of us were there nearly two thousand years ago! When Jesus died, he took our place. We were there, sold unto sin, and the wages of sin is death. Yet in God's amazing grace, Jesus came and offered himself for us. He paid it all, that everyone who trusts in him "shall not perish but have eternal life" (John 3:16).

Herein is the essence of the gospel. It is the blood—the all-conquering cross of Jesus Christ. Behold the Lamb of God! He has taken away the sin of the world! That is why we can celebrate with the hosts in heaven. We overcome by the blood of the Lamb.

Our Victorious Method

To this knowledge of Christ's triumph the voice from heaven adds a second reason for the victory of the church: "the word of their testimony."

Believing the gospel commits one to proclaim it. Built into the saving message is the principle of reproduction. The blood that brought us to God cries out for all to come. Jesus gave his life for the world, and he bids us go and tell everyone who has not heard. To keep this good news to ourselves would be, in effect, to repudiate its validity for others.

All who believe, therefore, are appointed to pass the word along. We do not have to be trained theologians or gifted preachers. We simply declare what we have seen and heard, not as a credal statement, but as a personal, living experience. In this witness, every Christian becomes a minister of the gospel.

An Asbury College student who one day was going to Cincinnati, Ohio, on an interstate bus typified this spirit beautifully. Having some time to relax, she decided to read her Bible. After a while the man seated next to her commented that he had never before seen anyone read the Scriptures in this kind of setting. The remark gave the young co-ed a natural opportunity to share her testimony. (There is a lesson in this for us all. Let our manner of life create a mystery so that others will want to know why we are different.)

When the young woman had finished, the man was so impressed that he wanted his friend to hear what she had to say. So they switched seats and the girl proceeded to tell her story again. Before long, the elderly gentleman in front turned around and asked her to speak louder for he was having difficulty getting every word. By this time the woman across the aisle was interested. So the co-ed asked if they would like her to speak so that everyone could hear. They nodded.

She got up, stood behind the driver's seat, and gave her testimony to all the passengers. About that time the bus pulled into the Cincinnati terminal. But before opening the door, the driver turned to the girl and asked, "Young woman, do you have anything more to say?" She responded, "All I want to say is, 'Hallelujah!'"

Have you noticed that when the shine is on your face and the love is in your heart, this tired, aching world will listen when you declare

77

the praise of a mighty Savior? Not that you will do it like that college student, of course. Our temperaments and personalities are all different, and the way we share our testimony reflects that uniqueness. But when was the last time that someone heard you, in your own way, say a good word for Jesus?

The relationship between the triumph of the church and your testimony may be seen in Peter's confession at Caesarea Philippi, when he affirmed that Jesus was the Christ, the Son of the living God. This pleased the Lord, though he reminded Peter that his insight was a divine revelation, not a human deduction. Then he declared, "on this rock I will build my church, and the gates of Hades will not overcome it" (Matt. 16:18).

Some think that the rock refers to Christ; others relate it to Peter as the spokesman of the church, or to the orthodoxy of his statement. Be that as it may, the fact remains that Peter proclaimed his experience of the living Christ. Only after he bore his testimony did Jesus mention the conquest of hell.

Evangelism is the heartbeat of the church's life. If Christ is not made known, how can the church come into existence? It is by hearing the Word that persons believe. Without the faithful witness of God's people, the church would soon become extinct.

But we can be assured that whenever the Son of God is lifted up by his followers, men and women will be drawn to the Father. As they in turn tell others, the victorious gospel is destined to spread from person to person, until everyone has heard. Through this simple process of multiplication nothing in this world can keep the church from storming the gates of hell. We overcome by the word of our testimony.

Our Victorious Commitment

What makes the testimony so undefeatable is the willingness of the witness to die for it, which the voice mentions as the final reason for the victory of the church: "They did not love their lives so much as to shrink from death." The clause may be translated, "not by loving their own lives, they were willing to die." We are not to forget the condition for powerfully communicating the gospel of the slain Lamb.

Significantly, in the New Testament the word "witness" translates the Greek word "martyr." That is exactly what we become in following Christ. "If anyone would come after me," Jesus said, "he must deny himself and take up his cross and follow me" (Matt. 16:24). It is a call to complete obedience—to live in abandonment to the will of God.

We hear a lot today about self-fulfillment, but very little about self-denial. Even in the church we seem more preoccupied with protecting our own rights than renouncing them for Christ's sake. His call to martyrdom, to be his "witnesses" (Acts 1:8), has not been quite forgotten, but it has been relegated mostly to the verbalizing of beautiful hymns and emotionally charged choruses. Little wonder that so few church members have a spring in their step.

I cannot forget an inscription I saw on a church door not long ago. It read: "Enter his gates with thanksgiving and his courts with praise" (Ps. 100:4). Reflecting on these words from the hundredth psalm, I realized that immediately before that verse, the psalm states, "we are his people, the sheep of his pasture" (v. 3).

Suddenly it occurred to me that there was only one reason why sheep would be taken out of the pasture and led through the gates of Jerusalem to appear in the courts of the holy temple. They came to be offered as sacrifices on the altar. Yet they were to come with gladness, with rejoicing, with praise.

God is talking about us. We are his sheep. We must understand that in embracing Christ we must die with him. "Therefore," Paul wrote, "I urge you, brothers, in view of God's mercy, to offer your bodies as living sacrifices, holy and pleasing to God—this is your spiritual act of worship" (Rom. 12:1).

That which is laid upon the altar becomes God's possession. Inherent in this separation is sanctification. A saint is one set apart for God, one owned by him.

Such sainthood appears from the beginning of the Christian life. We should always be fully committed to Christ. The cross allows no compromise. Of course, as we grow in grace and learn more about our Lord, our experience of consecration will enlarge. There is never a foreclosure on our progress.

That which the Spirit of God shows us to be contrary to the Word of God must be confessed and nailed to the cross. This includes that pestering disposition of selfishness—sometimes called carnality—which is usually not recognized until it comes into conflict with the life of grace.

The principle of obedience applies all the way through the Christian life. Those who follow Christ "have crucified the sinful nature with its passions and desires" (Gal. 5:24). We count ourselves "dead to sin but alive to God" (Rom. 6:11). "If we live, we live to the Lord; and if we die, we die to the Lord. So, whether we live or die, we belong to the Lord" (Rom. 14:8).

That is the kind of dedication that has always confounded this world—that joyous commitment to go with Jesus whatever the cost. It is an inward experience of the cross. Our understanding of its meaning deepens as we follow our Lord, but at any time we should be willing to respond to all that we do know of his will. And in this daily abiding in him we know the triumph of his resurrection. When the battle is won on the inside, we can face confidently the battle raging in the world around us. Regardless of the circumstances, nothing "will be able to separate us from the love of God that is in Christ Jesus our Lord" (Rom. 8:39). We overcome because we, too, do not "love [our] lives so much as to shrink from death."

In the third century Cyprian, bishop of Carthage, wrote a letter to a friend in which he set forth a timeless observation:

> If I could ascend some high mountain and look out over this wide land, you know very well what I would see. Robbers on the high roads, pirates on the seas, in the amphi-theaters men murdered to please applauding crowds, selfishness and cruelty, misery and despair under all roofs.
>
> It is a bad world—an incredibly bad world. But in the midst of it, I have found a quiet and a holy people who have learned a great secret. They are the despised and the persecuted, but they care not. They have overcome the world. These people are called Christians, and I am one of them.[1]

Such are Christian witnesses in every age. Though buffeted by many foes, we care not, for we have overcome the powers and principalities of this world.

Though what we will be is not yet fully revealed, we know that when our Lord comes in his glory, "we shall be like him, for we shall see him as he is" (1 John 3:2). In that day every knee shall bow before him, and every tongue confess to the glory of God the Father that "Jesus Christ is Lord" (Phil. 2:11).

This is more than a hope. It is the unshakable assurance that "now have come the salvation and the power and the kingdom of our God, and the authority of his Christ" (Rev. 12:10). Jesus has conquered the enemy of our souls. No longer do we have to endure the insults of Satan. We do not even have to listen to his recriminations.

Do you hear that mighty shout resounding from the throne of heaven? It echoes across the earth and to the farthest star. "The Lord God Almighty reigns! He has overcome every foe, and with him, we, too, can live in triumph by the blood of the Lamb, by the word of our testimony, and because we love Christ even unto death."

7

Sinclair B. Ferguson

————◆————

A graduate of the University of Aberdeen with the M.A., B.D., and Ph.D. degrees, Sinclair B. Ferguson was ordained in the Church of Scotland (Presbyterian). He served a pastorate in the Shetland Islands, and was an associate at historic St. George's-Tron Church in Glasgow. He joined the faculty of Westminster Theological Seminary, Philadelphia, Pennsylvania, as professor of systematic theology in 1982. Since 1976 he has also been associate editor of the *Banner of Truth* journal.

A prolific author, Ferguson has written *A Heart for God, John Owen on the Christian Life, Kingdom Life in a Fallen World, Know Your Christian Life,* and a *Commentary on the Book of Daniel* in the Communicator's Commentary series; he also edited the *New Dictionary of Theology, Pulpit and People,* and *The Collected Writings of William Still.*

————◆————

All preachers must preach one final sermon. Indeed, in theory at least, we all recognize that we should preach our next sermon as though it were our last. It may be; and it is statistically even more likely that it will be the final sermon for one of our hearers. In this sense all of our preaching should express the spirit of Richard Baxter's *bon mot* that we should preach "as never sure to preach again, and as a dying man to dying men." But actually *knowing* that this would be one's last sermon is a different matter! My immediate reaction to such a prospect is to ask if there are some guiding principles.

For myself, the following principles would be important to have in mind in preparing a "last sermon":

1. It should point the hearers specifically to Christ, express his office as Savior, and set forth his grace and graciousness.
2. It should be rooted in the exposition of Scripture.
3. It should seek to provide nourishment for all one's hearers, including oneself (perhaps oneself most of all).
4. A final, perhaps idiosyncratic consideration would be that if I *knew* this to be my final sermon, it would be of some importance to me that the message should be relatively simple and easy to preach, and what the old divines used to call "sweet" and "Christful." As preachers know, that is not always the case with our preaching!

In view of these considerations, the sermon that follows is an exposition of Psalm 23. The passage readily lends itself to each of the principles outlined above.

I Shall Not Want

The LORD is my shepherd, I shall not be in want.
  He makes me lie down in green pastures,
he leads me beside quiet waters,
  he restores my soul.
He guides me in paths of righteousness
  for his name's sake.
Even though I walk
  through the valley of the shadow of death,
I will fear no evil,
  for you are with me;
your rod and your staff,
  they comfort me.
You prepare a table before me
  in the presence of my enemies.
You anoint my head with oil;
  my cup overflows.
Surely goodness and love will follow me
  all the days of my life,
and I will dwell in the house of the LORD
  forever.

Psalm 23 NIV

It has taken me a long time to appreciate and love this great psalm of King David.

No doubt that has been partly due to my own spiritual insensitivity. But it is also due, I suspect, to being brought up on what I now think of as "the child's storybook version" of Psalm 23.

I can still see the cover of the copy I was given as a child. David is sitting on a rock, his shepherd's crook neatly in place beside him. He looks about thirteen. His hair is curly and his cheeks are ruddy from his outdoor life; his eyes are bright and sparkling. Nearby—

"in green pastures"—graze some pure white sheep. Beyond runs a river of sparkling, clean water; above, the sky is clear blue, with only wisps of clouds floating in it to add to the beauty of the scene. This is an ideal world. All is well. David lacks nothing.

But almost everything about this "child's storybook version" is a misunderstanding of the psalm. For one thing, the world in which it was written was far from ideal. In fact it was full of dark places, "the valley of deepest darkness" (as v. 4 would be more literally translated), and sinister figures (the "enemies" of v. 5). This is a world of harsh and painful reality. Not only so, but David himself is no wide-eyed youngster, naïve and innocent of this world's darker side. He has lived long enough to know failure and fear, to make enemies, and to need comfort in the valley of the shadow of death.

There is, however, an even more basic misunderstanding about this psalm. It is the assumption that one day, as he watched his sheep, the idea dawned on David that God is like a shepherd, and so he began to think about the ways in which this is true.

But that is to overlook what lies behind David's confession. For King David was not the first person in the Bible to say, "The Lord is my shepherd." These words are found first of all on the lips of his ancestor Jacob. Jacob—the twister who by God's grace became a prince.

Do you remember that, at the end of Jacob's life, Joseph came with his sons Manasseh and Ephraim for the old man's blessing? The aged patriarch said:

> May the God before whom my fathers
>   Abraham and Isaac walked,
> *the God who has been my shepherd*
>   *all my life to this day,*
> the Angel who has delivered me from all harm
>   —may he bless these boys.
>
> Genesis 48:15–16, emphasis added

Jacob is saying that the God of the covenant, the God of Abraham and Isaac, had also become his God. The divine Shepherd had pursued him as a lost sheep and rescued him, had led, disciplined, and guided him throughout his life. It was not on shepherding so much as on the narrative of Scripture that David was meditating when he exclaimed, "The Lord is my shepherd!"

Later, at the burning bush, Moses would learn that the same covenant-keeping God of Abraham, Isaac, and Jacob, would be his God (Exod. 6:1–10). As the Shepherd of Israel, he would lead his chosen people like a flock out of Egypt and into the promised land (Ps. 77:20; cf. Ps. 80:1). Later still, Ezekiel would make use of this same idea of the Lord as a shepherd who would gather and lead his people (Ezek. 34:11–16).

Centuries later, this great revelation of God's grace would take on new meaning when Jesus spoke of his mission as that of a shepherd come to seek lost sheep:

> Suppose one of you has a hundred sheep and loses one of them. Does he not leave the ninety-nine in the open country and go after the lost sheep until he finds it? And when he finds it, he joyfully puts it on his shoulders and goes home. Then he calls his friends and neighbors together and says, "Rejoice with me; I have found my lost sheep."
>
> Luke 15:4–6

Eventually Jesus would remove all doubt about the identity of the divine shepherd described in the Old Testament when he declared: "I am the good shepherd" (John 10:11).

David's confession, therefore, is one of the links in a long chain of revelation that will lead eventually to our Savior, Jesus Christ. The psalmist is not drawing lessons from shepherding so much as he is applying a great text of Scripture to his own life. He is saying: "I have proved the truth of what Jacob confessed; this is how I have discovered the power of Scripture for myself." He had tasted the grace that would be fully and finally revealed in the Good Shepherd, Jesus Christ.

How did David discover this? How can we, now that the Good Shepherd has appeared? Let me underline only some of the great affirmations David makes. What does it mean to have Christ as your shepherd?

If the Lord Is My Shepherd, He Will Supply All My Needs

The LORD is my shepherd, I shall not be in want.

verse 1

This kind of confidence evokes the admiration and even the envy of others, doesn't it? It is the reason many people read this psalm as wishful thinkers. Sometimes they will even say to Christians, "If only I had your faith." But David's emphasis is not on his own faith. "It is not so much my 'faith' that you need," he would surely say, "but my Lord." My faith only draws on his gracious resources. It is because he is all-sufficient that I know my needs will be met.

Do you know the old mnemonic for faith that Christians used to be taught? *F*-orsaking *A*-ll, *I* *T*-ake *H*-im. Faith means having Christ. It is but the eye that sees Christ as the Light of the World; the mouth that feeds on Christ as the Bread of Life. It contributes nothing to him, but takes everything from him. Thus Christ fills us with all we need. This is God's promise: "My God will meet all your needs according to his glorious riches in Christ Jesus" (Phil. 4:19); "My grace is sufficient for you" (2 Cor. 12:9); "in all things God works for the good of those who love him" (Rom. 8:28). Feast your soul on these promises! But it is one thing to know these words, another to be so deeply persuaded of their truth that we share David's confidence in the Lord. Martin Luther said that true religion consists in being able to use personal pronouns; "The Lord is *my* shepherd, *I* shall not be in want. He makes *me* lie down . . . he restores *me* . . . he leads *me*."

It is not a coincidence that even in this statement David seems to be applying Scripture to himself. He is echoing Moses' words in Deuteronomy 2:7: "These forty years the LORD your God has been with you, and *you have not lacked* anything." David uses exactly the same verb when he says "I shall not be in want." As in many other psalms, he had learned to think things out: if the Lord can be the shepherd of a multitude in the desert, and supply all their needs, surely he can do the same for me.

What is the reason for David's tremendous assurance? It is rooted in the character of the shepherd. There are two things about him with which David was familiar. Jesus underlines both of them when he identifies himself as "the Good Shepherd."

The Good Shepherd knows his sheep (John 10:14). I had a friend in my native country of Scotland who had been a shepherd before he was called into the Christian ministry. Here is what he wrote about a shepherd's knowledge of his sheep:

The mark of a good shepherd is that he knows his sheep. If he does not know his sheep, he does not last long as a shepherd. He has to know his sheep as individuals. . . . I have known men who knew their sheep so well that they could recognize them anywhere. One man I remember had sold a hundred lambs in Oban and, travelling in a train three weeks later, he passed a big flat plain called "the Carse of Stirling," where lambs are fattened and then sold (often at a fat profit). When he got back home, this fellow said to me, "You know, Douglas, I saw my lambs." "Where did you see your lambs?" I asked. "In among about three thousand other ones in a field at Stirling," he said. . . . I didn't even think of saying to him, "How did you know they were your lambs?" . . . The man would have looked at me and said, "Are you daft?" He knew his lambs.[1]

Do you see what David is saying about his Lord? This shepherd knows his sheep better than they know themselves! Jesus "knew all men. . . . he knew what was in a man," says John (John 2:24–25). He knows your past; he knows your heart, desires, motives, ambitions, disappointments, sins—everything. He knows you better than you know yourself. He knows your future, too, just as well as he knows your past! Nothing about you is hidden from him. Stop frequently and think hard about that. He knows exactly what you need and will provide it.

The Good Shepherd also cares for his sheep. To know that Christ has unrestricted, intimate knowledge of us and our needs would be terrifying if we did not also know that his care for us is as great as his love for us. And it is! He is willing to lay down his life for us (John 10:15).

But the Lord's care is not always obvious to us. David's friend, Asaph, the director of music, knew that. It seemed to trouble him often. Then he began to understand a little of the mystery of God's ways, as he points out in Psalm 77. Describing how God led his people "like a flock by the hand of Moses and Aaron," he comments: "Your path led through the sea, your way through the mighty waters, though your footprints were not seen" (vv. 19–20). Here is a fine description of God's providence in our lives: he is present in the storm, but invisibly. Footprints are not visible in the sea! So discovered William Cowper, that Asaph of eighteenth-century England:

God moves in a mysterious way
His wonders to perform;
He plants his footsteps in the sea,
And rides upon the storm.

Ye fearful saints, fresh courage take;
The clouds ye so much dread
Are big with mercy, and shall break
In blessings on your head.

Judge not the Lord by feeble sense,
But trust him for his grace;
Behind a frowning providence
He hides a smiling face.

We have to learn to trust God even when we do not fully understand his ways. Then we will discover how much he really cares.

Do you remember how the disciples learned this when they made their eventful crossing of the Sea of Galilee? They say that fishermen can smell a storm brewing. I have often wondered whether a man like Simon Peter was not tempted to dig his heels into the shore and tell Jesus pointedly, "Jesus, what do *you* know about Galilee? There's a storm coming; it would be foolhardy to try to cross in the next few hours. You are just a carpenter from Nazareth; we are seafaring men. Listen to me! I know best!"

But Christ knew best, didn't he? He always does.

How impoverished Peter's knowledge of his Savior would have been if Jesus had not led them into the storm. He would never have seen his Master's glory displayed in his power over the winds and the waves. He would have missed discovering that Jesus knew better; that he knew what the disciples needed if they were to grow strong in faith. It is the same with us. Nothing has changed.

Have you begun to grasp this? Perhaps few of us would ever say it openly, but we have spoken the disciples' complaint privately: "Lord, don't you care if we drown?" (Mark 4:38). Then he reveals himself to us, even to our weak faith, to assure us that he knows what we need, that he cares. In the end nothing else matters. Knowing and trusting the Lord in this way is life-transforming. It means that in every situation, no matter how painful, we rest in the assurance that he knows what is best for us and is working everything together for our good. His purposes are full of love. We say, "He means this for my good."

That was how David had learned to live—in trust. Is that how you live? He can be trusted implicitly. Trust him. He knows what is best for you, and he cares.

If the Lord Is My Shepherd, He Will Restore Me When I Fall

I once had the opportunity to visit a Rembrandt exhibition. I remember one small self-portrait in particular. Such remarkable light seemed to shine out of it that I wondered if some kind of artificial illumination was being used. Somewhat clandestinely I examined the frame and the wall on which it was hung. I even glanced behind the painting to find the origin of this extraordinary light! I should have known better, shouldn't I? The light came from *within* Rembrandt's painting itself. That is one of the things we admire about his work. Part of his artistic genius was that he was able to display the quality of light by the way he employed shadows and darkness.

The same is true of Psalm 23. Its power to help us lies, partly, in the way in which it uses darkness to highlight the grace and goodness of God.

In fact, the psalm is full of shadows. David has felt the engulfing darkness of the valley of the shadow of death (v. 4) and the menacing shadows of his enemies (v. 5). In verse 3, however, he mentions a shadow on his life that seems to have been deeper and darker than these. He is very guarded in what he says about it. We know of it only because he was delivered from it.

All David is prepared to say in public about this is: "He restores my soul." But the verb he uses is significant. It is one of the most important and frequently used verbs in the Old Testament. It means to turn back, or to return. It is the great verb for repentance. Here it means to restore what was lost, to restore to an earlier condition.

David speaks to us as a man with a past. Although he is a believer, that past has continued to haunt him. The memories of his disappointments continue to pursue him; the recollection of pain and loss is still there.

Even more obviously in David's case is the haunting memory of his sin and the paralysis of guilt it produced. In Psalm 25:7 he writes of this in a heart-rending cry to God: "Remember not the sins of my youth and my rebellious ways." As Samuel Rutherford would later write, "The old ashes of the sins of my youth are a new fire of sorrow to me."[2] From nowhere, it would seem, memories of his sin and shame would invade his mind, stunning him, paralyzing his spirit, and, worse, exposing him to the assaults of Satan. ("How can someone with your past have the arrogance to think he is a true believer?" "What would people say if they really knew the truth about you?" "How can you sing praises, or preach, or pray, when *that* is in your biography?") Have you heard that voice?

But David had discovered this: there is more grace in God's heart than there is sin in our past. He abounds in mercy. There is forgiveness to cover all of our sins against all of God's commandments!

Have you taken that in? Or do you still harbor a suspicion that at best the Lord forgives only grudgingly? I have become more and more convinced that such mistrust of God's grace lies deeply embedded still in the hearts of many of God's true children. Look again at Jesus' description of himself as the shepherd returning home with his lost sheep, now restored: "When he finds it, he *joyfully puts it on his shoulders. . . . he calls his friends and neighbors together and says, 'Rejoice with me'*" (Luke 15:5–6, emphasis added). Or listen to Zephaniah 3:17:

> The LORD your God is with you,
> he is mighty to save.
> *He will take great delight in you,*
> he will quiet you with his love,
> *he will rejoice over you with singing* (emphasis added).

This is the shepherd whom David had discovered.

I think I can guess what you may be thinking. David needed to. He was guilty of shameful sin, including adultery and premeditated murder. But the seeds of these and other sins are in your heart, too! Surely on occasions you have caught a glimpse of what would be possible for you to do, left unhindered by providential restraints on your life. "You are the man!" for you, too, have sinned (2 Sam. 12:7). The dark shadows of guilt haunt you, too. The issue is not whether or not you need restoration. You do. The question is this: Do you know that there is more forgiveness available for you in Christ than the burden of guilt that presses down on your conscience and sometimes seems to crush you to death?

Can you, too, sing, "O Jesus, full of truth and grace, More full of grace than I of sin," or have you allowed past guilt to silence the joy of his pardon? If you have fallen, know this: he can restore your soul. And he wants to.

How wise of David to hint that such restoration is neither easy nor painless. He tells us that the Lord's purpose is to lead us in the "paths of righteousness," to teach us to live "for his name's sake" (Ps. 23:3). He has set his heart on making us faithful, obedient, and holy. His love is not cheap. It is all-consuming, allowing no rivals. He wants to embrace you and make you his own property so that "for his name's sake" will be written over all you are and do.

The Good Shepherd's grace is free, but he is not tame or domesticated. He is also the Lion of the tribe of Judah (Rev. 5:5). Isn't that marvelous? Christ is a lion. He destroys sin in order to restore and to build new lives—nothing less. All the more reason for gasping with amazed gratitude, "He restores my soul!"

If the Lord Is My Shepherd, He Will Surprise Me with His Grace

Clearly this psalm shows us that the Lord will provide all of our needs and will restore us when we fall. But in what sense does it teach us that he will "surprise us with his grace"? As we read on into verse 5 of the psalm we notice how David had begun to learn that in our relationship with the Lord, we must be prepared for the unexpected.

Many commentators on Psalm 23, understandably, think that two sets of imagery are used in it. They argue that in verses 1–4 David draws on the world of the shepherd and his sheep; whereas, in verses 5–6 he employs the picture of the host and his guests.

There is an obvious reason for thinking that a change of scene takes place. No ordinary shepherd would lead his sheep into the presence of their enemies. That, however, is perhaps the point. This is no ordinary shepherd. What to us may seem to be incongruous, to him may be the right path to bring us to the destiny he has appointed for us. Think again of those disciples caught in the storm on the Sea of Galilee. Why were they there in the first place? Because they had obeyed Jesus!

Mark's Gospel describes what happened in a telling sentence: "they took him [Jesus] along, *just as he was*" (4:36). Taking Jesus just as he is leads us into all kinds of unpredictable situations beyond our control.

How superficial our understanding of the Lord would be if we thought that he always does things in the easiest and most comfortable fashion for us. Would that produce strong, well-tested, and enduring faith? How foolish we are when we imagine that the way of faith and obedience cuts out all difficulties. On the contrary, the disciples were in the storm precisely because of their obedience. Jesus now intended to expose their "little faith" (Matt. 8:26), but in such a way that they would see his glory in the midst of the storm and be strengthened. In the presence of these enemies in the natural order, Christ displayed his all-sufficiency.

If Jesus had not led these men into the storm, they never would have seen his glory. That is the surprise. He takes us where we would not naturally go and shows himself to us in ways we would never expect. He is full of surprises!

Can you see this Good Shepherd lead his flock into enemy-occupied territory? Do you see the sheep tremble? Their hearts fill with fear and their minds flood with questions as he opens the picnic hamper and spreads before them food and drink. See them glance anxiously at him as they hear the wolves baying and hostile beasts coming so near to them that their shadow almost touches the cloth on which the food is laid. Why has the shepherd brought us here? To show us that he has the power to preserve us, to provide for us, even to give us joy in the most menacing of circumstances.

Have you experienced Christ that way yet? Do you know what it is for the situation you most dread actually to happen? To lift the telephone and hear the news you feared, or open the letter that brings a life-shattering message?

Many of us already know what that is like. It may happen to us again. But here is something the Lord's people discover: He shows himself to us in new ways in situations so dark that our only light is that which shines from his face. But because the Lord makes his face shine on us, we have peace (Num. 6:25–26). He anoints my head with oil; my cup overflows (Ps. 23:5). "He has taken me to the banquet hall, and his banner over me is love" (Song of Sol. 2:4).

It is as though Christ reserves the best of his blessings for the darkest hours. He gives us experiences of his power, a sense of his nearness, and a consciousness of his love that surpasses our ability to describe and is almost too real and intimate for us to speak of to others.

The saints in every generation have known this. Christ surprises us with his grace. He knows he has the power to work everything together for the good of those who love him, and he does. Trust him, won't you?

If the Lord Is My Shepherd, He Will Be with Me Now and Always

I still vividly remember a "call-in" broadcast on a Christian radio station to which I listened on a car journey some years ago. One of the callers was in great need because of the terminal illness of her husband. The evangelist told her what she needed: a miracle of healing that would prolong her husband's life. That was all he had to say.

Everything within me wanted to call out into the airwaves, "No! My dear woman, you need something more than that!" A "miracle of healing" would prolong her husband's life—until the next crisis. Her greatest need was for something that would take her through every crisis, even through the "valley of the shadow of death." It was not the "miracle" Christ could do that she most needed; it was Christ himself.

David grasped that. "You are with me," he said. "I will fear no evil" (Ps. 23:4). The Lord had been with him in the past. More than that, he would be with the Lord in the future. "I will dwell in the house of the LORD forever" (v. 6). But there is a third dimension to

95

the Lord's presence. He would be with David at every point and stage between the past and the future. So David joyfully affirms, "Surely [your] goodness and love will follow me all the days of my life" (v. 6).

There is something unavoidably attractive about the suggestion that David here continues the shepherding metaphor, for the Hebrew verb "follow" has the sense of "pursue." It is almost as though David was saying that the heavenly Shepherd has sheepdogs, trained to work on behalf of his sheep to bring them safely into the fold. Their names are "Goodness" and "Mercy"! "Other men pursue good, and it flies from them; they can never overtake it," wrote the Puritan pastor John Flavel, "but goodness and mercy follow the people of God and they cannot avoid or escape it."[3] Our Good Shepherd has promised he will work all things together for our good!

As Allen Gardiner, a nineteenth-century missionary to Patagonia, lay dying, he took refuge under an upturned boat. There he managed to pen a few closing entries in his journal. He wrote: "I am lying under an upturned boat and out of reach of the sea. I am dying, but I am in peace; my chief discomfort arises from a strong feeling of thirst." A later entry in a weaker hand reads as follows: "Last night it rained heavily and by thrusting the corner of the sail under the greenwale, and getting it drenched, I have been able to allay the almost intolerable pangs of thirst." Then comes this final entry: "I am overwhelmed with a sense of the goodness of God."[4] "Surely goodness and love will follow me all the days of my life, and I will dwell in the house of the Lord forever!"

How may we know such assurance? The Good Shepherd has given his life on the cross as a sacrifice for his sheep (John 10:15). In him the ancient prophecy has been fulfilled in which God had said, "Strike the shepherd . . ." (Zech. 13:7; cf. Mark 14:27).

No one saw this more clearly or expressed it more eloquently than the prophet Isaiah. He saw that the shepherd would bear God's judgment against the sins of the sheep. He wrote:

> Surely he took up our infirmities
>   and carried our sorrows,
> yet we considered him stricken by God,
>   smitten by him, and afflicted.

96

> But he was pierced for our transgressions,
>> he was crushed for our iniquities;
> the punishment that brought us peace was upon him,
>> and by his wounds we are healed.
>> We all, like sheep, have gone astray,
>>> each of us has turned to his own way;
>> and the LORD has laid on him
>>> the iniquity of us all.
>
> Isaiah 53:4–6

This is why we trust and love, obey and follow our Shepherd.

Throughout my Christian life I have returned again and again to the great argument Paul uses to prove that God is for us and nothing can therefore ultimately be against us. This is how he puts it in Romans 8:32: "He who did not spare his own Son, but gave him up for us all—how will he not also, along with him, graciously give us all things?" He works "all things" together for our good. This is the promise of one who did not hold back his Son in order to save us. He will stop at nothing in order to bless us.

And all this we know if the Lord is our shepherd.

He was certainly David's.

By his grace, I know he is mine.

But is he yours?

Are you able to say, in faith and joy, "The Lord is *my* shepherd"?

Say it to him, now: "Lord, you are my shepherd!"

8

Joel C. Gregory

———✦———

Joel C. Gregory has served eight Southern Baptist pastorates in Texas, most recently at the huge First Baptist Church of Dallas. He has also been an assistant professor of preaching at Southwestern Baptist Theological Seminary, Fort Worth. A preacher of international repute, he is a frequent speaker at conferences, conventions, college commencements, seminaries, and missions at home and abroad. In 1990 he delivered a plenary address at the Baptist World Alliance meeting in Seoul, Korea. He was appointed permanent "Baptist Hour" radio preacher, and is also heard on the National Baptist Hour television broadcast. He earned the M.Div. degree at Southwestern Baptist Theological Seminary, and the Ph.D. at Baylor University.

Gregory has published articles in many periodicals and journals. His books include *James: Faith Works!*, *Growing Pains of the Soul*, and *Homesick for God*. He is co-editor of *Southern Baptist Preaching Yesterday* and *Southern Baptist Preaching Today*, and a contributor to *A Passion for Preaching*, edited by Stephen Olford. He has produced video studies of New Testament books and topics and one entitled *Contemporary Biblical Preaching*.

———✦———

Traveling across the nation, I have discovered that American Christians typically suffer from one of two theological extremes. Many lack balance in their understanding of the critical doctrines of justification and sanctification. Accordingly, they spend their days of service to the kingdom hopelessly hindered by an unhealthy sense of inadequacy or a repugnant attitude of superiority. An overemphasis on the insufficiency of people to save themselves often leaves evangelicals with a morbid feeling that they are of no more use to God than a mere worm. On the other hand, an inflated view of our own importance in the eternal purpose and plan of God usually produces an overbearing spirit that makes a mockery of the example of the Savior.

The proper balance needed for an effective Christian walk is to be discovered in the apostle Paul's discussion of the "treasure in earthen vessels" in 2 Corinthians 4:7. I would take this text for my "last sermon," because it proclaims the value of the treasure given to us, while countering the tendency to overvalue ourselves as containers. Only when this important truth is comprehended can we become effective instruments of God for the evangelization of the world in this generation. As we grasp the value of the treasure, we are motivated to reach the world for Christ. As we recognize our expendability, we are compelled to give glory for our successes to God. The very truth of our Christian existence is that we do, indeed, possess a heavenly treasure in an earthen vessel.

━━━◈━━━

Strong Treasures—Weak Containers

⟫•◆•⟪

But we have this treasure in earthen vessels, that the excellence of the power may be of God and not of us. We are hard pressed on every side, yet not crushed; we are perplexed, but not in despair; persecuted, but not forsaken; struck down, but not destroyed—always carrying about in the body the dying of the Lord Jesus, that the life of Jesus also may be manifested in our body. For we who live are always delivered to death for Jesus' sake, that the life of Jesus may also be manifested in our mortal flesh.

2 Corinthians 4:7–11 NKJV

We have a treasure in an earthen vessel. Earthenware vessels, clay pots, jars. That's an unusual description for believers, yet it always helps me when I encounter the life of a genuinely recognized, acknowledged, all-world Christian hero or heroine who is nevertheless willing to admit that when all is said and done, "I am only an earthenware jar, a clay pot, fragile, insignificant, holding a great treasure." One such world-class, recognized, modern-day saint is Elisabeth Elliot. Elisabeth Elliot became a household name in evangelical circles when in 1956 her husband was speared to death by the Auca Indians in Ecuador. But both before and after that, she was willing to admit honestly, "I am at best an earthenware vessel, a clay pot holding a treasure." As a senior in college, she surrendered to go to the foreign mission field; but giving herself to God she told him, "I do not want to go alone. I want to go with a husband." She met and fell in love with Jim Elliot, but in the providence of God they both went separately to Ecuador as missionaries. One on one side of the Andes, and the other on the other side. For five years they exchanged letters, which took six weeks to travel back and forth. They never even saw each other. During the first year on the mission field Elisabeth worked on inventing a language for the Colorado Indians in Ecuador. Her only informant was murdered so no one could

101

tell her about the language and customs. All of her notes, manuscripts, and vocabulary compilations were stolen, and she had no record of them. Meanwhile, Jim Elliot's mission station was swept away in one night by a flood. All of that in their first year. Elisabeth as much as said, "We were left before God like earthenware vessels, clay pots, empty, only knowing that we had a treasure."

Finally God permitted them to marry. Three years into their marriage, Jim was speared to death by Auca Indians as he tried to take the gospel to them. Elisabeth went home; but then she came back to the Auca Indians, and then went to the Chacaw Indians. She then married a widower seminary professor only to watch him disintegrate, ravaged by cancer. Some years later in a very honest article she said, "My grandfather had on his desk a great Christian motto. It said, 'Not somehow, but triumphantly.' If I really told the truth about my life, I would have to say, 'Not triumphantly, but somehow.'" There are warped versions of Christianity that present it as something other than having a treasure in an earthen vessel.

The apostle Paul recognized in his letter to the Corinthians that he was no more than a clay pot with a treasure in it. Using the first-person plural of the apostles he said, "We are jars of mud with a treasure inside." James and John, with terrible tempers, called the "Thunderstorm boys" by Jesus; Peter, vacillating so much that he could claim to die for Jesus one moment and curse him the next; Thomas, a doubter. Clay jars with treasures in them. What about you? Have you ever said, "I'm simply too weak for God to use me"? Would you consider with me the possibility that you are not yet weak enough for God to use? When we vaunt our strength, flaunt our ego, and pretend that we are something more than clay jars, then God can never make his strength conspicuous in us. God conquers in those lives that know all too well, "I am nothing but a clay jar with a treasure inside." Our weakness is the only stage on which God can display his strength.

The Weakness of Humanity Contains the Strength of the Gospel

The apostle does say, "we have this treasure in *clay pots.*" That's what the word literally means, "jars of mud, earthenware vessels."

In the biblical world treasures were kept, were hidden, were preserved in earthenware, ceramic, fragile, common containers. In Matthew 13:44 Jesus told the story about a man who found a treasure buried in a field. What he had in mind was a treasure buried in a ceramic pot, a clay jar. Plato, the philosopher, and Herodotus, the historian, also tell us that in the ancient world it was common practice to keep expensive, valuable treasures in worthless, valueless, commonplace, unattractive clay jars. It is that very figure of speech that sets off the contrast of Paul's words in verse 7. An uncommon treasure in a common jar. An attractive treasure in an unattractive container. A durable treasure in a container that is already perishing. A treasure of great value contained in something of no inherent value at all. This is a great reality about the Christian life. And the great reality is that we do have a treasure. To the extent that you know the Lord Jesus Christ, you recognize that a treasure, indeed, has been lodged with you. Jesus even called it a "pearl of great price." You may ask, "What is that treasure?" That treasure is the knowledge of the saving power of God in Christ. It is the knowledge of the gospel that rescues us. More specifically in verse 6, it is the light of the knowledge of the glory of God in the face of Christ. It is being able to look up to an unclouded sky, to an ungrieved, unquenched Holy Spirit and see the glory of God reflected in the face of Jesus Christ and reflecting in my life. Paul says, "That's a treasure." "Treasure" is not an adequate word for this possession. But it's the best word we have. So he says, "We have this treasure." But we have that treasure in a clay pot, in an earthenware vessel. Paul does not say, "We have a treasure of gold in a treasure chest of silver." Not at all. He says, "The treasure we have is in a clay pot," and his readers immediately knew what he meant, because a clay pot suggested something about strength, attractiveness, and value. As to strength—weak. As to attractiveness—insignificant. As to value—valueless.

The picture was of something fragile, breakable, and weak. It portrayed something that was inherently unattractive, common, and insignificant. And it described something that was basically and inherently worthless. The apostle Paul says, "The treasure that we have in Jesus Christ is in clay pots."

The Old Testament presents this fact in many places. In Psalm 31:12, when all of the friends and neighbors of the psalmist had abandoned him, he cried out to God, "I am forgotten like a dead man, out of mind; I am like a broken vessel." When God judged King Jehoiakim, Jeremiah said, "Is this man Coniah a despised, broken idol? Is he a vessel in which is no pleasure?" (Jer. 22:28). In the biblical world to say that you had a treasure in a clay pot or earthenware vessel was the same as confessing that you had a thing of value contained in a thing of valuelessness. You had an attractive thing in something that was essentially insignificant.

What in the world is Paul trying to say to us when he says that we have this treasure, the gospel, the power of Jesus Christ, in clay pots? Someone may suggest that he is talking about our physical bodies. Indeed, to one extent he is. Whatever we know of the power of God resides in our feeble, frail, and inevitably perishing physical bodies. But that's not all he means by this imagery. He means further that our whole person—our personalities, our mind, our emotions, our will, even our moral life—has the characteristics of frailty and insignificance. Paul explains autobiographically in Romans 7:19 that "the good that I will to do, I do not do; but the evil that I will not to do, that I practice." He said, "When you take me as a whole person and look at me, body, mind, soul, spirit, even my moral life, I am little better than a clay pot, an earthenware jar."

Actually he was agreeing with his Corinthian critics. You may wonder, "Did they criticize Pastor Paul?" Did they! Look at 2 Corinthians 10:10. Quoting what he had overheard from some of the believers in Corinth, Paul recounts: "'For his letters,' they say, 'are weighty and powerful, but his bodily presence is weak, and his speech contemptible.'" Basically, they attacked him by declaring, "Paul, you're unimpressive. More than that, you can't even talk well." In 11:6, he acknowledges that very fact: "Even though I am untrained in speech, yet I am not in knowledge." It's almost pathetic—the way he had to say it. In 12:7 he says, "a thorn in the flesh was given to me, a messenger of Satan to buffet me." Basically Paul says, "You there at Corinth say that I am an unattractive person. I am. You say that I don't speak well. I don't. You say that I suffer physically and am weak. That's true. Everything you say about me is true. I am just an earthenware vessel, I'm just a clay pot." Paul was able to make life's second greatest confession. Life's greatest confession is the confession that Peter made about Jesus at Caesarea

Philippi, "You are the Christ, the Son of the living God" (Matt. 16:16). What's life's second greatest confession? It's the confession that Paul made at Lystra in Acts 14:15, when the people came out to him and Barnabas and said, "You are gods!" The priest of Zeus wanted to offer a sacrifice to them. But Paul said, "Stop! We are only men just like you." You want to ask, "Why two thousand years later are we reading what Paul wrote? Why two thousand years later does his life explode on the world with power in a thousand congregations?" Because he was willing to confess that when everything else is said and done, "I am nothing more than a clay pot, an earthenware vessel. But inside of me there is a treasure."

There's a reason for putting a treasure like this in such a container. Jewelers don't display the value of diamonds by putting them against a backdrop of other diamonds. Jewelers display the value of diamonds by putting them against a comparatively worthless black cloth. Over against the backdrop of that worthless black cloth, the beauty, lustre, and value of the diamond are seen. How does God display his power? Does he display his power by finding people who inherently are strong? By discovering people who are strong in and of themselves: their personality, their cleverness, their education, their ability, their overwhelming personal magnetism, their commanding presence? No! God delights to display his power in those who are inconspicuous and who, because of their weakness and frailty, become a backdrop so that when everyone sees them, they can say, "That is not he. That is not she. That is the power of God in life." God has always delighted to do it that way.

You say, "I'm weak." Good. Then God might be able to do business in your life. When people look at that which is essentially unattractive and they see attractiveness in it, when they look at that which is essentially weak and they see a supernatural power in it, when they look at that which seems to be common and they see something uncommon in it, then they might say, "That is the power of God!"

The phrase "excellence of the power" in 2 Corinthians 4:7 translates a word that means more than enough power, power that is emotional power. How do people look at us and see that about us? How is it that we can look at it and see it ourselves? When we're willing, along with the apostle Paul, to say, "Look, I'm no more than a clay pot, an earthen jug made out of mud, earthenware," then God can make his power conspicuous in our lives.

You know, it's always like God to work that way. You can do a survey of Old Testament 101 in one minute and discover this truth. Look at Abraham and Sarah. Abraham, ninety-nine years of age, Sarah, ninety. Weak? Yes! Impossible? Indeed! Then Isaac is born so that everyone would say, "Jehovah is great." Moses, eighty years old, a tongue-tied shepherd throwing down the rod of God in front of Pharaoh or splitting the Red Sea with it. An eighty-year-old tongue-tied shepherd with a wooden stick. Yet God used him to pull off an exodus.

Joshua, with a rag-tag army of slaves marching around a walled Canaanite fortress city. Ridiculous! They blow trumpets and the wall falls down so that everyone will say, My, what a strategist is General Joshua! No! The Canaanites looked down on him from the walls and laughed. But then they said, "Jehovah is great."

Gideon with his army of three hundred men, trumpets in one hand, torches in the other, and, of all things, clay pots. There against the Midianites, breaking those pots. What a ridiculous way to fight a battle! But everyone said, "The victory belongs to God."

I don't care who it is. If it's Elijah with his cloak, David with his slingshot, or the little lad with loaves and fishes, God delights to take that which is inherently inconspicuous, weak, and fragile, and so act in it with power that everyone will say, "That reveals the power of God."

Let me apply that to me, to you, and to our church. There are two ways that I can look at my life, my ministry, my person. On the one hand, there's the way of the world. In fact, the way the world commends people in our generation more than any other way is with unabashed egoism: "If you've got it, flaunt it." And I might say, "Now look here, Gregory, you have earned three degrees: B.A., M.Div., and Ph.D. You have spent twenty years getting from tiny churches in unknown towns to one of the great churches in this country. Why, you speak to thousands of people. You must be very gifted. They write you letters now and then. You have more opportunities offered than you can accept, more doors to enter than you can go through. You're highly visible, on and on, ad nauseam." You know what God says to that kind of attitude? He says, "Very well. If that's what you think, verily, verily, I say to you, 'You have your reward and my power will never be manifested in your life.'" But, on the other hand, if I tell the truth about myself, if I am willing to say, "Gregory, you're just a clay pot. Physically, you don't have half enough stamina to do what you are supposed to do every week. Emotionally, you are often on the edge, sometimes just about to lose it. Spiritually, you preach to hundreds of people who are better Christians than you would ever think about being." If I tell the truth about myself and say, "I am just a clay pot, an earthenware vessel," then God might be able to do something to manifest his strength in my life.

What's true of me is true of you. If you are willing to say, "I am no more than an earthenware jug with a treasure," then God might manifest himself in your life. But you know, that's true of our church, too. If we stand back and say, "We have an impressive and beautiful sanctuary, the finest group of people coming to church, millions of dollars given last year, expanding facilities, thousands coming," God will say, "Fine. Have it your way. You have your reward. But not my power." We have to be willing to say, "We're just a group of regular folks, a slice of life, with many facilities that are insufficient for the task, without enough resources to get the job done, without enough of anything we need to make any kind of impact on this world." If we are collectively willing to look up and say, "God, after all, we are just clay jars," then he might say, "I am able to do something to manifest my strength and power through First Baptist Church." I'm not talking about something marginal. I'm talking about something in the very center of whether or not we experience what God can do. If we are willing to say that we are clay pots, he is willing to say that he will give us a treasure. But if we say that we are treasures, then he will say that we don't even amount to a clay pot. He gives us strength in our weakness. But is that all? Look yet once again.

The Power of God Prevails in the Midst of Our Difficulties

If inwardly we are like clay pots, outwardly we are clay pots that are about to be cracked because of pressure. The apostle Paul looked from inside to outside. In verses 8 and 9 in four death strokes he tears open his heart and lets us see what it was like to be a great Christian, a great apostle. He says, "We are hard pressed on every side, yet not crushed; we are perplexed, but not in despair; persecuted, but not forsaken; struck down, but not destroyed." Four phrases. They are very interesting because they are phrases that literally come out of the arena of the soldier fighting on the battlefield or the gladiator in the arena at Rome. The language is taken from a gladiator in a fight like you may have seen in the movies, when suddenly a stronger opponent knocks the sword out of his hand, or the shield out of his other hand, and all of a sudden he is perplexed. He is knocked down, but suddenly he stands up to fight again—and not only to fight, but to prevail. That's the language that Paul uses in these four phrases. Notice in each of the four, the first part of the phrase mentions a human weakness, and the second part identifies a more than compensating divine strength. In verse 8, the human weakness is, "we are hard pressed." But look at the last part. God's strength is "not crushed." Look again. Human weakness is "perplexed." God's strength, "we are not in despair." In verse 9, the human weakness is "persecuted." God's strength, "not forsaken." "Struck down," human weakness; "but not destroyed," God's strength.

You want to say, "How does God's strength prevail in my life?" Well, we can prevail in outward pressure. Look at that first statement. "We are hard pressed." The word means to be pressed like wheat ground on a millstone or grapes crushed in a winepress. In fact, the Greek New Testament says, "We are hard pressed in everything." Paul said, "I face multilateral pressure all of the time." And he did. Read 2 Corinthians; it's like a catalog of everything that he faced. Hard pressed, crushed. No! He says, "Even though we are hard pressed, we are never crushed." The word means to be confined, to be in the straits, to be cornered in a narrow place. He probably took it from the Silician Gates, a narrow mountain pass near his hometown of Tarsus that was sixty feet wide. He had seen armies defeated because they were cornered, hemmed in, and caught in the straits. Paul said, "Yes, I am always pressured but because of the power of God, I am never crushed." Let me tell you something very honestly. You may be thinking, "Well, I want to be a Christian so I can get away from the pressure." Not on your life! You just get into it. I maintain that those who try to stand up and live for the Lord Jesus Christ are those who throw themselves into not only the pressure of the earth, but all the pressure that hell can bring against them. The apostle Paul said, "No, not that I get out of pressure. I am hard pressed." Where's the power of God in it? "I'm never crushed!"

He went on to say in the third part of this statement, "persecuted, but not forsaken." That word "persecuted" means, "I am hunted. I am harassed." It refers to somebody who is hunted like game. Paul felt like he was quarry, with everybody after him. But he said, "I'm not abandoned." Not abandoned by God. Humanly, always chased. But by the power of God, never abandoned! That's what it means for God's strength to show through in our weakness.

Somehow we imagine that the great super-saint Christians of the ages lived in some other kind of world and walked in some other kind of atmosphere than the one we get up in and live in and walk in every day. We think that they were three feet off the ground and never faced what we face. Nothing could be further from the truth. Consider John Wesley. Wesley was one of the super saints of all the ages. He was a Christian whose name and fame will live as long as the church stands. Wesley started a worldwide Christian movement and saved England from a disaster similar to the French Revolution. He was the founder of Methodism. He lived into his eighties. He rode 250,000 miles on horseback preaching. He preached more than 50,000 times, often five times a day. But do you know what? All the while Wesley lived in a domestic hell. He made a very unwise choice in his marriage. He married Molly Vazeille, the widow of a London merchant who was already the mother of four children. When Wesley's brother, Charles, heard about it, he went and shut himself in his room and cried, because he knew it wasn't going to work. The woman was so insanely jealous, she dogged John Wesley everywhere he went to see what he was doing. She went to his study and tore up his papers after rifling through them. She would never allow her husband to have any friendships or guests in their home. Perhaps the most telling incident was related by one of his preachers, John Harrison, who said that he happened on the two of them in Northern Ireland one day, and when he opened the door, Mrs. Wesley was in a rage and Mr. Wesley was on the floor. She had drug him there and she held in her hand the locks of his gray hair that she had just pulled out. Now, when you think about John Wesley, you think about a man whom God used to shake this planet for the gospel of the Lord Jesus Christ. Yet all of it was achieved in spite of a background like that. The power of God was manifested in the life of John Wesley even though he lived in the midst of a domestic hell.

Examine the life of David Livingstone. In England, Livingstone ranks somewhere between St. Francis of Assisi and the apostle Paul. The greatest missionary of the ages, he was almost canonized in the nineteenth century as a Protestant saint. He wanted to go to China but the door was closed. So God led him to Africa. The great missionary Robert Moffatt, stretching the truth, had said, "At Kuriman there are a thousand villages that have never heard the gospel." When Livingstone went there he didn't find a thousand villages. He found practically nobody there but a group of missionaries who were so mean and cantankerous that he said they had no more love for one another than an ox had for its grandmother. Discouraged, he went to Mabosta, where he was unable to get along with the only other missionary there. So they parted company. After that, on a lion hunt, a lion attacked him and so ravaged his left arm that he was wounded and crippled for life. Finally, he went to a third mission station in Chanwaine. There he married. Soon after, there was a drought. He had to leave when his fourth child was born. The child died, his wife was paralyzed, and on top of all that, his in-laws wrote him letters that were so angry, brutal, and nasty that they almost make the paper burn when you read them today. Yet in spite of all of that, David Livingstone was one of the greatest missionaries of the ages.

You need to understand something: for God's power to be manifested in your life doesn't mean that somehow you live three feet off the ground, above contradiction. No! It means that you are willing to say, "I am pressed but not crushed, I am persecuted but not abandoned, I am perplexed but not in despair. I am knocked down but not knocked out. And in the middle of all of this God's power is manifested in my life." That's what it means.

You ask, "How was Paul mentally?" Struggling with inward pressures, he said, "I am perplexed, but not in despair." That's a figure of speech that means, "I am at my wit's end, but really not out of my wits." He said, "I'm almost over the edge, but not quite. I'm about to lose it, but I haven't yet." He said, "That's the power of God." The great climactic statement in these verses is this declaration, "Struck down, but not knocked out."

Ludwig von Beethoven was born in 1770 in Bonn, Germany. His education was meager, and that hurt him all his life. Socially, he was awkward, inept, and rude because of his upbringing. Personally, he was irascible and unpredictable. Yet his personal journals reveal an overwhelming sense of responsibility to God for the gift he had been given. At twenty-eight years of age, in 1798, he began to go deaf. Out of that deafness, out of that weakness, he composed music supernaturally powerful in its sweetness and its thunder. One day in Vienna he presented for the first time his ninth symphony. Already deaf, he took his place before the orchestra. Someone told the orchestra and the choir, "Look at him but don't follow him, because he's as deaf as a stone." What a pathetic sight to see him standing there waving his baton—the orchestra and singers watching him but not following him because he couldn't even hear the music. At the end of one of the movements, the whole place broke with thunderous applause. The audience knew they had heard one of the masterpieces of all the ages, but the great composer never heard them. He simply turned over the pages of his score, until a musician pulled his sleeve and pointed to him to turn around. Then he saw that the whole place was in pandemonium because of the greatness of what he had done. But in his deafness, he couldn't even conduct the music or hear the applause. You say, "What a tragedy!" No! No! Who knows? Had he not been deaf there might never have been a ninth symphony. His biographer, Thayer, said, "Who can say that the world has not been the gainer by a misfortune that stirred the profoundest depths of his being and compelled the concentration of his powers in one direction." Out of his weakness, there came an overwhelming strength.

Death to Self Releases the Life of Christ

Paul drops the figure of speech and says, "Let's stop talking about clay pots and let's get straight to reality." He's been talking in a figure of speech but in verses 10 and 11 he drops it and says, "Here's what I am talking about, if you want to get to the center of it. We always carry around in our body the death of Jesus so that the life of Jesus may be real in our life."

Then in verse 11 he says the same thing but in different words. He writes, "We who live are always delivered to death for Jesus' sake, that the life of Jesus also may be manifested in our mortal flesh." For many of us that kind of statement is very, very strange. There are some disturbing passages in the New Testament. One of them is 1 Corinthians 15:31, where Paul says, "I die daily." Another is Romans 8:36, where he says, "We are killed all day long." Another is Philippians 3:10, where he says that he was "being conformed to His [Christ's] death." He says, "Let's stop talking about clay pots for a minute and let's get to the center of the truth." He says, "I carry around in my body the act of dying of the Lord Jesus Christ." The word "necrosis" means, literally, the act of dying. He says, "My act is a perpetual Passion play. It is a mystical martyrdom every day. I die." Paul means that physically. He means, "If I am marked for martyrdom, so be it." We may have to say that someday. Meanwhile, all of us need to say it spiritually. "If I want to experience the release of the life of the Lord Jesus Christ in my life, I must be willing to say, 'I die daily.'" That's what it means to be a clay pot.

Joseph Ton is a world-famous Romanian pastor. He served the largest Baptist church in Romania. As you might expect, he is sometimes a controversial man. A time came when a communist edict in Romania said, in effect, that the people could have church, but that they couldn't. The communists didn't make the church illegal, but they so restricted it that it was completely neutralized. They said, "You can't baptize; you can't disciple; you can't train young people." Obedience to that law would have destroyed the church. Joseph Ton went to the mountain, and while he was walking and talking with God, God told him, "You do not have to keep that communist law." After studying martyrdom in the Bible, he came to understand that he might be called on to be a martyr. And it was settled that day. He died on that mountain. Oh, he was still alive, but he died. He went back down the mountain and told his wife. As is often the case, she had a harder time with that message from God than he did, because she did not look forward to being a widow with children in a communist country suffering persecution. But finally she accepted the possibility and the matter was settled. Then Pastor Ton went to his church and told the members and the other pastors. They said, "No, no, don't do it! You fool, they will kill you." But he said, "It's settled." The inevitable day arrived when the Minister of the Interior came to Joseph Ton and said, "You must keep these laws." "I cannot keep them and I will not keep them," he replied. The communist official said, "Do you know what I can do to you? Do you know what I must do to you?" Then Pastor Ton spoke words I just can't forget. He said, "Your greatest weapon is killing me. My greatest weapon is dying. If you use your greatest weapon on me, I will use my greatest weapon on you." The official was so shocked that he went back to the Central Committee and said, "Don't kill Ton. He wants to die. He's crazy." From that moment on Pastor Ton experienced an anointing on his life and ministry that he had never known before: power for living and, if necessary, for dying.

I recognize that many people probably think I am reaching the stratosphere. But I want you to understand this: For me, for you, to be a clay pot is ultimately to say, "I die daily." That really sets you free. When you insult someone who is dead, that person doesn't retaliate. If you say that you die daily, the establishment in your community may ridicule you or reject you; they don't care. But you will have settled the biggest question of all. Because of that, the life of Christ's resurrection power can be released in you. And do you know what? If even a nucleus of us contemporary American Christians would truly say with Paul, "I carry around in my body the dying of Jesus," the power of God would explode upon us just as it did on the early church, as the Book of Acts tells us. Our world would never be the same.

⇒•◇•⇐

9

Kenneth S. Hemphill

———<>———

Kenneth S. Hemphill received the M.Div. and D.Min. degrees from Southern Baptist Theological Seminary, and the Ph.D. from Cambridge University in England. He became director of the Office of Church Growth, Home Mission Board, and Baptist Sunday School Board in 1992, after a pastorate of more than ten years at First Baptist Church, Norfolk, Virginia, where Sunday morning services were televised weekly. His earlier experience included ministries in five Southern Baptist churches in Kentucky, North Carolina, and Virginia, and an interim pastorate in Little Stukeley, England. He was a teaching fellow at Southern Baptist Theological Seminary, and an instructor in religion at Wingate College, Wingate, North Carolina.

Hemphill is the author of four books: *Spiritual Gifts: Empowering the New Testament Church*, *The Official Rule Book for the New Church Game*, *The Bonsai Theory of Church Growth*, and *Mirror, Mirror on the Wall*, co-author of *Growing an Evangelistic Sunday School*, and a contributor to *Evangelism in the 21st Century* and *Authentic Worship: Exalting God and Reaching People*, among others.

———<>———

"One sermon to preach" is certainly an intimidating thought for any preacher. My first inclination was to choose a message with a primary focus on Jesus. Biblical preaching should always exalt Jesus and such a decision would certainly place me on a solid foundation. The Word promises that when Christ is lifted up he will draw people to himself. Besides, for eleven and a half years at First Baptist Norfolk, I stood behind a pulpit with a plaque that read, "SIR, WE WOULD SEE JESUS." Immediately I thought about Philippians 2:5–11 or Colossians 1:13–20 as a text for my message.

Yet as I prayed about this assignment I couldn't escape the thought that one of the central themes of my preaching ministry has been a serious commitment to the church. If I had only one message to preach, I would want to challenge those present to be all they were called to be as Christ's body, the church. As I reflected on this theme, and with the affirmation of my wife, I returned to a passage that has been pivotal in my own life and ministry at several crucial junctures: Ephesians 3:14–21.

As I studied this passage again to prepare this message, I was thrilled to be reminded that when the church receives glory, it is glory to Christ. It is his body and his bride. What man does not like to hear someone honor his wife? Later in this same letter Paul compares the husband's relationship to his wife with Christ's relationship to the church. "So husbands ought also to love their own wives as their own bodies. He who loves his own wife loves himself; for no one ever hated his own flesh, but nourishes and cherishes it, just as Christ also does the church, because we are members of His body" (Eph. 5:28–30).

May Christ be exalted as we focus on the church.

Let the Church Be the Church

——⟫◆⟪——

For this reason, I bow my knees before the Father, from whom every family in heaven and on earth derives its name, that He would grant you, according to the riches of His glory, to be strengthened with power through His Spirit in the inner man; so that Christ may dwell in your hearts through faith; and that you, being rooted and grounded in love, may be able to comprehend with all the saints what is the breadth and length and height and depth, and to know the love of Christ which surpasses knowledge, that you may be filled up to all the fulness of God. Now to Him who is able to do exceeding abundantly beyond all that we ask or think, according to the power that works within us, to Him be the glory in the church and in Christ Jesus to all generations forever and ever. Amen.

Ephesians 3:14–21 NASB

It was a beautiful spring morning in the mountains. The kind of morning that makes you want to be out-of-doors after the rigors of a cold winter. I had just assumed the pastorate of my first full-time church, and I was anxious to make a good impression. I had decided to greet "my people" as they entered the building for Sunday school. I had noticed that most of the men drove under the portico to let their families out before they parked their cars. So I stationed myself outside this particular door and opened the car doors for the ladies and children, at the same time welcoming them to church. My good intentions were met with mixed reactions as I frequently interrupted those "going-to-church family conversations." Topics such as whose fault it was that the family was late, the church envelopes had been left at home, and other such edifying topics.

One particular Sunday morning I noticed a rather animated conversation between a dad and his young son. The lad was struggling with his collar and tie, which he obviously considered too tight. The father, on the other hand, was quite comfortable in his loose-fitting knit shirt. The son was dressed for church; the dad was dressed for golf. I surmised that the young boy was pleading with his dad to let him accompany him, instead of going to church. As they approached the entrance to the church the conversation became more desperate and heated. I could image the child's argument.

"Please, Dad, let me go with you. Why do I have to go to church, and you don't?"

When they arrived at the door, they were so engrossed in the dialogue they didn't notice that I had opened the door. I overheard the last few volleys in the verbal battle.

"Dad, are you sure that you went to church when you were a little boy?"

"Son, that's enough! If I've told you once, I've told you a thousand times. I went to Sunday school and church every Sunday when I was your age. Now go on in and no more fussing."

"Okay, Dad, I'm going," sulked the boy, "but I bet you it won't do me any more good than it did you!"

I had to wonder what went on in that home that had convinced the boy that church had not helped his dad. What had been missing in the church that had caused this young professional to conclude that church was good for kids but irrelevant for adults? Do we sometimes think that church "won't do us any good"? Do you ever hear yourself saying, "These people will never change"? "We'll never make that budget"? "My spouse will never be any different"? All of those statements imply that the transforming power of the living Christ doesn't affect the people in church.

One of the greatest tragedies of our day is people going through the motions of "playing church" without any concept of *being* the church—the body of Christ, fully empowered to be on a mission for the redemption of the world.

One of the most critical challenges of the 1990s is for the church to be the church—embracing its mission, living up to its heritage. It is essential to the purpose of God in the world today for the church to be the church. Since the beginning of time God has always used human instrumentation to accomplish his work on earth. That plan will continue until Jesus returns for his bride, the church.

The apostle Paul issued his greatest challenge to the church in the Letter to the Ephesians. This letter was written as a companion to the Letter to the Colossians. Both were aimed at counteracting heretical teaching that had spread throughout Asia Minor. False teachers challenged the unique role of Christ as the only way of salvation. In so doing, they reduced the church to little more than another mystery religion. They forgot that our convictions about the uniqueness of Christ and the authority of the church will always be inextricably bound together since he is our head, our husband, and we who comprise the church are his body, his bride.

Paul addressed this heresy directly in Colossians, declaring that "it was the Father's good pleasure for all the fulness to dwell in Him" (Col. 1:19). In the Ephesian letter he applies all the great doctrinal truths, underscored in the Colossian letter, to the church, declaring, "He put all things in subjection under His feet, and gave Him as head over all things to the church, which is His body, the fulness of Him who fills all in all" (1:22–23). In his incarnation, it was Christ alone who was the fullness of God, but since his resurrection and ascension the fullness of God is experienced through his body, the church.

Read the entire Ephesian letter. Notice that each chapter begins with an emphasis on the individual believer, but concludes by focusing on the church. For example, in the first half of chapter 1 Paul identifies the many blessings God has conferred on the believer in Christ, but at the end of the chapter he reminds the reader that God has done all of this for the church. In chapter 2 Paul begins by discussing the wonderful transformation process that we call the new birth. We who were formerly children of disobedience were saved by the grace of God and made his workmanship (vv. 1–10). Yet the focus of the second half of chapter 2 is on the formation of one new body out of Jew and Gentile, a community built on the foundation of the apostles and prophets, with Christ as the corner stone. God saved us that we might be a holy temple, a community indwelt by his Spirit (vv. 11–22).

That brings us to chapter 3. Here Paul begins by talking about his personal calling to be a minister of the gospel. He was overwhelmed by the knowledge that one of the least of all the saints (v. 8) could be used to preach to the Gentiles the unfathomable riches of Christ. Paul was staggered to think that God could use him to reveal the mystery that had been hidden for ages, "that the Gentiles are fellow-

119

heirs and fellow-members of the body, and fellow-partakers of the promise in Christ Jesus through the gospel" (v. 6). The mystery that Paul was privileged to reveal was God's plan for the church, a new community made up of Jew and Gentile as fellow-members.

God's purpose in creating this new community was to hold it up before all the world as his demonstration of his manifold wisdom (v. 10). We all enjoy demonstrating our workmanship. Parents of young children are often proud recipients of numerous pieces of sometimes unidentifiable artwork. Our children never grow tired of showing us what they have drawn, and we never grow weary of admiring their pictures. I think refrigerators were invented to provide an art gallery for our children's drawings.

With that picture of a proud parent in mind, allow this truth to challenge you. The God of the universe holds us, his church, up before all the spiritual powers of the universe as his handiwork, the clearest picture of his manifold wisdom. While the universe, the creation of God, presents ample evidence of his power and glory, it is the church that stands at the zenith of his creative activity. It is the church that reveals him most clearly. Listen to verses 10–11: "in order that the manifold wisdom of God might now be made known through the church to the rulers and the authorities in the heavenly places. This was in accordance with the eternal purpose which He carried out in Christ Jesus our Lord."

The phrase "the rulers and the authorities" refers to spiritual powers, both good and evil. Paul was saying that God is actually educating the spiritual powers by means of the church. The angels themselves learn of the manifold wisdom of God as they view the church. The demons who recognized Jesus when he was here on earth and acknowledged his authority, look at the church and see once again the manifold wisdom of God.

It must grieve the Father when persons who call themselves Christians treat the church with casual disdain. We do so when we allow petty hurts to disrupt our fellowship and paralyze our ministries. We do so when we are lackadaisical about our commitment in giving, or teaching, or serving. We do so when we doubt that "it'll do us any good." We must fully become what we are called and empowered to be. Through our faith in Christ we have been caught up in God's divine purpose that spans eternity. Just as the redemptive work of the cross was an accomplished fact in the heart of God before the foundation of the world, so the founding of the church was in the heart of God before the foundation of the world.

Notice in verse 12 that it is the knowledge of who we are in Christ that gives us boldness and confidence in prayer. If the One in whom we have access to the Father is also the head of the church and we are his body, we have great boldness to ask whatever we will. Too much is at stake in every generation for the church to fail to be fully empowered and enable it to live up to its heritage.

Why, then, do we see so few churches that "make a difference"? Why are we so impotent in our ministries? What will be required for the church to be the church in this decade?

To answer these questions we look now at Paul's second prayer for the church in Ephesus.

Strengthened with Power in the Inner Man

So much was at stake that Paul modeled bold and confident prayer. The intensity of his prayer is seen in the phrase, "I bow my knees." Standing was the usual posture of prayer for the Jews. Kneeling for prayer was an expression of deep emotion or earnestness. The prayer begins with an individual focus, "that He would grant *you*" (v. 16), but quickly moves to the corporate community as seen in the phrase "with all the saints" (v. 18). The point is this: the church—your church—will begin to realize its potential only when the individual members of that church appropriate all that is available to them in Christ. We can flip the coin and look at the obverse of this truth. We will experience individually what God has in store for us only in the context of community. To know fully God's empowering in the inner man we must learn to live in community with one another.

Paul's first prayer request was for strength in the inner man. "Spiritual strength" was actually the topic of Paul's first prayer for this church as found in Ephesians 1:15–23. Who among us would not admit the need for greater spiritual strength? I often hear people confess, "I'm just serving the Lord in my poor, weak little way." I want to shake them and exhort them, "Well, quit it now! You need to serve Christ in his mighty power." One of the reasons the church in the

121

twentieth century is so impotent is that we are attempting to serve him in our weak human strength. The work we are called to do for Christ is supernatural work and thus requires divine empowerment.

Paul used several synonyms to suggest the great wealth of power available to the believer. Lest there be any confusion about the abundance of the resources available, Paul reminded his readers that this power is "according to the riches of His [God's] glory." The Greek here is very precise. The verb translated "to be strengthened with power" speaks of being made strong or capable. The apostle was speaking of power that enables the believer to stand firm in the spiritual battle and to serve the Lord victoriously. This power for meaningful ministry is available to every Christian. This is your heritage! Your calling!

This empowering was experienced in the "inner man." The "outer man" refers to the body that is destined to pass away. The "inner man" refers to the true enduring self that delights in the Law of God and experiences daily renewal (2 Cor. 4:16). Thus the empowering in the inner man is nothing less than the infilling of the Holy Spirit. This inner strength is an enduring strength. It doesn't fade in the face of conflict or difficulty.

I learned about the value of enduring strength early in grade school. Do you recall how teachers wrote comments on the back of your report cards? Most kids received comments like: "It is a pleasure to teach your son." Or, "Sue has such a sweet spirit." Not I! My collection of comments was not as complimentary. One report card was different. The teacher wrote, "Ken's greatest attribute is his tenaciousness." Sounded good to me, even though I had no idea what the word "tenaciousness" meant. I could only hope that it was positive.

I had a simple strategy. I would hand Dad the report card and step back to a safe distance. If he smiled, I would ask for a definition. If he frowned, I would beat a hasty retreat and discuss the whole matter with Mom when she got home. My plan progressed as planned with one slight hitch—my dad read the comment without the slightest change of facial expression. By now curiosity overcame my intimidation and I asked, "Dad, what does 'tenaciousness' mean?" With aged wisdom and years of experience he looked at me and responded: "Son, I could tell you, but that wouldn't do you any good. Why don't you look it up?" Now that I am the parent of three school-age children, I know precisely why he had me look it up. He didn't have the slightest idea what tenaciousness meant either.

I took down the dictionary and half-heartedly began my search. I finally found "tenaciousness," but the definition was not all that illuminating. It read, "the act of being tenacious." I backed up to "tenacious" only to discover that the first several definitions used words I had never seen. Finally, with Dad's help I came to a definition I could understand. It read: "has an attitude like a bulldog." I didn't know whether I was being commended by my teacher or not. My dad assured me that it was a positive comment. She was saying that I was determined. Tenaciousness is the stick-to-it attitude that grabs on and refuses to let go. Like a bulldog, it endures.

We have this tenacious strength in Christ. We are empowered to live victoriously and serve God effectively. Yet we so often fail to exhibit this strength, because we passively remain in the familiar territory of our own proven ability. We're asked to serve in a new capacity, to teach a Bible study or to chair a long-range study committee, and we respond that we're not able. We're afraid we might fail. We're challenged to dream a new dream for our church's outreach ministry, and we recoil because it's new and untried. Until we individually and corporately dare to push ourselves beyond the barriers of our natural ability, we will forfeit our opportunity to experience this supernatural empowering for service.

Indwelt by the Living Christ

An obvious and close connection exists between the empowering of the Holy Spirit in the inner man and the indwelling of the living Christ. We are empowered by the Spirit in direct proportion to the union that we have with Christ. The daily infilling of the Spirit for ministry comes through our surrender to Christ.

The word "dwell" means to take up residence. Paul prayed that we would allow the living Christ to take up residence in our hearts. The heart is the very center of one's being. Children use "heart" in this same manner when they come home and announce: "Dad, I love him with all my heart." They mean that they love that person with the very essence of their being.

123

Could it be that we are missing out on spiritual empowerment because we call Christ "Lord" with our tongues but have never permitted him to be Lord of our hearts? We talk a great deal about the implications of lordship, and we sing songs pledging our allegiance to Christ as Lord. We meet in our mission groups and Sunday school classes and discuss the profound implications of lordship. "If everyone in our church tithed . . . If every member of our church would lead just one person to Christ . . . If everyone just did his or her own part . . ." We play the "lordship game" with no expectation or intention that this will ever occur in our church.

The "lordship game" that we play reminds me of an on-the-field conversation I had with my dad after one of our college football games. I played football for Wake Forest University. I was recruited with an outstanding freshman class, and everyone expected great results when we graduated to the varsity level. We had hoped to move to a new stadium during our sophomore year. The building of the stadium was delayed, but we entered the season with great enthusiasm. Our new uniforms, featuring old-gold helmets with a modern logo, crisp gold pants, and gleaming white jerseys with gold-on-black numerals, made us look invincible.

There was one small hitch. We weren't playing well and we weren't winning. I remember one particular game when the score grew more lopsided as the game progressed. Nothing we tried worked. The enthusiasm of the fans began to wane and the stands were only sparsely filled by half time. When I say the enthusiasm of the fans was dampened, there was one exception: my dad. He was the epitome of a fan. He never left and never gave up. He was the eternal optimist, always looking for something deserving of a compliment.

As the seconds on the clock ticked toward a merciful end to the slaughter, I began to watch my dad. I knew from experience what he would do. He would make his way onto the field and congratulate me with some positive comment on our performance. Believe me, I knew it would take the height of optimism and a wealth of creativity to find something positive to say about our performance that day.

The horn sounded and I sprinted for the clubhouse hoping to get inside before my dad could find me. No such luck! He beat me to the clubhouse. He found me and threw his arm around me, declaring excitedly: "You guys looked great!" I couldn't believe my ears.

Not even my dad could think that we had looked great. What game had he been watching? Then, after a short pause, he finished his sentence—*"in the huddle."*

His concluding phrase caught me unprepared. He was right. We did look good in the huddle. We had crisp new uniforms, and mine for one, wasn't even dirty. When we lined up in the huddle we looked good. We broke the huddle crisply, and we even hustled to the line of scrimmage. It was precisely at this point that everything broke down. When the ball was snapped and the play began, we looked a shambles.

Isn't this the problem we face in the church? We get on our mission committee and talk about our strategy for winning the world to Christ. Our long-range planning committee has a contingency plan for every possible occasion. Our deacons talk about "what could be" if we reached our missions budget. We meet in our Bible study huddles and talk about the power of God to change lives, then stand by helplessly as divorce destroys the families in our classes. Our churches are well organized; we have crisp new buildings; we know all the right plays; but we encounter tremendous difficulty when the ball is snapped. We have grown so familiar with defeat that we limp back to the line of scrimmage, not expecting anything to change. We must turn rhetoric into reality and promise into practice. It's not enough to look good in the huddle. The church of the living God must become all that it is empowered to be.

To turn our talk into reality requires faith. Did you notice those two little words in verse 17: "so that Christ may dwell in your hearts *through faith"*? God's power is unleashed "through faith." Christ waits for us to be willing for him to come in with the fullness of his blessing. We must believe his word and abandon ourselves to his infilling. We must move expectantly at his command, trusting that he is sufficient to supply all our needs according to the riches of his glory. What area of your life requires an obedient response so that you know the indwelling presence of the living Christ? Will you "through faith" surrender that to him today?

Know the Love of Christ

Paul's third concern was that his readers might come to know, in an experiential way, the love of Christ. Not only is the language of this request arresting—we do not usually speak of love in terms like breadth, length, height, and depth—but the paradox of Paul's request is breathtaking. He prayed that we might come to know the love of Christ "which surpasses knowledge."

Paul's use of terms of measurement to describe Christ's love alerts us to the inadequacy of human vocabulary to describe the love of Christ. These words are to be experienced by the heart, rather than calculated by the mind, as we confront the many dimensions of Christ's love made available to us.

This experiential knowledge of the love of Christ is the very foundation of the Christian experience and of the Christian community. Paul uses two different word pictures to communicate this truth. The word "grounded" pictures the foundation of a building that provides the stable platform on which the superstructure is built. If we have no foundational knowledge of the love of Christ, we have nothing on which to build our Christian experience. "Rooted" visualizes a tree with a root system that deeply penetrates the soil, providing both nurture and stability. The personal knowledge of Christ's love is the platform and root system on which both personal growth and church growth are built.

But how do we resolve the paradox of being encouraged to know that which surpasses knowing? The clue is in the context. It is "with all the saints" that we are able to comprehend the love of Christ. It is here in the Christian community with all of its ragged edges, bumps, and bruises that we truly experience the love of Christ.

One Father's Day morning, I was standing by the door of the church receiving the "due accolades" for my stirring message on a father's love. I had talked about the special relationship I had with my dad and how that had helped me comprehend the love of God as my Father. Everyone seemed impressed by my sermon except one young lady about fifteen, who approached me with head bowed and tears in her eyes. She looked at me and commented: "Preacher, how can I understand the love of God? My dad is gone and my step-father beats me." I stammered some feeble answer and headed for a quiet place to think. How could I help her understand God the Father's love when she had never seen an earthly model?

That's when this passage came alive for me. It is here in the family we call the church that she had the possibility of seeing a father's love that is not clouded by abusiveness. In the body, I can know through experience one facet of God's love, while you might know another, and so on throughout the congregation. For example, I know of a rich dimension of God's love through my joyous experience of loving parents. Perhaps you have not known that love, but you may have experienced a different facet of God's love. Perhaps you have walked through the trauma of the death of a spouse or child, and have discovered the sustaining power of God's love. Perhaps you have experienced the tragedy of divorce, yet you have found God's love to be steadfast. I have not known those particular dimensions of God's love, but I can learn from you as we walk together in community. It is only when we bring the entire body together that we can know God's love that surpasses knowing for any individual believer.

I feel for people who pretend that they are so spiritual they can't find a church deep enough or pure enough for them. I am equally concerned about people who call themselves "Christians" and yet believe that they can get along without the church. Certainly, there are times of conflict in the church when we feel that we could manage the Christian life well enough, if it wasn't for some of the Christians we have to put up with. However, we are family! And it is in the context of God's family that we experience and learn to express the love of Christ.

The stability of our spiritual existence and the roots of our Christian life are discovered in the experience of Christ's love in community. We must, for our sake and that of the body, renew our commitment to the body of Christ.

Filled with the Fullness of God

Paul's concluding request is that his readers would be "filled up to all the fullness of God." The theme of fullness plays a significant role in Ephesians and in its twin letter, Colossians. Apparently the term was used in the popular vocabulary of Paul's time to refer to the experience of deity, somewhat like the use of the word "force" in the *Star Wars* movies. Paul grasped this popular term and filled it with new meaning. For example, in Colossians 2:9, he affirmed that in Christ "all the fulness of Deity dwells in bodily form." For that reason it is in Christ that the individual believer has been made complete (v. 10). In Ephesians 1:23 Paul prayed that the Christians in Ephesus would come to understand that the church is "the fulness of Him who fills all in all." In our present passage Paul took his initial request a step further and prayed that his readers might individually and collectively be filled to the fullest extent that God desires.

If you want to understand the fullness of God, look at Christ. If you want to experience the fullness of God, cling to the church. It is through the church, the body of Christ, that individually we come to know the fullness of God. Thus this final request is a fitting and practical conclusion to Paul's prayer for believers in Ephesus and for believers today. God desires to express himself fully on earth through the church. For the church to become all that God intends it to be, we must individually become all that God calls us to be.

The fullness of God is not a specific gift or attribute, but is everything we need in order to be made complete. It is the full indwelling of God himself. Is it any wonder that God would boldly choose the church to showcase his manifold wisdom to the rulers and authorities in the heavenly places?

Those who believe that they can experience the fullness of God and yet treat the church with casual disdain, are caught up short by this passage. Christ expresses his fullness through his body. We need nothing else to be made complete: no New Age enlightenment, no second blessing, no subsequent baptism of the Spirit. We are made complete in Christ. Now we must fully appropriate the empowering of his Spirit as we surrender ourselves fully to his lordship.

In case you think this prayer is too bold for the average Christian and is certainly beyond your grasp, listen to Paul's concluding benediction. "Now to Him who is able to do exceeding abundantly beyond all that we ask or think . . ." What is your greatest dream for your spiritual life or for your church? What is your boldest request? God is able to do more than you can ask or think.

It's easy to find ourselves swept up by the sheer majesty of this prayer and miss a final arresting phrase: "according to the power that works within us." It is through us, his church, that the lordship of Christ will be demonstrated on earth. We serve a sovereign, omnipotent God who desires to give his church the fullness of himself, so that his manifold wisdom can be clearly seen. Notice the connection between Christ and his church. The glory seen through the church is simply a reflection of the glory of Christ. God loves to see the church abound because it is his Son's bride.

Why do we sell ourselves so short? Why do we behave as if the church today is impotent? Before you argue that this prayer was intended only for the first-century church, notice that its impact extends to "all generations forever and ever."

In my early ministry we were blessed with a great harvest. Soon the church outgrew my ability. The Sunday school director and I headed off to a growth conference hoping that we could figure out what to do next. We learned many helpful principles and we were challenged to set bold, even supernatural, goals for the church.

On the drive home we discussed the conference and decided that we needed to involve the Sunday school leaders in setting goals for enrollment growth in Bible study. In a few weeks all the class goals were in and the grand total came to 840. This figure represented more than 68 percent of our present growth goal of 1,200. I didn't realize that such a goal was impossible for a church our size, so I nodded approval. The goal was announced, banners were placed throughout the church, and we embarked on a new Sunday school year.

In the ensuing weeks I began to notice that other churches our size were announcing "more reasonable" goals of about an 8 to 12 percent increase. I called the Sunday school director into my office and asked what he was thinking when he set such an impossible goal.

He replied, "Preacher, didn't you tell us to dream a great dream? You told us God could do beyond all that we ask or think."

Caught by my own sermon! I gritted my teeth and thought, "Great dreams are one thing, but this is crazy!"

Calmly he continued. "I think we can do this. All the teachers think the goals are reachable. Let's give it a try."

We left the banners up and went for it. When the end of the year rolled around, we discovered that we had actually exceeded our goal. What caused such a surge in growth? It certainly wasn't excellence in pastoral leadership. Rather, the church dared to dream a dream and to trust that God could do more than we could ask. We experienced the supernatural empowering of God.

A church living out its heritage gives glory to God. We cannot afford to play church. We cannot afford to live in the realm of the natural, afraid to trust ourselves to the supernatural. If we are going to express the manifold wisdom of God, we must know his fullness. What is the area of your need? What is the fear that keeps you from knowing his fullness? What commitment do you need to make to experience the fullness of God in your life and in the church?

James B. Henry

———⟫◈⟪———

James B. Henry earned his M.Div. degree at New Orleans Baptist Theological Seminary, and was awarded an honorary D.Sac.Theol. degree by Southwest Baptist University. After serving Southern Baptist churches in Alabama, Mississippi, and Tennessee, Henry became pastor of First Baptist Church, Orlando, Florida, in 1977, where Sunday morning services are regularly aired on television. He is a popular speaker at assemblies, pastors' conferences, evangelism conferences, and colleges and universities, and has preached on several occasions at the Billy Graham School of Evangelism. In addition to numerous articles in Southern Baptist publications, his writings include the books *Heartwarmers* and Broadman's *The Pastor's Wedding Manual*.

———⟫◈⟪———

I first preached this message in North Carolina in the summer of 1971. By the next year, I had preached it on eight other occasions at a number of different places. It quickly won a place in my heart. Five years later I wrote a book of favorite sermons and included this one. I've preached it at least once a year, nearly every year since the first time that warm June morning in the Blue Ridge Mountains. When I was invited to contribute a sermon to this book my mind quickly came to this favorite. I like it because it comes as close as I am able to come in capturing something of the majesty and marvel of the person and work of our Lord Jesus Christ. Usually I feel my effort to express some of his glory is like taking a picture of the universe with a miniature camera. I can relate to the apostle John when he wrote: "Now, there are many other things that Jesus did. If they were all written down one by one, I suppose that the whole world could not hold the books that would be written" (John 21:25 GNB).

This version is considerably different from my first effort. I pray that it reflects something of my own maturing in the faith and knowledge of our Lord Jesus Christ. Yet the basics are the same, for he is the same "yesterday, today, and forever." This is a topical message, although my usual style is expository. But the central truth—the wonder of Jesus—is the thesis, as he must always be whatever the method. If I had a thousand lives to live, a thousand tongues to preach, I would give them all over to Jesus, my Savior God, my Lord, my King. I count it all joy to be a servant in his vast court.

⸺⸻◈⸻⸺

King Jesus

⊰◈⊱

Therefore God exalted him to the highest place and gave him the name that is above every name, that at the name of Jesus every knee should bow, in heaven and on earth and under the earth, and every tongue confess that Jesus Christ is Lord, to the glory of God the Father.

Philippians 2:9–11 NIV

Dr. R. G. Lee was probably one of the greatest preachers in this century. He had a brilliant mind and was a spellbinding orator. Some years ago, Dr. Lee came to our church and preached. When we pulled up in front of the church, he turned to me and asked, "What do you want me to preach?" Well, I'm the kind of preacher that has to work on my sermons, get them in mind, get them in heart, get them ready. I just can't drive up to the church and ask, "What do you want me to preach?" I looked over at him and thought, "He's one of the greatest preachers in the world and he's asking me what to preach!" Before I could reply, he said, "I've got two sermons on my mind. One of them just covers the whole world and the other just talks about Jesus." I said, "Well, let's go with Jesus." He said, "You can't beat Jesus, can you?"

Paul must have had that in mind when he wrote the words of Philippians 2:9–11. They are some of the greatest verses in the Bible. Didn't John have this in mind when he penned Revelation 19:11–16?

I saw heaven standing open and there before me was a white horse, whose rider is called Faithful and True. With justice he judges and makes war. His eyes are like blazing fire, and on his head are many crowns. He has a name written on him that no one knows but he himself. He is dressed in a robe dipped in blood, and his name is the Word of God. The armies of heaven were following him, riding on white horses and dressed in fine linen, white and clean. Out of his mouth comes a sharp sword with which to strike down the nations.

"He will rule them with an iron scepter." He treads the winepress of the fury of the wrath of God Almighty. On his robe and on his thigh he has this name written: KING OF KINGS AND LORD OF LORDS.

Paul and John, in writing these Scriptures, clearly delineate the lordship, the kingship, of Jesus Christ. He is, indeed, King Jesus! He alone is worthy of our praise, our service, our love, our worship. Why is this so?

Jesus Is Superior in His Uniqueness

Jesus is unique. When you ask people about what they believe, whom they believe, and what their religion or faith is, there are three questions you can ask quickly to see if their faith is genuine.

First, what do they believe about the uniqueness of the Bible? Is it the inerrant, infallible Word of God above all other books? Second, how does one come to salvation? Is it through faith, repentance, and confession of the Lord Jesus Christ, and through him alone? Third, is Jesus the unique Son of God, fully God and fully man? If anyone is off on any of these three, that person is off base altogether. If anyone is on target with those three, that person is probably going to be on target with most everything else.

Jesus is unique in his manhood. Jesus is God and Jesus is man. When Jesus was here on earth, he was as fully human as anyone can ever be. He was the perfect man. In his deity, he was also as fully God as God can ever be. Jesus is the God-man.

Manuel Scott, the great preacher, said that when Jesus came to earth the Celestial became terrestrial. The God out there became the God down here. The Supernatural became naturalized. Jesus stands out in all of history as God's unique person. He did everything we were intended to do, except that he did it perfectly and we don't.

Years ago, when Lawrence of Arabia was trying to persuade the Arabs to join the Allies in the Great War, they told him, "We'll fight with you, if you'll do one thing. If you will live like us, eat like us, drink the water we drink, live in the tents we live in, and fight like us, and do it as well as we do, if not better—we'll join you." In a way, that's what Jesus did. He came among us, he lived like us, he lived with us, he drank the water we drink. He wore clothes like we wear. He did everything we do, except that he did it better than anyone else ever did.

Jesus is superior because of his uniqueness. He is God in the flesh. "The Word was made flesh, and dwelt among us (and we beheld his glory, the glory as of the only begotten of the Father)" (John 1:14 KJV). Jesus is unique. He is so unique that God gave him the name that is above every name. In the Old Testament, God said there is no other name except his name. But here, in his revelation to Paul, God says, "I'm giving Jesus a new place as far as man is concerned. I'm giving him the name that is above every name. I'm giving him the name Jesus, an exalted name."

Jesus is unique. He is superior in his uniqueness.

Ask the angels what they think of Jesus: "a Savior has been born to you; he is Christ the Lord" (Luke 2:11).

Ask the Roman centurion: "Surely he was the Son of God!" (Matt. 27:54).

Ask the demons: "What do you want with us, Son of God?" (Matt. 8:29).

Ask John the Baptist: "Look, the Lamb of God, who takes away the sin of the world!" (John 1:29).

Ask the beloved disciple: "the bright Morning Star" (Rev. 22:16).

Ask Judas: "I have betrayed innocent blood" (Matt. 27:4).

Ask Paul: "I consider everything a loss compared to the surpassing greatness of knowing Christ Jesus my Lord" (Phil. 3:8).

Ask Peter: "God has made this Jesus, whom you crucified, both Lord and Christ" (Acts 2:36).

Ask Pilate: "I find no basis for a charge against him" (John 19:6).

Ask Thomas: "My Lord and my God!" (John 20:28).

Jesus is superior in his uncommon offices. He is a prophet, priest, and king. Moses said that he was going to be a prophet (Deut. 18:15), and he is. The writer of Hebrews said he is a priest after the order of Melchizedek (Heb. 6:20), and he is. Pilate asked him when he stood before him to be questioned, "'Are you the king of the Jews?' 'Yes, it is as you say,' Jesus replied" (Matt. 27:11). Jesus is prophet, priest, and king, all wrapped up in one person.

Jesus is superior in his undeniable character. Even his enemies couldn't find fault with him. Judas said, "I've betrayed innocent blood." Pilate said, "I can't find any fault in this man." He is unimpeachable in his character. His enemies had to trump up charges to say that something was wrong with him, and they were all lies. Jesus is superior in his flawless character.

Jesus is superior because of his unprecedented mission. Why did he come? He came to die. All of us come to live. But Jesus came into the world to die. That's why John described him as "the Lamb that was slain from the creation of the world" (Rev. 13:8). His death was voluntary (John 10:17–18).

When I was in Scotland some time ago, I learned that our neighbors were shearing sheep. They had some beautiful black rams, and they invited me over to watch them and take some pictures. The rams weighed 120 to 130 pounds. They looked pretty tough with their big horns. When the men were ready to shear, one man would get in the pen, grab a ram, and separate him from the others. He would flip the ram over and prepare him for the shearer. All of a sudden that ram became as helpless as a little baby and just fell back into the shearer's arms. The ram lay there passively as the shearer removed that beautiful black wool. As I watched, I thought, "That's what Jesus did. He suffered as the Lamb of God, the holy sacrifice." He didn't say a word of protest when he died for us. He had an unprecedented mission. He came into the world to save sinners. That's what we are, and that's why Jesus came.

Jesus is superior in his unceasing ministry. Do you know what he is doing today? He is seated at the right hand of the Father. That means he intends to remain there for a while. As he is seated at the right hand of the Father, he is praying and making intercession for us. Jesus is praying for you today. Get that into your mind and heart. Jesus is living to intercede with the Father for *you* (Rom. 8:34). No wonder he has been given a name that is above every name. *He is superior in his uniqueness.*

Jesus Is Unique Because of the Salvation That He Brings

No other name can save us (Acts 4:12). Napoleon can't save us. George Washington can't save us. Abraham Lincoln can't save us. The greatest, finest person you know can't save us. But Jesus will save us. God has no grandchildren, only children. Augustine said, "The Bible is written up in personal pronouns—a man and his God." Do you know Jesus? That's why he came—to save us.

Isn't it wonderful to see how Jesus is saving people today? I want you to know he's doing it! He is doing it on a scale that is unbelievable.

I visited the home of a young couple. The wife was a Christian. Her husband, a successful Naval Academy graduate, was lost without Christ. A lengthy discussion and witness led to a return visit. I pressed the claims of Christ on Rusty, asking him if he would open his heart and accept Jesus as his Lord and Savior. He looked intently in my eyes, and after pausing for what seemed like five minutes, he softly said, "Yes." We bowed our heads to pray and he invited Christ into his heart. Joy and peace flooded his face and he shared a statement I'll never forget: "Tonight, I feel like I've found a soft pillow to lay my weary heart on."

Jesus is the name that is above all names because of the salvation that he brings. He is God's rescue squad in one person!

Jesus Is Unique Because of the Sense of Personhood That He Brings

So many people today are looking for their identity. A swiftly changing world, job uncertainty, and dysfunctional families have led to a paralyzing loss of personhood. Many ask, "Who am I? Why am I here?" But when we accept Jesus, he gives us a sense of belonging, of identity, because he comes to live in our hearts. We realize God loves us so much that he has made us his sons and daughters (2 Cor. 6:18). We are adopted into the family of God! When that happens we feel that we are somebody.

I remember when I was in high school. I attended the Hopewell Baptist Church with my grandparents and my mother. I was converted in that wonderful church. An anniversary celebration was to be held there. I persuaded my parents to let my cousin and me thumb our way out to the church, which is about thirty miles from Nashville. We wanted to be there for the dinner on the grounds and to hear the special speaker.

On the outskirts of Nashville, we stood beside the road with our thumbs out. In a few minutes we were approached by a big, black

Oldsmobile. As the car drew nearer I noticed the hat of a state trooper. My heart froze. The brakes screeched as the car stopped. I feared he might arrest us. As we ran up to the car, I noticed that the license plate displayed the number 1. The thought quickly ran through my mind that this must be a very important person to have a number 1 on his license plate.

The patrolman rolled down the window and said, "Where are you boys going?" I introduced myself and replied, "We're going up to my grandparents' church for a special service." Surely, I thought, he won't throw us in jail if we're going to church. He said, "Jump in! We're headed that way, and you can ride with us." We climbed into the back seat amid briefcases, papers, radios, and other important-looking items. The man seated in the back said, "Hello, Jimmy. I'm Frank G. Clement, governor of Tennessee. I am going up to the Hopewell church to speak. I will be glad to give you and your friend a lift. Buckle your seat belts! We're running a little late, and we need to get there in a hurry."

Well, that patrolman let the hammer down on that big, black Oldsmobile. We reared back in the seat with the governor, and the closer we got to Hopewell, the bigger and more important we felt. In my mind's eye I envisioned the scene when we arrived at the church. My mother and daddy would be there, and my younger brother, Joe, plus the friends and neighbors that I had known through the years. Imagine what they would think when they saw Jimmy Henry riding with the governor of Tennessee! Sure enough, the vision soon became a reality.

As we rounded the corner and came near the church at the top of the hill, we saw a great crowd of people awaiting the arrival of the governor. The patrolman stopped amid the popping of gravel, the swirling of dust, and the swishing back and forth of the aerials on top of that shiny, black Oldsmobile. The crowd enveloped the car. The first one out was me. I jumped out, tipped my hand in the governor's direction, and said, "Thank you, Governor. I sure did appreciate and enjoy the ride. God bless you." I can assure you that I was the envy of my brother and all my buddies from that moment on. I was somebody!

As I have grown older and think back on that exciting moment, I realize that as wonderful as it was, there is something even more precious to recognize: I am a child of the King and can have an audience with my Father at any time! King Jesus gives a sense of personhood and dignity to a person no one else can.

Tom Skinner, the late great preacher, said that when he lived in Harlem, he had to struggle with the questions of who he was and why he was here. What was the purpose in living? Listening to the radio one night, he happened to catch an unscheduled gospel program. The preacher was the most uncouth and uneducated one he had ever heard. But as he preached about the cross and the power of Christ to forgive every sin and radically transform a person's life, Skinner asked Jesus to come into his heart. And he did! Here he was, a young man not knowing who he was, searching for meaning and purpose in life, for an identity—and all of a sudden he had it. He wanted to be somebody. He was leader fo the tough Harlem Lords. His one ambiton was for his gang to become the chief gang in Harlem. That night Tom Skinner discovered that he was a person of far greater importance than he had ever imagined he could be. He was nothing less than God's child. No longer did he need to walk arund with his head down—ashamed of his status, ashamed of where he lived, ashamed of everything about himself, his family, and everything else. The president's kids can only say, "My father is President of the United States." The Queen of England's kids can only say, "My mother is the Queen of England." But he could stick his head up now and walk around with his shoulders back and his chest out because he could say, "I am a member of the royal family of God, which puts me in the best family stock there is in the world." He discovered his identity at last. He really was somebody!

Isn't that what Professor Higgins reminded Eliza Doolittle of in *My Fair Lady?* "You're a Duchess! Think like a Duchess! Talk like a Duchess!"

Whatever your background; wherever you've come from; whether your dad was an alcoholic; whether you were abused or ridiculed in school; or whether you've been put down on the job; whatever your circumstances may be—just keep remembering that when you are in Christ, you are somebody!

Jesus is unique because of the sense of personhood that he brings. Isn't it a thrill to feel that we're important? That we are somebody?

Jesus Is Unique Because of the Subjection of Sin That He Brings

According to Paul in Romans 6, Jesus brings sin into subjection. We are no longer slaves to sin. He doesn't say we can't sin. He says we're no longer bound by sin (Rom. 6:22). We can't read the Bible without being overwhelmed by the way Christ transforms lives and subdues besetting sins—Zacchaeus's greed, Peter's cowardice, the prostitute's immorality.

From time to time I hear of men and women who are homosexuals and lesbians who say they have been born that way, that they can't help themselves, and that's why they have to be that way the rest of their lives. No, they don't! Why? Because when we come to Christ, we're no longer slaves to sin. That's what Paul said in 1 Corinthians 6:9–11, when he wrote of people who were in the church at Corinth. He said that some were homosexuals, some were adulterers, some were liars, some were stealers, some were idolaters, and some were slanderers. He made a list of ten moral failures and then added, "such were some of you." What happened? They met Jesus. When they came to Jesus they put those things in the past tense. Did that mean they weren't tempted any more to be homosexuals? No! Did it mean they weren't tempted any more to steal? No! Did it mean they weren't tempted any more to slander? No! Did it mean they weren't tempted sexually? No! What happened? They were at one time controlled by these lusts, but the indwelling Christ gave them power to put sin into subjection.

So the homosexual can say, "Yes, I'm tempted to go back to that lifestyle, but Jesus gives me the power over it." The man who is tempted to commit adultery can say, "Yes, I'm tempted by that woman, but Jesus puts that temptation into subjection." Jesus can do this because his name is above every name. God has highly exalted him, and he has put sin into subjection in our lives.

The British have a unique expression. When a person in political office is defeated or needs to resign, they say that he's going to "stand down" or he should "stand down." He shouldn't hold that office anymore; therefore, he's not going to run for that office—he's going to "stand down." I thought about that. That's what Jesus does to sin. He says, "Stand down. I'm going to put you down. You can't win, so stand down. Stand down, adultery! Stand down, thievery! Stand down, power! Stand down, greed! Stand down, cheating!" Stand down, because the King of Kings and Lord of Lords reigns in our hearts! These sins have got to stand down before Jesus.

I'll never forget a man who came to my house once. He was an alcoholic and had a beautiful family. He had tried everything to get that devil off his back. He had been to every group and sought help from many sources. We talked for a long time and then we knelt to pray. On his knees he said, "Dear Lord, I can't overcome this, but you can. Help me be the man you intended me to be." And the Lord did.

Jesus is unique because of the subjection of sin that he brings. He is the only one who can empower us to be persons he intended us to be.

Jesus Is Unique Because of the Sure Victory That He Will Bring

Jesus is going to win the final round! That's great news to know, isn't it? There are many celebrations on the Christian calendar. Some churches observe Lent. That's the season when we recall, among other things, Jesus' temptation in the wilderness. We note Good Friday when Jesus endured his passion and suffered for our sins. Then on Easter morning we celebrate Jesus' resurrection from the grave. I remember Dr. Lee saying that on that wonderful Sunday morning when Jesus' body was lying in the grave, the Father spoke out and said, "Son, you've done everything I've asked you to do. Now let's get out of here!" And he rose up from the grave! His body was resurrected! We celebrate that! We celebrate Pentecost Sunday when the Holy Spirit came on the church and indwelt the believers.

But that's not the end. Someday King Jesus will come back to take his church, his bride, to be with him. Then, after a period of time, he will return again, and on that day every knee shall bow to King Jesus. The person who won't bow to Jesus now, on that day will. All those in heaven—the cherubim, the archangels, all the old saints, and every believer in glory—will bow their knees. All those on earth—every man, every woman, all who thumb their noses at God now, every person who has neglected his Word—all of them are going to bow. All those under the earth—every demon, every evil spirit, even Satan himself—they, too, are going to bow at the name of Jesus on that day! He's the King of Kings! They can't stop him!

So don't get discouraged. When things seem to be going the wrong way in your home, in your work, in our country, don't get discouraged. We know the final chapter. That doesn't mean we pull in the walls and say, "Oh, hold the fort, Lord! We're holding on until

Jesus comes!" Go out and get on the offensive! This is the time to be doing that. The King is coming! You can't stop him!

You can try fire, but he'll quench it. You can try water, but he'll walk on it. You can try the wind, but he'll make it wrap around his feet like a puppy dog. You can try the grave, but he'll break the seal of the tomb. You can try the United Nations, but he'll make it fall at his feet. You can try atheism, humanism, and secularism that say he never lived, that the Bible is a lie, that he is irrelevant; but the King of Kings and Lord of Lords will ultimately conquer them. You can't stop him. He has the name above every name—the name *Jesus*.

One of our missionaries was serving in Indonesia. One day while he was walking down the street with his ten-year-old boy, they ran into a Muslim funeral procession. In order to get out of the flow of the crowd and with nowhere else to go, they slipped through the open doorway of a nearby mosque. All was quiet. They could hear nothing. Though his parents were missionaries, the boy had never been in a mosque before. He just stood there and looked around at that massive building in awe. In a few minutes, the imam climbed to the minaret of that mosque and called the people to prayer. In the native tongue he called out these words, "Allah is god, and Mohammed is his prophet." You could hear the words echo all around that big mosque. "Mohammed is his prophet . . . Mohammed is his prophet . . . Mohammed is his prophet . . ." They listened, and before the father could say anything, his son cupped his hands and shouted, "God is God, and Jesus is his Son!" All through that mosque you could hear it echo, "Jesus is his Son . . . Jesus is his Son . . . Jesus is his Son . . ." Then it became quiet again. They stood there, not knowing what to expect. Finally, the boy, holding his dad's hand, said, "Daddy, they can't stop him, can they?"

No, they can't stop him! They'll never stop him! No one will ever stop him! No political machine will ever stop him! No government will ever stop him! No philosophy will ever stop him! Because "God exalted him to the highest place and gave him the name that is above every name, that at the name of Jesus every knee [shall] bow, in heaven and on earth and under the earth, and every tongue confess that Jesus Christ is Lord, to the glory of God the Father." He is, indeed, King Jesus!

—◆—

II

Richard Kent Hughes

⟾◆⟸

After holding two pastorates in California and serving as an adjunct professor in Greek and homiletics at Talbot Theological Seminary, Richard Kent Hughes became pastor of College Church, Wheaton, Illinois, in 1979. His preaching ministry has included addresses at URBANA, Moody Bible Institute Founder's Week, Moody Pastors' Conference, Slavic Gospel's Annual Conference in Austria, and HCJB's Annual Conference in Ecuador. Hughes earned his M.Div. degree at Talbot Theological Seminary, and his D.Min. at Trinity Evangelical Divinity School.

He is the author of *Behold the Lamb* (Exposition of John 1–10), *Behold the Man* (Exposition of John 11–21), *Blessed Are the Born Again, Liberating the Ministry from the Success Syndrome, Disciplines of a Godly Man,* and the *Preaching the Word* series.

⟾◆⟸

If I had one sermon to preach to the contemporary church it would certainly be "Not Far from the Kingdom," because I am convinced that this is the condition of many in evangelical churches who are not truly "born again." They know the great doctrines and publicly confess them. They have mastered Christian vocabulary and can correctly mouth the expected shibboleths. They subscribe to Christian ethics and social conventions. Some can even boast of an enviable Christian heritage. But when all is said and done, they are not truly regenerate—"unsaved evangelicals," we might say.

For such people, Jesus' words in Mark 12:28–34 are graciously surgical, just as they were for another unconverted churchman, John Wesley, who upon becoming aware that he was "not far from the kingdom," was by that very discovery prepared to meet Christ.

This exposition cuts through the cant and religiosity of contemporary Christianity, clearly showing the way of grace.

⟫⬦⟪

Not Far from the Kingdom

One of the teachers of the law came and heard them debating. Noticing that Jesus had given them a good answer, he asked him, "Of all the commandments, which is the most important?"

"The most important one," answered Jesus, "is this: 'Hear, O Israel, the Lord our God, the Lord is one. Love the Lord your God with all your heart and with all your soul and with all your mind and with all your strength.' The second is this: 'Love your neighbor as yourself.' There is no commandment greater than these."

"Well said, teacher," the man replied. "You are right in saying that God is one and there is no other but him. To love him with all your heart, with all your understanding and with all your strength, and to love your neighbor as yourself is more important than all burnt offerings and sacrifices."

When Jesus saw that he had answered wisely, he said to him, "You are not far from the kingdom of God." And from then on no one dared ask him any more questions.

Mark 12:28–34 NIV

Few people have so affected history that its very epochs are marked by their births—let alone their spiritual rebirths! John Wesley was one of the few. Had it not been for Wesley's conversion and the ensuing revival with its social impact, England would probably have undergone something similar to the French Revolution. John Wesley's coming to faith was one of the important historical events in the Western world.

John Wesley was born in 1703, the fifteenth child of Samuel Wesley, the rector of Epworth, and his wife, Susanna. He enjoyed a good upbringing under his unusually talented and dedicated mother. He had a brilliant career at Charterhouse and Oxford, where he was elected fellow of Lincoln College in 1726. After serving as his father's assistant on two occasions, he was ordained a priest in the Church of England in 1728.

145

Returning to Oxford, Wesley joined a group of undergraduates led by his brother, Charles, and the later-to-be great evangelist, George Whitefield. This group, which was dedicated to building a holy life, was derisively nicknamed by other Oxonians the "Holy Club." Though Wesley was not yet truly converted, he met with these men for prayer, the study of the Greek New Testament, and devotional exercises.

He set aside an hour each day for private prayer and reflection. He took the sacrament of Holy Communion each week, and resolved to conquer every sin. He fasted twice a week, visited the prisons, and assisted the poor and the sick. Doing all this helped him imagine he was a Christian.

In 1735, still unconverted, he accepted an invitation from the Society for the Propagation of the Gospel to become a missionary to the American Indians in Georgia. His ministry was a great fiasco. He utterly failed as a missionary—undergoing miserable conflicts with his colleagues, and almost dying of disease. When he returned to England, he wrote: "I went to America to convert the Indians; but, oh, who shall convert me?" His mission experience taught him the wickedness and waywardness of his own heart.

Not all, however, was lost. In his travels aboard ship he met some German Moravian Christians whose simple faith made a great impression on him. When he returned to London, he sought out one of their leaders. Through a series of conversations, to quote Wesley's own words, he was "clearly convinced of unbelief, of the want of that faith whereby alone we are saved."

Then on the morning of May 24, 1738, something happened that Wesley would never forget. He opened his Bible and his eyes fell on the text of Mark 12:34: "You are not far from the kingdom of God." The words reassured him. Before he went to bed that night, he crossed that invisible line into the kingdom of God. This text was to become Wesley's life verse, a reminder of the shape of his life for the first thirty-five years of his existence. "You are not far from the kingdom of God."

Beautifully, not only the verse, but its setting (the Lord is conversing with a scribe, a lost clergyman of the house of Israel), bears remarkable parallels to Wesley's own lostness. Both were clergymen. Both were highly educated. Both were Bible scholars who knew the Scriptures inside and out. Both were confronted with Christ, who said to both, "You are not far from the kingdom of God."

Near the Kingdom of God

The exchange, of which our text is a part, began with a question from the scribe: "One of the teachers of the law came and heard them debating. Noticing that Jesus had given them a good answer, he asked him, 'Of all the commandments, which is the most important?'" (v. 28). The scribe initially had come to witness the confrontation between Jesus and the Sadducees. Though he disliked the Sadducees' doctrine, he came rooting for them because they, like he, had a religion of human achievement. Jesus was a threat to his belief-system. However, as he witnessed the breathtaking intelligence of Jesus in answering the resurrection question, refuting the Sadducees with a quotation from Exodus 3:6 (from the very heart of the Torah), he found himself inwardly applauding Jesus and subconsciously drawn to him. Before he knew it, he was impulsively asking a question, and it was *his own* question. It came from the scribal mind-game of trying to reduce religion to a single axiom. Rabbi Hillel, for example, was promised by a Gentile that he would convert if Hillel could give him the whole Law while he stood on one foot. Hillel answered with a version of the Golden Rule: "What you yourself hate, do not do to your neighbor; this is the whole Law—the rest is commentary. Go and learn it!"[1] This is the kind of answer the scribe was looking for from Jesus. He was standing heart-to-heart with eternity.

The scribe was not to be disappointed, for Jesus' reply was consummately brilliant: "'The most important one,' answered Jesus, 'is this: "Hear, O Israel, the Lord our God, the Lord is one. Love the Lord your God with all your heart and with all your soul and with all your mind and with all your strength." The second is this: "Love your neighbor as yourself." There is no commandment greater than these'" (vv. 29–31).

The first part of Jesus' answer was known to everyone. It is from the Shema Israel, "Hear, O Israel," the opening sentence of every synagogue worship service, taken from Deuteronomy 6:4. It was repeated by every pious Jew every morning and every evening. In fact, it was worn by the devout in a tiny leather box, called a phylactery, on the forehead and on the wrist during prayer. Godly households also hung the Shema on their doors in a small round box called a mezuzah. Everyone knew this part of Jesus' answer. It was the creed of Israel. Heart, soul, mind, and strength were not intended as a breakdown or a psychological analysis of human personality. They simply mean that one's whole being is to be devoted to loving God. It does not take much of a man to be a believer, but it takes all of him there is.

The second part of Jesus' answer is taken from Leviticus 19:18, "love your neighbor as yourself." This also was familiar to all Jews. So where was the genius in Jesus' answer? It was in this: The thought of loving God and loving humankind had been voiced by other rabbis and scribes, but this was the first time any rabbi had fused these two specific Scripture references together.[2]

The brilliance of Jesus' answer lay not only in its formulation, but in its implications. First, it summarizes the first four commandments, which have to do with our love for God (Exod. 20:2–11). The second part summarizes the final six commandments, which have to do with our love for humankind (Exod. 20:12–17). Jesus' answer is comprehensive to the "nth degree."

Second, Jesus' double answer shows that love for God and love for humankind cannot be divided. This teaching had a powerful impact on the subsequent teaching of the apostolic church. Later the apostle John wrote, "Whoever loves God must also love his brother" (1 John 4:21; cf. Rom. 13:8–9; Gal. 5:14; James 2:8).

Third, Jesus' command to love your neighbor "as yourself" radicalizes the call to human love. None of the earlier formulations included this qualifying clause. Including "as yourself" provides us with a conscious and conscience-convicting standard, because we sinners all love ourselves, despite our psychological demurrals. Just how radical Jesus' demand is can be seen in the story of the Good Samaritan, where he portrayed a neighbor not as a fellow Jew, as any Jew would have expected, but as an enemy, a Gentile—from the world next door (Luke 10:25–27).

What powerful teaching this was! This marvelous symmetry of devotion—loving God and loving humankind—could not be disputed. Nobody had ever put it so well, or so scripturally, until now! It was brilliant! It was perfect! It truly encompassed the whole Law. And the obvious ethos of Christ's own person (he was living it!) made it so compelling.

How would the scribe answer? Remember, his cronies were standing by, watching. The New Testament scholar C. E. B. Cranfield says that the opening words in verse 32, which our text renders, "Well said," should really be an exclamation[3]—perhaps "Beautifully said, teacher! What a beautiful answer!" The scribe told Jesus, "You are right in saying that God is one and there is no other but him. To love him with all your heart, with all your understanding and with all your strength, and to love your neighbor as yourself is more important than all burnt offerings and sacrifices" (vv. 32–33). Our Lord was clearly pleased with his response: "When Jesus saw that he had answered wisely, he said to him, 'You are not far from the kingdom of God'" (v. 34). Jesus' answer was tantalizingly ambiguous. He was after the scribe's soul.

This was a *compliment*. From the scribe's response, Jesus saw that the man was capable of thinking for himself. He saw that the scribe understood that the Law was more than a system, that it was essentially spiritual. So he complimented him: "The way you're thinking, you're not very far from the kingdom of God." Some people are far from the kingdom of God, some at the threshold. The scribe was *very close*.

This was also a *warning*. Though he was close, he was decisively separated. It is possible to be within an inch of heaven, yet go to hell!

Here Jesus' point was positive: The man was near! How so? He realized that loving God and humankind "is more important than all burnt offerings and sacrifices." This tells us much about his heart, for he speaks of the entire ceremonial system as not being as important as loving God. What he was saying was light-years beyond the place at which many people have arrived today who imagine that their good works will suffice. The scribe was near!

The scribe was also a thinking man. Jesus complimented him for this by telling him that he had "answered wisely." He was intellectually convinced that Christ was right. Samuel Johnson said: "If a man thinks deeply, he thinks religiously." In a world that is about as shallow as a bird bath, those who enter the kingdom are those who are willing to pause and truly think about eternal things.

The scribe was also near because he faced head-on the implications of the fact that the love of God is the highest priority of all. Squarely faced, this is a sobering reality, because by nature we do not love God with all our heart, no matter how hard we try. There has to be a radical change inside us in order for us to do this. This is a work of the Spirit of God. By embracing the necessity of love the scribe drew near to heaven's door.

He was also near because he was honest. He was a scribe, and naturally sided with his fellow scribes and Pharisees. But he did not let his natural allegiance keep him from acknowledging the truth. There is always hope for a person who will break ranks to keep his or her conscience. The scribe was nearer than most.

He was also near because he was not a coward. He was willing to risk mocking in order to step up to the door of the kingdom of God. Lack of courage and love of approval have been fatal to many souls. This man was so near to the kingdom—so near!

John Wesley was like that. Sitting at the feet of one of England's most famous mothers, he was taught that the love of God was the highest priority of all. Susanna Wesley's own testimony was that she spent regular time with each of her nineteen children, instructing them in the things of God.

Wesley was a thinking man if there ever was one! He was famous for his unadorned clarity in a day of ornamental obfuscation. He brought all his intelligence to bear on eternal things. Wesley was honest—in personal matters and in spiritual matters. After his experience in America, he bared his soul without guile to those he thought could help him. Wesley was also brave and refused to be a "people-pleaser."

With all of this he was so near, but still not in the kingdom. His biggest problem was understanding the inward nature of Christ's requirements.

Wesley was a master of external discipline (fastings, prayers, and good deeds). Yet, as he later explained, after he stood in the face of death his religious exercise gave him little comfort, and no assurance of his acceptance by God.

Far from the Kingdom

If we are to believe God's Word first and then the testimony of John Wesley as well, we must take to heart this truth: While the scribe and his clerical counterpart, John Wesley, were not far from the kingdom, they were still outside. Being almost there is not being there!

Perhaps you recall some years ago that stuntman Evil Knievel tried to jump the Snake River in his jet-motorcycle. He went up with a burst of power, then fizzled out across the canyon, ignominiously pulling the ripcord of his parachute. Making it halfway, or even all but an inch, is not making it.

Today, in some circles, it is fashionable to talk about "spiritual pilgrimages." That is okay in the context of a regenerated life. We are certainly part of a growing experience. However, if the word "pilgrimage" is used to sanctify or baptize the state of not arriving at something good, it is a deception. Being on a pilgrimage can sound so humble. It implies that you do not have the proud audacity to say you have arrived. It means that you are not an "absolutist"— something akin to a fascist or racist in the relativistic thinking of the world. But being a pilgrim must not be an end in itself. You must make it into the kingdom or your pilgrimage is of no use at all.

Did the scribe ever make it into the kingdom? We do not know. The Scriptures are silent.

Getting into the Kingdom

If the scribe finally did enter the kingdom of heaven, it was because he submitted to the logic of his own words. Loving God is more important than the entire ceremonial system. Perhaps he attempted to love God with all his heart and failed, thus realizing that he could never achieve the moral excellency of the Law and that he was a lost sinner. Finally seeing himself for what he was, he may have cast himself on the mercy of God, and thus found salvation.

When a religious man sees and acknowledges the profundity of his sin, it is a great day. Sir James Y. Simpson, the discoverer of chloroform, used to say that the greatest discovery he ever made was that he was a sinner and that Jesus Christ was the Savior he needed. Such a discovery will lead to the casting of one's self on the mercy of God, and thus receiving the gift of faith, repentance, and salvation.

This is what happened to Wesley. His experience in America had brought him to the end of himself. His honest interchange with the Moravians who witnessed to him brought further conviction of his inner failure. On one occasion as he talked with them, he heard them speak of their personal faith as a gift from God. When he asked how this could be, they replied that this faith was the free gift of God. They assured him that God would unfailingly give it to everyone who earnestly and perseveringly sought it. Wesley wrote after the meeting that he resolved to seek it to the end.

Finally, on May 24, 1738, as Wesley opened his Bible, he read that beautiful statement that in nine words condensed the progress of his spiritual pilgrimage: "You are not far from the kingdom of God." Then came evening, and the famous statement in his journal tells the story. "In the evening I went very unwillingly to a society in Aldersgate Street where one was reading Luther's preface to the Epistle to the Romans. About a quarter before nine, while he was describing the change which God works in the heart through faith in Christ, I felt my heart strangely warmed. I felt I did trust in Christ, *Christ alone,* for salvation; and an assurance was given me, that He had taken away my sins, *even mine,* and saved me from the law of sin and death."[4]

The rest of the story is well-known history. Wesley became a dreamer. He preached in Saint Mary's in Oxford. He preached in other churches. He preached in the mines. He preached in the fields. He preached on the streets. He preached on horseback. He even preached on his father's tombstone. *John Wesley didn't tire!* "John Wesley preached 42,000 sermons. He averaged 4,500 miles a year. He rode sixty to seventy miles a day and preached three sermons a day on an average. When he was eighty-three, he wrote in his diary, 'I am a wonder to myself, I am never tired, either with preaching, writing, or travelling!'"[5]

As we all know, the church has never been the same. Wesley's disciples, including Francis Asbury, were mighty powers in evangelizing England and frontier America. Read his life and the lives of his circuit riders and you will find chronicled the most amazing love for Christ and a tenacious love for lost souls. Their lives are among the great glories of the Church Universal.

What are the lessons for us? First, it is entirely possible to have grown up in the church, to have consistent, godly parents, and yet never have come to a saving knowledge of Christ.

Second, it is also completely possible to have studied theology and have never become a true Christian. One can know the Scriptures in the original, as Wesley did, and know more than the preacher, yet be unregenerate still.

Third, it is possible to have heard the grace of Christ preached all your life and still be resting on your own goodness.

Fourth, it is possible to become gospel-hardened, and so seal your damnation even within the church. It is possible to fool everyone and have the preacher conduct your funeral and assure everyone that your soul is resting in heaven—when it really is in hell.

Fifth, it is possible to be within just an inch of the kingdom of God.

The abiding truth is this: Convictions not acted on die; truths not followed fade; lingering can become a habit; and we can either go in or go farther away.[6]

Are you near to the kingdom of God, but not in? There are times when a single step makes all the difference. When a man or woman stands at the entrance to an airplane, one step and the person is on the way to a new destination. But one who fails to act will never go anywhere.

———————————

12

D. James Kennedy

———◆———

D James Kennedy, senior pastor of Coral Ridge Presbyterian
Church (PCA), Fort Lauderdale, Florida, which he organized
in 1959, is one of America's best-known television preachers.
Founder and president of Evangelism Explosion International, he
is the designer of an evangelistic method and program that is uti-
lized by thousands of churches in many denominations throughout
the United States and around the world.

Kennedy earned his M.Div. degree from Columbia Theological
Seminary, his M.Th. from Chicago Theological Seminary, and his
Ph.D. from New York University, and is the bearer of five honorary
doctorates, including the D.D. from Trinity Evangelical Divinity
School, and the D.Sac.Theol. from Southwest Baptist University.

He is the author of *Evangelism Explosion, Truths That Transform, Why I Believe, Your Prodigal Child: Help for Hurting Parents,* and *Turn It to Gold.* He received the George Washington
Honor Medal, Freedoms Foundation of Valley Forge, 1971, 1976,
and 1980; and Clergyman of the Year Award, Religious Heritage
of America, 1984; and was named International Clergyman of the
Year by Civitan International, 1986.

———◆———

The reason I chose this message is that I believe it has the potential
for accomplishing the greatest good for the kingdom of Christ on
this earth.

The New Testament secret of evangelizing the world is spiritual
multiplication. We are told that three thousand were *added* to the

church at Pentecost, and five thousand more were *added* shortly thereafter. Next we are told that the disciples *multiplied,* and then we read that they *multiplied exceedingly.*

It is only through equipping the saints to evangelize and through training others to do the same that spiritual multiplication can be effected. This is the essence of Evangelism Explosion International and is, I believe, our greatest hope of reaching the multiplying masses of the world.

———>·◆·<———

Change Your Conduct or Change Your Name

——❖——

Go ye therefore, and teach all nations, baptizing them in the name of the Father, and of the Son, and of the Holy Ghost: Teaching them to observe all things whatsoever I have commanded you: and, lo, I am with you alway, even unto the end of the world.

Matthew 28:19–20 KJV

A young man had just graduated from Oxford. He returned to say goodbye to his favorite professor, who invited him in and asked him to take a seat. "What are your plans, young man?" he asked.

"I'm going into law," replied the young man.

"That's fine, and what then?"

"I hope to advance to the presidency of our firm."

"Excellent! And what then?"

"Then I hope to be elected to Parliament and become a member of the House of Lords."

"That's excellent. And after that, what then?"

"Well, I have some very excellent ideas for England and I hope to present them to the legislature."

"Wonderful! What then?"

"Well, I haven't thought too much beyond that. I suppose I'll retire."

"Yes, and what then?"

"I'll enjoy myself for a few years, I suppose."

"Fine, and what then?"

"Well, I don't know. I suppose I'll die."

"Yes. What then?"

"Well, I haven't given that any thought at all. I don't know."

"Young man, you are a fool! Go home, and think life through."

A lot of people in this world, both young and old, fit into that same category. They have never really thought life through. Have you? Have you taken a long look at life and what God really has for you? Perhaps you have been reading the Four Spiritual Laws to a lot of people and you have said to them, "God has a wonderful plan for your life." But have you given much thought to what that plan is for *you*? Have you really thought of the will of God in this matter? Have you really abandoned yourself into the hands of Jesus that his plan might be worked out fully in your life?

A survey of young people in our church revealed that over 50 percent of them had never seriously considered or surrendered themselves to serving Christ in some full-time capacity. Have you ever come to a place in your life when you have said, "Lord, if you want me in the ministry, if you want me on the mission field, if you want me working in some full-time capacity, if you want me to be in Christian education or youth work, then I am willing"? I wonder if you have considered this for yourself—not only considered it, but come to the point at which you are willing to be used in whatever way the Lord sees fit to use you.

I asked a group of young people one time what plans they had for their lives. They said they planned to be lawyers, and doctors, and butchers, and bakers, and candlestick makers. Then I asked them if they had considered being used in some full-time work for Christ. Again, less than half had really considered it. I said to them, "If you are a Christian, you have no right whatsoever to make any plans to be a housewife, a teacher, a doctor, a lawyer, a businessperson, a banker, or anything else until you have considered first of all whether or not Christ may be so condescending as to use you in full-time Christian service. That body that you are sitting there in is not your own! You don't own it. That mind that you are making your plans with doesn't belong to you. You don't own it. Those hands that you're going to use in your occupation don't belong to you. You don't own them. The Bible says we are bought with a price—the precious blood of Christ. We are not our own. We belong to him."

I have a number of books that I own, but I do not possess them. They have been borrowed by various people over the years who have forgotten to return them. I own them but I do not possess them! I don't get any use from them. I don't learn anything from them. They are of no service to me. Yet I bought them. I own them. But I don't possess them.

Does the God who bought you and who owns you, possess you? Have you really yielded yourself to him completely? God has called us to a wonderful life and he does have marvelous plans for all those who are his own. Many people in this country spend most of their time, as one person described it, "digging for clams in the mudflats of materialism." But God has called us to the stars, has made us for eternity, and has summoned us to greater things.

In all of eternity, this is the one and only chance that you have—right now. Everything else depends on it. Everything! Hundreds, billions, of centuries from now depend on whether you have received Jesus Christ as Lord and Savior of your life. Also the rewards that God has offered, he has promised to give to those who serve him faithfully. Everything depends on *now!*

Do you remember Casey at the bat? Do you remember this mighty batter when the home team in Mudville was one run behind in the last of the ninth inning and there were two outs? The bases were loaded and the mighty Casey came up to bat. Everybody knew that the score was soon going to be changed and Mudville was going to win the game! The first pitch was thrown. Casey looked at it with a scornful eye. It went right by him and the umpire cried, "Strike one!" He watched the next one go by and the umpire cried, "Strike two!" Then Casey tightened his muscles and the third pitch came. The mighty Casey swung his bat and *whop* . . . "Strike three!" There was gloom in Mudville that night, for the mighty Casey had struck out.

We have only one time "up at the bat" in all eternity—one single time. A familiar little couplet states it so well:

> Only one life, 'twill soon be past;
> Only what's done for Christ will last.

That little couplet can haunt you throughout your life. I remember thinking at times about what God has done in calling young people to his service. Who knows—there could be another David Livingstone, Martin Luther, John Calvin, Billy Graham among us through whom God could change the world.

Jim Elliot was class president and the most popular man on campus at Wheaton College. He was a wrestling champion and an amateur poet. He was a man who was at home with God, a man with

159

great devotion who gave his life to serve Christ on the mission field. In the 1950s he and four other missionaries went to the jungle in Ecuador to witness to the Auca Indians. After much preparation they landed, and Jim Elliot and the others faced these natives who came out with their spears. Every one of those missionaries was armed, but they didn't use their guns. Their bodies were found floating down the river with eight-foot Aucan spears through them.

When he was a senior in college, Jim Elliot wrote words in his diary comparable to Hamlet's soliloquy. I have never known any other words that have haunted me more in my own ministry than these. This young man who soon was to be plunged through with a spear was contemplating giving his life to Christ. He wrote:

> "He makes His ministers a flame of fire." Am I ignitible? God deliver me from the dread asbestos of "other things." Saturate me with the oil of the Spirit that I may be a flame. But flame is transient, often short-lived. Canst thou bear this, my soul—short life? In me there dwells the Spirit of the Great Short-Lived, whose zeal for God's house consumed Him. Make me Thy Fuel, Flame of God.[1]

"A fool! Threw his life away!" some perhaps would say. But he also said in his diary as he contemplated the prospects of losing his life, "He is no fool who gives away that which he cannot keep to gain that which he cannot lose." I hope you will seriously, this week, consider God's plan for your life. Whether you are called into full-time service or not, God calls every single Christian to be a faithful witness for him.

The greatest heresy that has ever plagued the church is the idea that somehow it is the minister's task to win people to Christ. I think one of the brightest lights on the horizon is the younger generation that is not afraid to speak out for Christ. When I was converted to Christ over three decades ago, I began reading the Scriptures. It was so clear that Christians were supposed to witness. But I looked and didn't see this happening anywhere. None of the churches that I knew anything about were doing this. I said to some people, "Aren't we supposed to share with other people, to witness, to evangelize?" Their reply went something like this: "Oh, that's the preacher's job. Just sit down and shut up." I couldn't understand it. There were so few who were not afraid to speak out.

It makes my heart sing to see the abundance of Christians who are willing to witness for Christ. Of course, it is one thing to witness when there are thousands of us together—but how about when you go home? Is your life really laid out for Christ? Are you really surrendered to him?

I hope that in your witnessing you will make very plain what Jesus said when he announced the entrance requirements into the kingdom: "Repent and believe the gospel." These are the twin requirements, the two sides of the same coin: repentance and faith. There never is true faith without true repentance; and there never is true repentance without true faith. God grants both or neither. I hope that you will call people to repent of their sins; that you will make clear that this is a renunciation of their will—a surrender of their will to God.

I remember reading about the conclusion of a war when the commanding general came to the other general to surrender and said, "I want to compliment you for your magnificent strategy and the way you waged this war." The other general said, "Lay down your sword!" God doesn't want compliments; he wants surrender! Lay down your sword! Men are at enmity with God. God calls you to repent: "Except ye repent, ye shall all likewise perish" (Luke 13:3).

Repentance is a determination of mind that leads to a change of life; a determination to turn from all the ways of past disobedience and to walk in the new ways of obedience. Jesus said, "He that hath my commandments, and keepeth them, he it is that loveth me" (John 14:21). We live in an exceedingly lawless age just as the Bible said would come. The mark of a Christian is the willingness and desire to live under the Law of God and to call it a delight and rejoice in it, because we know it comes from a loving Father for our good.

Satan is going to tempt you. That is going to be the test. How about that secret sin in your life? How about that sin concerning which the devil has said, "Well, you might get rid of everything else, but there's still that sin." You know what I'm talking about. God requires the axe be laid at the root of that sin. You must truly repent if you are going to be cleansed of that sin.

We read in Acts 8:4, "they that were scattered abroad went every where preaching the word." In the Greek text the term *euangelid-zōmenoi* is used, which means "evangelizing." Those who were scattered abroad went everywhere evangelizing. When Jesus gave the Great Commission in the first chapter of Acts, he said, "ye shall be witnesses unto me both in Jerusalem, and in all Judaea, and in Samaria, and unto the uttermost part of the earth" (v. 8). What did his followers do? They stayed in Jerusalem. Then persecution came because of the preaching of Stephen. Now the Christians were scattered abroad and they went everywhere evangelizing.

It is interesting to note how persecution has been connected with Christian witnessing. It wasn't until persecution came that the first Christians began to obey the Great Commission.

Richard Wurmbrand, a Lutheran minister, spent fourteen years in a communist prison in Eastern Europe. Terrible, terrible things happened to him. He was tortured every other day, and once was crucified for four days.

He was a guest at one of our church services. After the congregation had sung "How Great Thou Art," he said, "That was beautiful singing and that is a beautiful hymn. But that is not the most beautiful hymn I've ever heard. The most beautiful hymn I've ever heard was sung only behind the Iron Curtain. In the West you don't know what it is. But we used to hear it frequently in prison in those iron cells with those great openings that went down story after story. We could hear the hymn reverberating all night long, sung by different prisoners. You have never heard anything like it. I don't have much of a voice, but I will try to sing a little bit of it for you." I'll never forget this tall, gray-haired man who bore in his body the marks of years of torture. He said, "It goes something like this"— and he screamed a blood-curdling scream. All night long a million Christians were singing that hymn in communist prisons!

It wasn't until persecution came that they witnessed. I asked him if in Eastern Europe, where one could spend fifteen years in Siberia for witnessing, many Christians witnessed. His eyes sparked as he said, "Did many Christians witness! *I never met a Christian who didn't witness!*" But it took persecution to bring that about. What is it going to take here in America? I pray to God it won't take that.

In the account in the Book of Acts, who was doing the witnessing? Some people say, "It was the apostles who were doing it, wasn't it?" But a text without a context is a pretext, so look at the first verse of chapter 8. There we read, "and they were all scattered abroad throughout the regions of Judaea and Samaria, *except the apostles.*" Then Luke tells us in verse 4, "they that were scattered abroad went every where *preaching the word.*" This is how the greatest power in the history of the world was unleashed on the pagan Roman Empire. In less than three hundred years Christians completely overthrew the mightiest pagan force the world had ever seen and placed a Christian Caesar on the throne because believers everywhere were going out and witnessing to their Lord. By the middle of the second century Tertullian could say, "We are more numerous than anyone. We're in your army, your navy, your cities, your senate and palace; we are everywhere."

Then the whole empire was declared to be Christian by Emperor Constantine. Millions of pagans (who never knew Christ) were swept into the church. These "converts" in name only, of course, couldn't witness. The idea arose to "let clerical George do it." So today the "ecclesiastical general" gets up once a week and delivers the message to the soldiers. When he is finished, the whole army goes home for dinner, and the general puts his rifle over his shoulder and goes off to war—while hell laughs.

The fight for souls has been left to the clergy. This has been the story of the church for centuries. The result: there were two hundred million people when Jesus uttered the Great Commission. Today there are, by conservative calculations, well over ten times that many people who have never even heard the gospel.

The only hope we have is to marshal every Christian into the army of God. The problem is that we sing, "Like a mighty army, moves the Church of God," yet 95 percent of the army is AWOL.

I want to ask this question. How many of you know of one person who is a living, breathing Christian because you led that person to Christ? I don't mean someone who merely professes to be a Christian. Professing Christians and real Christians are two different things. The Great Commission is to go into all the world and make disciples, not just "converts." Many profess but they do not possess. How many of you can honestly say that you know one such person? I praise God for those of you who can.

Jesus made it very plain. He said, "Follow me, and I will make you fishers of men" (Matt. 4:19). Unless he is a liar, if you are really following him, he is making you a fisher of men. If you are not becoming a fisher of men, you are not following Christ. It is just that simple.

A story that has often challenged my heart concerns a man who was the great leader of an army. He led his army all around the known world. His soldiers followed him everywhere because he was not afraid to go out and lead them into battle and because he did more than he demanded of anyone else. He was not a Christian. His name was Alexander the Great. He conquered the world by the time he was thirty. He left a message that I think the church everywhere needs to hear today.

After he had conquered the world, Alexander was holding court in his vast palace with soldiers lining the marble walls. He was sitting on a golden throne. One after another of his soldiers was brought before him and sentenced by the king. There was no court of appeals. It was life or death, and nobody could deliver anyone out of his hand. Finally a youth of about eighteen—handsome, blonde, and blue-eyed—was brought before him. Everyone could see that Alexander was favorably impressed with him. The king said to the sergeant, "What is his crime?" He had turned and fled from the enemy, and was found crouching in a trench, hiding.

There was one thing Alexander could not stand and that was cowardice. He himself was always right out on the front line. All the Persian arrows and spears could not bring him down off his mighty steed. He could not tolerate cowardice in any of those who served as soldiers in his army. Alexander's features hardened. Finally, he breathed a sigh and said to himself, "The boy is so young." Then, his heart touched by the lad, he asked, "Son, what is your name?" "Alexander," the youth replied. The smile vanished from the king's face.

"What is your name?"

"Alexander, Sir."

The king turned red and exclaimed, *"What is your name?"*

The boy began to stammer, "Al . . . Alex . . . Alexander, Sir."

The king leaped from his throne and grabbed the lad by his tunic. With arms of steel he lifted him right off his feet, stared him in the face for a moment, then threw him on the ground. "Soldier," he shouted, "change your conduct, or *change your name!*"

164

"Man, woman, what is *your* name?"

"Christian, my Lord."

"What is your name?"

"Christian, my God."

You who have turned and fled from the battle, you who in craven, cowardly silence have kept your lips closed, how dare you take upon yourself the name of him who set his face like a flint toward Jerusalem and the cross? *Change your conduct or change your name!*

———⟫◆⟪———

13

Glen Charles Knecht

—◆—

G len Charles Knecht is senior pastor of First Presbyterian
Church (Associate Reformed Presbyterian Synod), Columbia, South Carolina. He previously served pastorates in
Pennsylvania and Maryland, and was a missionary evangelist with
the Presbyterian Church USA in Iran. He attended Fuller Theological Seminary, earned the B.D. and Th.M. degrees at Princeton Theological Seminary, did graduate study at Conwell School
of Theology, and was awarded an honorary D.D. by Covenant
College.

Knecht contributed a chapter to *The Preacher and Preaching:
Reviving the Art in the Twentieth Century,* edited by Samuel Logan;
and a sermon entitled, "The Principle of Substitution," to *Best Sermons 2,* edited by James W. Cox.

—◆—

It seems to me that whenever pastors approach a sermon opportunity, they need to look at it in the light of the urgency of time and
prepare themselves for ministry as if it were the last one.

So, in thinking about this book, I simply asked myself and the
Holy Spirit what I would bring to people if I had only one sermon
to preach. I then set about preparing the message, and passed it on
to the editor of this book. I think this way of approaching the pulpit will bring a seriousness to our preaching that will be lacking if
we act as if we have forever to teach and exhort our people.

167

In this message I wanted to encourage people to appreciate and enjoy all they have in Christ because all our resources are in him. The problem in the Christian life is not the lack of help but our failure to appropriate it. So we limp along with less than we need when we ought to be running and serving with great vigor and joy.

Possessing Your Possessions

———<>———

Every place that the sole of your foot will tread upon I have given to you, as I promised to Moses.

Joshua 1:3 RSV

If I had only one sermon to preach, what would it be? It is the principle of possessing your possessions. What a text it is! "Every place that the sole of your foot will tread upon I have given to you, as I promised to Moses." I get excited just thinking about the implications of it.

I remember a specific instance in my own life. The first piece of property I ever owned was now in my name—eight and one-half of the most beautiful acres you could ever want to see. There were streams and a quarry and thick underbrush and all kinds of interesting little places to explore. It was mine on paper, but not until the family and I tramped every inch of it, inspecting every rock and every tree, did we possess it. We had the title, indeed, but we didn't have the reality of it.

This text comes from a particular point in history, at the end of the mourning period for Moses. After being en route from Egypt to the promised land for forty years the Israelites are there on the brink. Everything on the way—all the struggles and the hardships—were for this moment of entrance into the promised land. And the possessing of the land would be done by the feet. Wherever they trod, that is where the possession would take place. So feet became sacred because they were the instrument of possession. The land wasn't really the people's until they had walked over it, claimed it, appropriated it, and made it their own.

Part of grasping this truth is to see the difference between position and possession. Position is the title one has that brings with it certain privileges and powers. Possession, on the other hand, is exercising those prerogatives, actually experiencing those powers and privileges. One can have one without the other.

169

Joshua, Moses' right hand and heir, had the position. But the position did not in itself bring the benefits and the reality with it. There must still be the actual taking of the land, a bonding with it, an appreciation of it, a gratitude for it.

Long ago God had determined that this land was to belong to the Israelites and had promised it to them. They had been moving toward it. Now the time had come to arise from their disciplinary wanderings, from their inactivity and unfruitfulness, to the dignity of their calling and to the strenuous toil that lay before them. It was time to possess their God-given possessions.

What is the relevance of this to our lives? You have a position in Christ. You are joined to him by faith. You are one with him, the Lord of the universe. You are an heir of the kingdom of God, a joint-heir with Christ, a child of God. You are seated with Christ positionally in the heavenly places. "All [things] are yours; and you are Christ's" (1 Cor. 3:22–23).

Yet your actual Christian life might be lived out in spiritual poverty, misery, coldness of heart, defeat, and worldliness. You have a position, but you may not possess the great spiritual benefits and realities that God has already given to you. That is, you have not yet claimed them, appropriated them, rejoiced in them, lived in their light, and said, "These things are mine."

What can we learn from this passage to help us possess these possessions, the use of which we need so desperately? What are some of the possessions we have as God's people, but which we may not have grasped as our own?

We Possess a Supernatural God

Joshua was confronted with the Jordan River, which at that time of year was swollen with current. No bridges, no boats. Two million people had to get across to the other side. He had seen what God did to the Red Sea. Was God still able? Could he do a miracle like that again?

God gave Joshua the solution: consecrate yourselves before the Lord. They got ready by purifying themselves and by praying. Then the priests carried the ark of the covenant down to the river, and when their feet touched the water, the waters upstream piled in a heap, until the whole nation had crossed over on dry ground.

170

This became a great sign to Joshua and the others. God's power had not changed. Joshua said to them, "Hereby you shall know that the living God is among you" (Josh. 3:10).

This God is alive today. He has not changed. He works supernaturally. He is not bound by the laws of nature. He can do whatever he wills in his world. "I will not fail you or forsake you," he says (Josh. 1:5). We are called to claim this God by faith, to depend on a great God instead of a weak God—a God who can do whatever he wills. This is the true God and the One we claim as our own.

We are to give him chances to display his power. We have forgotten the words of the three young Hebrews to King Nebuchadnezzar when faced with the ordeal of the fiery furnace: "Our God . . . is able to deliver us" (Dan. 3:17).

George Mueller of England delighted to exhibit God's power. On a trip to Quebec the ship on which he was a passenger encountered a dense fog that threatened to delay its arrival beyond the time of Mueller's speaking engagement. Mueller prayed and assured the captain that they would make it on time. "God made that appointment for me," he explained, "and he intends me to keep it." Mueller reached Quebec on time. God had miraculously lifted the fog and sped the ship on its way.

God is looking everywhere to find people through whom he can demonstrate his supernatural power. "For the eyes of the LORD run to and fro throughout the whole earth, to show his might in behalf of those whose heart is blameless toward him" (2 Chron. 16:9).

Christians should expect the impossible because of the kind of God they have. Our church desperately needed more room several years ago. After prayer and earnest effort we decided to purchase a nearby building for our work. By God's power we were able on the appointed day to walk over to the neighbor with a check for the full amount of the purchase.

Remember the words of the Lord Jesus: "If you have faith as a grain of mustard seed, you will say to this mountain, 'Move from here to there,' and it will move; and nothing will be impossible to you" (Matt. 17:20). Jesus was trying to teach us to claim and possess the God we actually have, instead of some puny god of our own imaginings.

How can we be afraid? "Be strong and of good courage," God commanded Joshua; "be not frightened, neither be dismayed; for the

LORD your God is with you wherever you go" (Josh. 1:9). The possession of a supernatural God makes all the difference in our Christian lives. Distrust makes us sluggish and useless. Faith and confidence in the God of the Bible inspire us with vigor and enthusiasm.

We Possess the Benefits of God's Covenant

Joshua was in sight of the enemies, but instead of fighting them, he reestablished the covenant sign on the men of Israel.

He had not circumcised the men born on the way since the Israelites' great rebellion against God forty years before. The sign of the covenant was withheld as a chastening of the Lord on them. Every time fathers saw their sons' naked bodies they realized anew the effect of their transgression. Their sin was keeping them from claiming their place as God's covenant people.

The covenant was God's promise to own Israel for himself. It was his pledge to them that he would make of them a great nation and that they would be a blessing to all the earth. He had committed himself in the most solemn way to it. The covenant was renewed at Sinai when he gave the Ten Commandments on the stone tablets. What great benefits belonged to the people by virtue of the covenant the Lord had established with them! What privileges waited to be possessed!

That same covenant is ours. Yet we have not claimed the benefits, like the assurance of our salvation, which are annexed to it. We ponder whether or not we are truly Christ's but possessing the benefits of the covenant would solve that question for us. We have not claimed or improved the blessings of our baptism. But it has great benefits stored up for us.

What are some of the possessions to be claimed in the covenant?

Peace with God. We have peace positionally but many Christians live without its present reality.

The Promises of the Bible. All these rich vows of God to assist us in temptation and in every situation wait to be claimed by us and made part of our lives. The fulfillment of God's promise to Moses had been delayed by forty years. But it was still a promise and would be fulfilled.

The Destiny to Be Like Christ. We have been predestined to be like him. That is our goal, but we are not realizing that potential in our daily experience.

The Gaining of Courage. Because of the covenant "no weapon that is fashioned against you shall prosper" (Isa. 54:17). What you are being called to do is part of God's covenant arrangement for you and that carries his promise with it. Take heart!

All these riches are in our covenant sign of baptism, but we have left them largely untouched. Even when we witness a baptism we are seldom moved to possess the great privileges that come with the sacrament. "Every place that the sole of your foot will tread upon I have given to you." That surely includes covenant blessings.

We Possess the Forgiveness of Our Sins

The Israelites observed the Passover on the desert plains after the circumcision had taken place, because they could not do this in their uncircumcised condition. This was only the third observance of the Passover in forty years. It should have been an annual event. This great possession had been neglected.

The Passover lamb was an atonement for sin. Its blood was sprinkled on the doorposts of the Israelites' houses in Egypt, so as to cover the sin of those within. "When I see the blood, I will pass over you" (Exod. 12:13).

The lamb was eaten to signify the people's participation in the sacrifice—to show that the forgiveness of sins had been accepted and embraced. But without the Passover offering all these years, the Israelites could have no clear sense of the forgiveness of sins.

We have neglected these great riches as well. We have not claimed the mercy and grace of God as we ought. We have concentrated on reforming ourselves, instead of being cleansed in the blood of Christ. Or we have tried to shift the blame for our sin to others. We do almost anything rather than ask God to be forgiven.

Yet how abundant in mercy he is. He is more ready to forgive than we are to ask. What a treasure house this is! We ought to be running to it every hour and saying, "Father, I have sinned in your sight. Cleanse me with the blood of the Lord Jesus Christ."

"If we confess our sins, he is faithful and just, and will forgive our sins and cleanse us from all unrighteousness" (1 John 1:9). From this cleansing comes the clear conscience, which with faith is the great weapon of the Christian. So Paul said, "I always take pains to have a clear conscience toward God and toward men" (Acts 24:16). Claim your possession! The blood of Christ will cleanse you.

We Possess Communion with God as Our Own Privilege

In the midst of Joshua's perplexity about what to do with Jericho, a man with a sword appeared to him. Joshua did not recognize him; he did not know if this individual was a friend or an enemy. But it was an appearance of the Lord God in the form of a man— a "theophany." Joshua fell on his face before him, as any of us would, and began to commune with him and take instruction from him about the battle to come.

Communion with God has also been given to us. A great way of access to the heart of God has been opened through the blood of Christ. A great road to the mind of God has been opened by the Spirit of God speaking in the Holy Scriptures.

Now we can commune with God's heart in prayer and with his mind in Scripture. What a privilege for us to have fellowship with the One who made us! This is what we were created for. This is the aspiration of the human race from the beginning. And it is now granted to us. But are we claiming it? We hurry past the place of prayer on our way to many less important appointments.

We spend more time daily with the newspaper than we do with the Word of God. A great possession we have, but we are not possessing it—not storing it away in our hearts. Most of the troubles that Christians have come from their failure to possess this great possession.

What a great encouragement to trust in God's Word this opening chapter of Joshua is! Fourteen centuries before Christ we have a written "book of the law" (v. 8). Scripture was already being written and was seen as the Word of God. Those who claim that these accounts were only passed along orally and then subject to error have not read this chapter carefully. The written Word of God is a part of his good gift to us and is utterly reliable. Possess that possession of yours!

We Possess Victory over the World

There stood the city of Jericho. It looked invincible. Army, chariots, walls, guards, knowledge of the territory: everything was on the side of that great walled city.

That was the way it was for Dave Wilkerson when he went as a country preacher to the streets of New York City to work with the gangs there. The challenge seemed to him too formidable to tackle. Momentarily he had forgotten about God's victory over the world. Have you felt that hopelessness as well?

God told Joshua what to do. The strategy was God's. The instructions sounded very strange, demanding unquestioning obedience and trust. "On the seventh day you shall march around the city seven times, the priests blowing the trumpets" (Josh. 6:4). When at last the trumpets sounded for the walls to come down, it was like a long cry to heaven for God to do what he had said he would do.

So the Book of Hebrews says, "By faith the walls of Jericho fell down" (11:30). In that great act Joshua saw by faith God's victory over the world, especially his overthrow of all the Canaanite cities and their people.

Jericho stands for the world. It is arrayed against Christians. It seems impossible to live the Christian life, so we settle for defeat. Like Paul's co-worker Demas, we are overpowered by the world. We think, Who are we to stand against sin and the world and the devil? Are we a special breed of "holier than thou" persons who can be expected to do the impossible?

There *can* be victory over the world. You do not need to succumb to it. Whether you are a college student facing the ravages of an unbelieving teacher, or a homemaker standing up for your right to rear your children yourself, or a businessperson seeking to live above dishonesty and greed, you can be more than a conqueror through him who loves you! "This is the victory that overcomes the world, our faith" (1 John 5:4).

Jesus said, "I have overcome the world" (John 16:33). This means that in his name we can do the same. The victory over the world can be won. But it must be claimed to be experienced.

The Book of Revelation calls us "overcomers." Paul calls us "more than conquerors." No wonder! There is no reason why sin, or the

175

world, or the devil should defeat any of us. "He who is in you is greater than he who is in the world" (1 John 4:4). Claim your world for Christ. All things are yours—including this world. It is yours to take over for Christ. Claim that workplace, that home, that marriage, that child for Christ, and take possession of it in Christ's name.

To possess your possessions in Christ requires an act of the will. Nothing less than unconditional surrender to the Lord and application of Christian exertion to the task is required. We have been too weak and flabby to take on the world, the flesh, and the devil. We need to put forth energy sanctified by a living faith.

How few Christians really possess their possessions! They have left Egypt and made the journey to the promised land, but they have barely entered into it, not tasting the sweet fruits, not swimming in the wonderful waters, not climbing the beautiful mountains of the Christian life. The land they have taken is small and cramped. But with courage of soul they could possess the broad, rich land that God has prepared for them.

Translate your position in Christ—a king and a priest, a son or daughter of God, and a member of his household—into a present reality, into something you actually possess. Then the land flowing with milk and honey will become yours here and now. That is what the Christian life is meant to be. Rise up and possess it!

———◆———

14

Erwin W. Lutzer

—————◆—————

A Canadian by birth, Erwin W. Lutzer is senior pastor of the famous Moody Church in Chicago, Illinois, where Sunday morning services are broadcast weekly. Before assuming his present position, he was senior pastor of Edgewater Baptist Church in Chicago, and taught at Briercrest Bible Institute and the Moody Bible Institute. He received the B.Th. degree from Winnipeg Bible College, the Th.M. from Dallas Theological Seminary, and the M.A. from Loyola University, Chicago. He was awarded an honorary D.D. by Western Conservative Baptist Seminary, and an LL.D. by Simon Greenleaf School of Law.

A contributor to *The Encyclopedia of Biblical and Christian Ethics,* Lutzer has also published five books: *All One Body: Why Don't We Agree?, Exploding the Myths That Could Destroy America, Failure: The Back Door to Success, Keep Your Dream Alive,* and *Putting Your Past Behind You.*

—————◆—————

If I had only one sermon to preach, I would explain the gospel, magnify grace, and urge men and women to trust Christ alone for their salvation. Against all the man-made theories about salvation, the cross stands as a welcome beacon for those who despair of earning their own way to God, and a stumbling block for those who insist that their own knowledge and goodness can gain them special favor with the Almighty. This sermon is intended to bring unbelievers to saving faith and to motivate believers to worship the God whose Son died a painful but victorious death. And because he

177

lives, those who trust him participate in his triumph. Although I usually preach expository sermons, I chose the topical method here to bring together the various strands of my central point that the cross is both horrible and glorious. For on it, Christ was both loser and victor.

Dying a Winner

Being justified as a gift by His grace through the redemption which is in Christ Jesus; whom God displayed publicly as a propitiation in His blood through faith. This was to demonstrate His righteousness, because in the forbearance of God He passed over the sins previously committed.

Romans 3:24–25 NASB

He made Him who knew no sin to be sin on our behalf, that we might become the righteousness of God in Him.

2 Corinthians 5:21

The Roman poet, Horace, criticized the playwrights of his day for bringing a god on the stage too readily in order to untangle the problems developed in the course of the plot. He wrote, "Do not bring a god onto the stage unless the difficulty deserves a god to solve it!"

This earth is a stage on which a drama is being enacted. On this planet issues of good and evil, justice and injustice, God versus the devil—all of these themes are being played out according to predetermined rules. But it soon becomes apparent that the plot is hopelessly tangled; a dilemma unfolds that only God can solve.

On stage is Satan, a powerful being who made his decisive choice against the Almighty. He has tens of thousands of lesser spirits under his command to carry out his bidding. He and his underlings work feverishly to create as much opposition to God as possible. Though he knows he will fail, his hatred drives him to attempt to frustrate God's plan at every turn.

Also active in the drama are the descendants of Adam, billions of us who, thanks to our forefather, have chosen to side with Satan in rebellion against the Almighty. Yes, we also are on stage, caught in a squeeze between God and the devil. We think we can control our own destiny, quite unaware that our future is, for the most part, in other hands. We can neither lift the condemnation from our shoulders nor change our sinful nature.

The plot is hopelessly tangled.

In siding with Satan, we stand to reap the bitter consequences for our fallenness. We are not only born under the condemnation of sin, but choose to commit sins that are destined to lead us to an eternity of regret, humiliation, and pain. We cannot control these consequences, but must helplessly accept our inevitable doom. Like a swimmer striving frantically a hundred yards from the rushing water of Niagara Falls, we must accept the fearful end that awaits us at the final curtain call. We cannot reverse what is irreversible.

Enter God.

His justice prevents him from forgiving us. He cannot act as if we are clean when, in point of fact, we are guilty. He cannot accept people whose debts are unpaid.

He had at least two possibilities. He could simply have consigned both us and the fallen angels to an eternity of deserved punishment. This would have magnified his righteousness; his justice would have been meticulously displayed throughout all the ages of eternity. The curtain would have closed and God would have been declared the victor. His rivals would have been appropriately banished from his presence.

Or he could have initiated a plan that would not compromise his justice and yet restore rebellious human beings fully to himself. This would have involved a more complete demonstration of all that he is: love, grace, wisdom, and, yes, justice. Thankfully, this is what he chose to do.

Several conditions had to be met. First, this plan would have to be entirely of God, executed without human cooperation. We are spiritually dead in trespasses and sins, and therefore unable to play a role in giving ourselves spiritual life. Corpses cannot effect their own resurrection.

Second, none of God's attributes could be compromised. Holiness, justice, and integrity would have to be meticulously preserved. When the curtain falls at the end of the last act, every being in the universe would have to declare that God is just.

Third, God would have to follow the rules of redemption. If men and women were to be reconciled to God, a human sacrifice would have to be made to accomplish this feat. No angel or beast could die for them; only the Right Man could be a substitute for the human race. Since this rescue effort was entirely a work of God, only he himself could meet the criteria his own righteousness demanded.

He chose not to stage a media event. Press agents were not enlisted to inform angels, demons, and people that God was about to arrive as a human being on planet earth. There would be no "photo op."

Six miles south of Jerusalem in the sleepy town of Bethlehem, a peasant girl gave birth to a baby boy. This child was God incarnate; he had the nature of a human being and the nature of God. Yet we marvel for he was a helpless baby, nursed in his mother's arms.

When he became a man, he traveled incognito, unrecognized for who he was. Though he performed miracles proving his divine origin, he was largely misunderstood and hated. Attempts were made to kill him, and though these plots were initially unsuccessful, eventually he was nailed to a cross. From our perspective this was just possibly his finest hour.

But his enemies were elated, convinced that they had finally put an end to this man who irritated them by pointing out their hypocrisy. The religious elite were especially delighted that he and his movement had come to an inglorious end.

To the untrained human eye Christ appeared to be a loser, a dreamer whose plans and programs had been aborted by the crucifixion. His fearful friends witnessed the injustice he endured yet he did not seek vindication. In heaven he had become accustomed to hearing shouts of honor, praise, and worship. In his presence the angels had sung, "Holy, holy, holy!" But here on earth, people shouted at him in derision. We can hear their taunts. Instead of honor there was envy; instead of wonder there was hatred. His clothes were ripped, and people spit in his face. His friends on earth stood by helplessly, and even his Father in heaven was silent.

Nobody cared about what he had to say. He had no attorney to represent him. We read of him: "Like a sheep that is silent before its shearers, so He did not open His mouth" (Isa. 53:7). He became the proverbial doormat, allowing men to whip him, curse him, and drag him from place to place without any attempt to set the record straight.

False stories circulated that the crowds were only too eager to believe. Injustice ruled without the slightest hint of compassion or objectivity. A loser, indeed!

Later generations would romanticize the cross. We visualize a beautiful beam of wood sanded to perfection, stained, and varnished. Today the cross is a symbol of beauty, a martyr's dream. But a cross in those days was rough, a tree stump or a hewn log with a branch as a crosspiece. The nails were long and rusty. Christ was offered sour wine to deaden the pain, but he refused it so that he could die with all of his faculties intact. This was death without dignity.

Dying as a common criminal, the God-man stood toe to toe with death and said, "This time you win!" He chose not to fight back.

Three men were crucified that afternoon, and they all looked essentially alike. They writhed in pain, defaced by whippings and splattered with their own blood. To the untrained eye this event appeared to be nothing more than the crucifixion of three com- moners who deserved their painful fate.

But in the spirit world an incredible event was taking place. The most sinful man who had ever walked on planet earth was dying. The man in the middle was guilty of the wanton cruelty of a Hitler or a Stalin. He was guilty of sedition, hypocrisy, and rape. He was guilty of adultery, rebellion, and, yes, child molesting.

Recently, our newspapers carried a story of a five-year-old girl locked in a closet, whipped and beaten until she died. She had tried to call for help, but was punished by her cruel parents. Such crimes are too painful for us even to think about. And yet, that day, a child abuser died!

Little wonder this criminal was forsaken by God. "My God, my God, why hast Thou forsaken Me?" (Matt. 27:46), he cried out with horrid anguish. Even nature felt the jolt: "And it was now about the sixth hour, and darkness fell over the whole land until the ninth hour, the sun being obscured; and the veil of the temple was torn in two" (Luke 23:44–45). Why the darkness? To spare the sun the indignity of shining on Golgotha where this horrendous sinner was mercilessly punished. To spare humanity from beholding the most shocking anguish of a man forsaken by the God he so passionately loved.

No wonder the light of the sun was obscured and darkness fell over the whole earth! The most terrible of criminals was dying on a cross. The songwriter reminds us:

Well might the sun in darkness hide
And shut his glories in,
When Christ, the mighty Maker, died
For man the creature's sin.

God closed the curtains for three hours while his beloved only begotten Son became identified with the sins of the world. "He [God] made Him [Christ] who knew no sin to be sin on our behalf, that we might become the righteousness of God in Him" (2 Cor. 5:21).

The irony, of course, is that Christ had personally not committed a single sin. He was the innocent Lamb of God who had done nothing amiss. Yet on that day, he became legally guilty of the sins of the people who some day would be his forever. "All of us like sheep have gone astray, each of us has turned to his own way; but the LORD has caused the iniquity of us all to fall on Him" (Isa. 53:6).

This humiliation of God would eventually result in his exaltation. His death would result in eternal life for millions. Three days later he was raised from the dead. This was proof that God was on center stage all the while.

Men and angels would eventually admit that this indeed was God at his best—God redeeming sinners through making a sacrifice that would meet every demand of his justice. God stooped down and picked people up from the gutter without defiling himself.

Throughout history God is displaying his attributes. He is taking the ordinary historical details of the world and making them converge into a mosaic of beauty that will enhance his own glory. The death of Christ gives us a glimpse into the character of God, his perfect attributes that will be magnified throughout all of eternity.

Seven attributes of God were displayed that dark day in Jerusalem.

The Righteousness/Justice of God

Paul says in Romans 3:25, "whom God displayed publicly as a propitiation in His blood through faith. This was to demonstrate His righteousness." The first purpose of the cross was that God might vindicate his name and prove that he is totally righteous. He showed that he could not save human beings without a proper ransom. There had to be a sacrifice that would meet the demands of justice. Only then could men and women be reconciled to God. Christ, as the second person of the Godhead, personally became that Redeemer.

Many years ago some atheists published a tract in which they wanted to mock God. They scrutinized men of the Old Testament. They showed the flaws in their character and then wondered how a holy God could accept them. For example, they said that Abraham lied about his wife to save his own skin, yet he is called "the friend of God" (James 2:23). Jacob was a liar and a cheat, and yet is called "a prince of God." David was an adulterer and a murderer, and yet is called by God himself "a man after My heart" (Acts 13:22). The atheists asked, "What kind of a God would associate with these men and call them his friends?"

In their own perverse way, these unbelievers had a point. If we were to judge God by his friends, his reputation might be tarnished. But Christ's death on the cross, being a complete payment for the sins of the Old Testament saints as well as for all of us, vindicated God. His reputation was completely preserved. He could associate with the unrighteous without compromise.

In California a man was given a speeding ticket. He arrived in the courtroom, heard the charge, and pleaded guilty. The judge then pronounced the sentence, promptly left the bench, and stood with the defendant to pay his fine! So it is with God. He pronounced us guilty, but then in the person of his Son he himself paid our penalty. Those who believe on Christ no longer owe God any righteousness, for he met all of those requirements for us. The cross removed the scandal from God's name.

Paul argued that the cross displayed the righteousness of God, "that He might be just and the justifier of the one who has faith in Jesus" (Rom. 3:26). He became both just and justifier. He is both the message and messenger of salvation.

The Truth of God

One characteristic of truth is consistency. Another is that truth does not hide the facts but exposes reality.

The cross reminds us that God would never pretend that sin does not exist, or that it is not really serious. There was no cover-up, no attempt to look the other way. That's why someday we shall sing, "Righteous and true are Thy ways, Thou King of the nations" (Rev. 15:3).

Pantheism, the teaching that "God is all and all is God," cannot take evil seriously. After all, if God is everything, then God is evil. To circumvent this dilemma, most Eastern religions teach that evil is illusory.

Not so Christianity. Evil has an actual existence. God does not expect us to redefine evil to make it compatible with his love. Evil is real, but so is God's intervention in the midst of it. God judges according to truth. His assessment is honest, according to the actual facts of the case.

The Mercy/Grace of God

What is grace? It may be defined as "unmerited favor." Christ got what he didn't deserve, so that we might escape what we deserve! Since the provision God made for the human race was entirely of his own doing, it must of necessity be granted to us as a free gift. We are, says Paul, "justified as a gift by His grace through the redemption which is in Christ Jesus" (Rom. 3:24).

In bearing our sins, Christ absorbed the anger of God against sin. Because Jesus was punished, God can forgive us, welcome us into his family, and give us high honor. Indeed, he can exalt us as "heirs of God and fellow-heirs with Christ" (Rom. 8:17). Paul wrote that God did this for us "in order that in the ages to come He might show the surpassing riches of His grace in kindness toward us in Christ Jesus" (Eph. 2:7). What grace! What undeserved favor! What mercy! Forever!

The Love of God

Talk is cheap. When we say we love someone, proof of that is our willingness to sacrifice for that person's benefit. Redemption cost God plenty. Not one of us need ever wonder whether God really loves and cares. Redemption is free for us simply because it was so expensive for God. "Knowing that you were not redeemed with perishable things like silver or gold from your futile way of life inherited from your forefathers, but with precious blood, as of a lamb unblemished and spotless, the blood of Christ" (1 Peter 1:18–19).

Is salvation free? From our standpoint, yes, for Jesus paid it all. But from God's standpoint it was incredibly costly. God gave, God suffered, God purchased. "For God so loved the world, that he gave his only begotten Son, that whosoever believeth in him should not perish, but have everlasting life" (John 3:16 KJV).

God loved us while we were his enemies. Now that we are his friends his love is unfailing even when we sin. It is wrong to think that God would love us more if only we were better! He loves us in Christ and for Christ's sake. Indeed, we were loved from before the foundation of the world and will be loved for all of eternity (John 17:23–24).

The Power of God

God displayed his power in Christ's resurrection. This does not simply mean that he proved that he has the physical power needed to resurrect a dead body from the grave. Christ had already displayed that power when he raised Lazarus. Christ's resurrection proves his spiritual power over Satan who wanted to keep Christ in the grave. The resurrection is proof of God's power over death and hell.

The clearest example of God's power is his ability to subdue the human heart and bring us to salvation. The gospel is "the power of God for salvation" (Rom. 1:16). Indeed, even the faith by which we receive the good news is a gift of God. From beginning to end, "Salvation is of the Lord."

God does not find it more difficult to forgive big sinners than small ones. This does not mean that all sins are equal, for some are greater than others. It does mean that the gift of God's righteousness is often given to the most notorious sinners as proof that God's saving power is unlimited. Since salvation is God's work, it can be extended to the most undeserving.

The Wisdom of God

Think about this: Evil men gathered to crucify Christ. They acted voluntarily, yet they were doing the will of God. Satan instigated the hatred against Christ, yet this also was simply another strand

186

in God's providential plan. Peter said that evil people cooperated to kill Christ, "to do whatever Thy hand and Thy purpose predestined to occur" (Acts 4:28).

Incredibly, God the Father is also spoken of as the one who put Christ to death. "But the Lord was pleased to crush Him" (Isa. 53:10); and again, "whom God displayed publicly as a propitiation in His blood through faith" (Rom. 3:25).

Thus the perverse will of people, the deranged hatred of Satan, and the plan of God all converged to culminate in this event!

What ingenuity!

The cross was the greatest crime of history. Not only was an innocent man mistreated, unfairly judged, and nailed to a shameful cross, but this man was the sinless Son of God! And yet—and yet—this great crime has become the hinge of history, the most glorious event that we could ever celebrate. As Paul said, "May it never be that I should boast, except in the cross of our Lord Jesus Christ" (Gal. 6:14). Throughout all of eternity, the church will display the awesome wisdom of God before angels and redeemed humanity. The cross will never lose its wonder.

The Glory of God

Throughout two thousand years of history, the church has been plagued with heresy, moral defection, pride, and a host of other sins and failures. When she is finally redeemed, free from these sins and limitations, she shall sing: "To Him who sits on the throne, and to the Lamb, be blessing and honor and glory and dominion forever and ever" (Rev. 5:13).

Throughout all the ages God will receive the glory that he so richly deserves. His mighty power and authority in the universe will continue to amaze angels and humans forever.

If God had simply created the universe, that would have displayed his physical power. If he had consigned fallen human beings and angels to everlasting torment, we would have seen his justice. But through the plan of salvation, through the cross, we see the attributes of God converge in a kaleidoscope of beauty and everlasting wonder.

Perhaps this explains why we read that creation is the work of his fingers: "I consider Thy heavens, the work of Thy fingers, the moon and the stars, which Thou has ordained" (Ps. 8:3). But salvation was wrought by "His holy arm" (Isa. 52:10). Salvation gives us a better glimpse of who God really is.

In Luke's account of the cross two thieves speak with Christ. One of the criminals abused him, saying, "Are You not the Christ? Save Yourself and us!" (Luke 23:39). He spoke for most people in the world today. "If there is a God, why doesn't he take care of the war, hunger, and abuse in the world?"

But the other man answered with humility, confessing that he was dying justly, whereas Christ did not deserve to die. Repeatedly he said, "Jesus, remember me when You come in Your kingdom" (Luke 23:42). Christ replied, "Truly I say to you, today you shall be with Me in Paradise" (Luke 23:43).

Symbolically, these men represent the polarization of the human race. The real division of humankind is not between men and women, black and white, educated and uneducated, East and West. While these differences are significant, the real distinction is between those who respond positively to Jesus Christ and those who reject him.

Let us marvel at the faith of this thief! He put his trust in a man who was just as bad off as he himself was! Christ's wounds were just as deep; his pain just as great. To the casual observer he hardly looked like a Savior. Yet this dying criminal saw beyond Christ's weakness to his eventual triumph. And Jesus, dying there in apparent helplessness, was able to say to this sinner in confidence, "Today you shall be with Me in Paradise."

Beyond the apparent defeat of death, there awaits the glory of heaven. If we could see believers five minutes after their death, we would understand that there is triumph even in defeat. An apparent loss is a genuine victory.

No matter how fearful our own impending death appears in this world, we will triumph in the next. We can look beyond the pain, humiliation, and failure to the world that lies beyond the senses.

Meanwhile, we can offer hope to our decaying world. To the child molester who wrote to me recently believing that his sin could not be forgiven, I can affirm that the man on the middle cross bore the full weight of sin for those who believe. Only the cross can reveal the marvelous extent of God's love and mercy. As the words of the song express it,

Jesus paid it all,
All to Him I owe;
Sin had left a crimson stain,
He washed it white as snow.

When the plot was hopelessly tangled, God walked onto center stage—not to take sides but to take over. Because his Son eventually won, we also shall be winners when the curtain falls.

15

Calvin Miller

―――――◆――――――

C alvin Miller is professor of communication and ministry studies, and writer-in-residence at Southwestern Baptist Theological Seminary in Fort Worth, Texas. He served his first pastorate in Plattsmouth, Nebraska, then became organizing pastor of Westside Church, Omaha, Nebraska, which grew from ten members in 1966 to more than 2,500 in 1991, when he assumed his present position. He holds both the M.Div. and D.Min. degrees from Midwestern Baptist Theological Seminary.

Author, lecturer, and convention speaker, Miller has written the Singer Trilogy *(The Singer, The Song, The Finale), A Requiem for Love,* and *Spirit, Word, and Story: A Philosophy of Preaching.*

―――――◆――――――

I have never been as struck by the JOHN-ONE-ONE-NESS of God, as I have been by the ROMANS-EIGHT-TWENTY-EIGHT-NESS of God. Don't get me wrong. God cannot be God without both his divine eternality or his incarnate, saving humanity. Still, when I am through watching God thunder in Exodus, or weep in Jeremiah, I turn to Job to watch him salvaging sorrow and doing a face-lift on the terror of my worst hurt. It is his there-ness that reassures me. When pain has ripped our nervous systems to shreds, he comes. Usually when we shout our "Whys" at him, he gets oddly quiet. There is no use going on! God will not talk! Just when we are about to side with Voltaire, God, our still, silent, cosmic colossus, at last folds his legs and sits with us. Is he here? Yes, and he's pointing somewhere. Yes, Yes! With his light-year finger our Great Lover is pointing out across the ages. We strain to see what he is pointing at. We squint our eyes against the blue. Then we at last see it: a hill, a cross, his Son. Our hurt has instant companionship! At last our terrible reversals have an answer. Our God weeps, and in doing so has not answered our "Whys," but our being. By doing this he makes us know our sorrows will be usable in ways we could never have imagined. If I had only one sermon to preach and then was commanded nevermore to preach again, I would counsel those who swim in pain through their inverted existence, "As soon as your anger ebbs, sit with this silent God and see your reversals as glory!" That is what I have chosen to do here.

━━▷◆◁━━

Seeing Your Reversals as Glory

=>◆<=

Paul and Timothy, servants of Christ Jesus,

To all the saints in Christ Jesus at Philippi, together with the overseers and deacons:

Grace and peace to you from God our Father and the Lord Jesus Christ.

I thank my God every time I remember you. In all my prayers for all of you, I always pray with joy because of your partnership in the gospel from the first day until now, being confident of this, that he who began a good work in you will carry it on to completion until the day of Christ Jesus.

It is right for me to feel this way about all of you, since I have you in my heart; for whether I am in chains or defending and confirming the gospel, all of you share in God's grace with me. God can testify how I long for all of you with the affection of Christ Jesus.

And this is my prayer: that your love may abound more and more in knowledge and depth of insight, so that you may be able to discern what is best and may be pure and blameless until the day of Christ, filled with the fruit of righteousness that comes through Jesus Christ—to the glory and praise of God.

Now I want you to know, brothers, that what has happened to me has really served to advance the gospel. As a result, it has become clear throughout the whole palace guard and to everyone else that I am in chains for Christ. Because of my chains, most of the brothers in the Lord have been encouraged to speak the word of God more courageously and fearlessly.

It is true that some preach Christ out of envy and rivalry, but others out of good will. The latter do so in love, knowing that I am put here for the defense of the gospel. The former preach Christ out of selfish ambition, not sincerely, supposing that they can stir up trouble for me while I am in chains. But what does it matter?

The important thing is that in every way, whether from false motives or true, Christ is preached. And because of this I rejoice. Yes, and I will continue to rejoice.

Philippians 1:1–18 NIV

Jesus is the cornerstone in all the reversals of life. Philippians was not written by a man unacquainted with life. Its author wrote from a prison cell, yet tried to see, in every life circumstance, the sovereignty of God.

Some time ago a book was released entitled, *If God Loves Me, Why Can't I Get My Locker Open?* In most reversals of life we ask ourselves, "If God really loves me, why aren't things working out better?" Yet in Philippians we hear from a man who knows God loves him, and also knows that life is not working out all that well. Still, in the midst of his circumstances, he praises God! In Philippians 1:18, Paul says, "I rejoice. Yes, and I will continue to rejoice."

Novelist Peter De Vries went through a great time of sorrow with his daughter who had leukemia. The story of that difficult time passed naturally and autobiographically into his novel, *Nothing but the Blood*. De Vries fictionally discusses his daughter's death, telling of their last few weeks together. Only shortly before the fictional heroine dies, in her hospital room, father and daughter watch a Red Skelton rerun in which there is a pie-throwing contest. (This hospital, by the way, is located between a great church and a medical science building, suggesting the plight of the church today.) Father and daughter are fascinated by the slapstick cleverness that Red Skelton could bring into that kind of comic situation. Only a few short nights later, it's the girl's birthday and the father visits her in the hospital. Now his daughter is so weak, she can scarcely raise her head. Yet it is her birthday, and he has a huge birthday cake riding in the back seat of his car. He decides not to take the cake into the hospital, at least not immediately.

Inside the hospital, his daughter can no longer eat: her appetite is gone; there are tubes in her body. Her illness has become a nightmare to both of them. At length his daughter begins to cough and spit up blood, and then hemorrhage, and finally dies in his arms.

The father, who has grown incredibly hostile toward God, gets in his car, drives to the church on the far side of the hospital, gets out of his car, picks up that cake he had taken for her birthday, and enters the church. He stands at last in front of a great stone statue of Christ. In defiance he takes that pink-frosted cake and slams it into the face of the stone Christ.

De Vries's hostility speaks to one view of God: that view that we sometimes have, that God is an ogre, and is there to keep us from having fun or wholeness in what we do.

I once preached at a funeral service for a seven-year-old boy named Jason, who united two congregations with his boyish charisma. Jason lived in Lincoln, Nebraska, but received most of his treatments for leukemia in a hospital in Omaha. Thus people from two different cities became involved in ministering to Jason and his family during the final critical weeks of his illness. Though his funeral was in Lincoln, those present at the service were almost equally divided between people from Omaha's Westside Church and his own church family in Lincoln. To see two congregations joined around the memory of a needy child was so touching that people wept abundantly. I called my sermon "A Tale of Two Cities," and beneath this Dickensian umbrella of love we all celebrated Jason's story. As I looked at his parents, I saw in their towering grief a great love for God, and I asked myself, "What is missing in them? Where is the hostility they should have toward God? Why don't they want to throw a cake in the face of some stone Christ?"

They had another view of God. To them, God was sovereign with a sense of wholeness: the only meaning they found in the world at all. The children's choir singing "Jesus Loves Me" lifted the sights of us all to see beyond the happenstances of this world.

Again, I emphasize that Philippians was not written by a man who knew no pain. Consider 2 Corinthians 11!

What anyone else dares to boast about—I am speaking as a fool—I also dare to boast about. Are they Hebrews? So am I. Are they Israelites? So am I. Are they Abraham's descendants? So am I. Are they servants of Christ? (I am out of my mind to talk like this.) I am more. I have worked much harder, been in prison more frequently, been flogged more severely, and been exposed to death again and again. Five times I received from the Jews the forty lashes minus one. Three times I was beaten with rods, once I was stoned, three times I was shipwrecked, I spent a night and a day in the open sea, I have been constantly on the move. I have been in danger from rivers, in danger from bandits, in danger from my own countrymen, in danger from Gentiles; in danger in the city, in danger in the country, in danger at sea; and in danger from false brothers. I have labored and toiled and have often gone without sleep; I have known hunger and thirst and have often gone without food; I have been cold and naked. Besides everything else, I face daily the pressure of my concern for all the churches. Who is weak, and I do not feel weak? Who is led into sin, and I do not inwardly burn?

verses 21–29

Paul had known the reversals of life. But in those reversals, he came out with a triumphant spirit.

In the final chapters of Genesis, Joseph's brothers are insecure. They had beaten Joseph, stripped him of his coat, and dumped him in a dry well to be sold into slavery. His grieving father never knew what happened to him.

Finally, in a time of famine, they all meet Joseph again. His brothers who had abused and maltreated him are desperately afraid that he will pay them back for all their offenses against him. But Joseph tells them, "As for you, ye thought evil against me; but God meant it unto good, to bring to pass, as it is this day, to save much people alive" (Gen. 50:20 KJV).

Paul says that God has three glorious uses for all of our reversals in life.

Reversals Demonstrate Christian Character

First, when reversals come, as people view us, they see our Christian character as it really is. Character is built by circumstances. Paul says to the Philippians, "Now I want you to know, brothers, that what has happened to me has really served to advance the gospel. As a result, it has become clear throughout the whole palace guard and to everyone else that I am in chains for Christ" (Phil. 1:12–13).

The King James Version translates Paul's words this way: "The things which happened unto me have 'fallen out.'" Christians just

196

have things "happen" to them. God doesn't plan these things in order to test your mettle, or to make you weep in the night, or to make you "throw pies in his face." There is a principle of indeterminacy in life. One of our fine young people had an automobile accident on the way home from church last fall, and someone was terribly hurt. The young fellow didn't come to church expecting that! But indeterminacy was loose. It had its way.

Now God is there to help us make sense of the unplanned. Madeleine L'Engle tells about a woman who was once locked up inside a stingy Calvinism. The woman, when just a young girl, was convinced that she was one of those predestined to be damned. One evening she was having dinner with friends who tried to assure her that she was not damned. But she told them, "'I am as certain that I am damned as that this wine glass will shatter when I fling it to the stone floor.' She flung down the fragile glass. It did not shatter. She cheered up, married, and ultimately became a mother."[1] Christian character survives indeterminacy. Christian character says, "I will celebrate God, even when I don't understand the mess I am in."

We all wind up in messes sometimes, but we should celebrate God even when we do not understand it all. A lady in our church was dying of cancer. In a way, every visit I paid her strengthened my life. One day she said to me, "Every morning I wake up with the resolution that I will not be as weak as I was the day before, but by night I am even weaker, in spite of my resolutions." Yet she always concluded with the testimony, "Jesus is Lord." She knew a wondrous sovereignty over the reversals of life! We learn character through what we suffer. I've seen people in our church go through scandal. One family said, "We never woke up a day when we failed to find that our names were in the newspaper again. Each time we had to remind ourselves, 'This, too, will pass!' God is sovereign!" People all around us are constantly facing ostracism and pain.

Once while I was preaching in Wheaton, Illinois, a reporter for one of the Chicago papers took notes on what I said. The article he wrote was ultimately released to several papers. This clipping came from a Dallas paper. I can't believe I said it, because I am one of those people who is scared to death of pain. But here it is.

I think one of the things God has let happen to me, probably for my own good, is to let me succeed slowly. . . . I hope I never get over having setbacks, because in the pain of being rejected or having a manuscript turned down I learn what it is to hurt. I want to be a seeing person, one who looks for faces and hearts longing to be understood and touched.

I cry a lot. I don't like being criticized or rejected, but these are incredibly important to continue growing *(sic)*. I have learned far more about who I was *(sic)* in life from my critics than from my friends, who overlook my faults or don't see them or who, because they want to continue being my friends, overstate my strong points. My critics have told me what I really was *(sic)* like.[2]

If you ever develop character, real character, in this world, it will come about far more from the rejection you find in your pathway than from the acceptance. St. John of the Cross once said, "Don't pray that you may have friends. Pray that you may have enemies, for only when you have enemies will you retreat of necessity to the cross of Christ." This is what the gospel is all about. "The first lesson," Paul said, "is that character grows out of these reversals. People see my life," he said, "and glorify God."

Reversals Bring Encouragement to Others

"Because of my chains . . ." Think about Paul's chains a moment. The fetters cut into his wrists, the footlocks into his ankles, and he was in pain (perhaps) for as long as two years. But he writes, "Because of my chains, most of the brothers in the Lord have been encouraged to speak the word of God more courageously and fearlessly" (Phil. 1:14).

Proverbs 27:17 says, "As iron sharpens iron, so one man sharpens another." There is pain in being sharpened! The honing, the emery, the sparks, the friction! The philosopher Jean Paul Sartre said, "Hell is other people." But Proverbs says that other people are honing devices. The pain of interrelationships that God gives you helps sharpen and hone your character. Lee Iacocca described how he saved the Chrysler Corporation through "equality of sacrifice":

When I started to sacrifice, I saw other people do whatever was necessary. And that's how Chrysler pulled through. It wasn't the loans that saved us, although we needed them badly. It was the hundreds of millions of dollars that were given up by everybody involved. It was like a family getting together and saying: "We got a loan from our rich uncle and now we're going to prove we can pay him back!"

This was cooperation and democracy at their best. I'm not talking about a Bible lesson here. I'm talking about real life. We went through it. It works. It's like magic and it awes you.

But our struggle also had its dark side. To cut expenses, we had to fire a lot of people. It's like a war: we won, but my son didn't come back. There was a lot of agony. People were getting destroyed, divorced. Overall we preserved the company, but only at enormous personal expense for a great many human beings.[3]

You see, if you live through reversals wisely, and other people view what is happening in your life wisely, a spirit of courage builds up in them.

A Sunday school teacher was telling the story of how some youth had taunted Elisha and how they were punished when two bears came out of the wild and ate forty-two of them.

"And now, children," concluded the teacher, wishing to stress the moral point, "what does this story show?"

"It shows," said one little girl, "that after 21 kids apiece, bears aren't hungry."[4]

Still, it seems to me that when I look out at this world, I see only hungry bears. They are often ravenous! But these bears are, in a sense, the key issue when it comes to character. Character is picked up by those who observe. Therefore, your children need to see you, as a mother, succeed. They need to see you, as a father, succeed. Such observance will encourage them to try in life.

But your children also need to see you tackle a big problem and watch you lose, to see how you handle it. When your children see you lose with equanimity and come out saying, "Praise be to God" (or as Paul says in Phil. 1:18, "I rejoice. Yes, and I will continue to rejoice"), then they can learn to handle all of life in joy!

Rabbi Harold Kushner reached national fame because of his reflection on the death of his son. When the boy was three years old the rabbi learned that he had a rare disease that would claim his life in his teens. The disease would stunt the boy's growth and leave him largely hairless and wrinkled like an old man. It would steal the beauty of adolescence from him, and devastate his entire family as they lived with him through its last ravages. Kushner admitted that because of this tragedy he had become a more effective pastor and a more sympathetic counselor. In spite of that, he writes, "If I could choose, I would forego all the spiritual growth and depth which has come my way because of our experience, and be what I was fifteen years ago, an average Rabbi, an indifferent counselor . . . and the father of a bright happy boy. But I cannot choose."[5]

I suspect that Paul, if he had been given a choice, would have chosen a paneled office just off the Appian Way in which to write his letter to the Philippians. But the chains probably did for his human understanding what the son's disease did for the Kushner household. The Kushners discovered that in some ways a tragedy can make us more whole than we otherwise might be. Paul discovered that chains can make us freer than we otherwise might be.

Reversals Bring Glory to Christ

"It is true," Paul writes, "that some preach Christ out of envy and rivalry. . . . But what does it matter? The important thing is that in every way, whether from false motives or true, Christ is preached. And because of this I rejoice" (Phil. 1:15, 18).

Consider the great reversals that have stood us on our ear as a nation. They are embarrassing even to mention! Do you remember that awful year when we worked our way through Watergate? Night after night, week after week, for a solid year, people in high places went on incriminating others and being incriminated themselves. It seemed that there was never any good news.

Finally, it ended in the terrible debacle of the tapes. We all remember that short red carpet that stretched out to the helicopter, and a broken president who had endured all that he could. His shoulders were bowed in shame and rejection as he laid aside the burden and the honor of his office. He stepped into that helicopter, rose into the sky, and was gone. When I saw that, I thought, "It isn't just Nixon who pays. Will not history portray a whole proud nation wallowing in the scandal of this week?"

One of the men frequently in the news was Charles Colson. Following Watergate, he picked up a copy of *Mere Christianity* by C. S. Lewis. Reading it while working through his personal embarrassment and shame, he came at last to call Jesus Christ Lord! Others, too, came into a brand new life, having been born again out of the odd mix of political scandal and the writings of an Oxford don. The traumas and turmoils and explosions of life activate a vigorous and urgent preaching of Christ. Paul could say, "In this I glory!" There is no ultimate shame in any situation that ends in the exaltation of Christ.

Max Cleland graduated from college in 1967. In 1968 he was in Vietnam as a captain in the army. He was fighting with his detachment in the battle for Khe Sanh. Looking down on the ground in the thick of battle, he saw a grenade lying there. He thought the grenade had fallen from his own belt. He picked it up. No sooner had he picked it up than a blinding flash blew him backwards into a tree. When the smoke cleared, he opened his eyes again. He could see that where his arm had been a white bone was now protruding. He tried to stand, only to find that his legs were gone. Shrapnel had perforated his windpipe. He spent many months in the hospital.

Throughout long months of suffering and embarrassment, he had to face many things about himself. He felt he was ugly; he knew he was severely handicapped. All hope for a useful life had been detonated with a grenade. What could a thinking, sensible head ever expect a motionless torso to do? It seemed he was damned to watch the world move around him. But God is a cheerful economist, multiplying our decimal capabilities into large and powerful ones. By 1971 Max was elected as a high official in the Veterans Administration. In 1980 he was elected to public office in Georgia. He said that coming to Christ through these horrible circumstances, he heard one prayer ringing in his head again and again:

> I was given poverty, that I might be wise;
> I asked for power, that I might have the praise of men;
> I was given weakness, that I might feel the need of God.
> I asked for all things, that I might enjoy life;
> I was given life, that I might enjoy all things.
> I got nothing that I asked for—
> but everything I had hoped for.
> Almost despite myself,
> my unspoken prayers were answered.
> I am among all men
> most richly blessed.[6]

Would Max Cleland remit those circumstances? Would he say, "Dear God, damn that grenade. I would rather have another set of options fall out for me"? I don't think so. More likely, he might say, "I rejoice. Yes, and I will continue to rejoice" (Phil. 1:18).

One of my favorite poets puts it all in perspective:

> Watch His methods, watch His ways,
> How He ruefully perfects
> Whom He royally elects,
> How He hammers him and hurts him
> And with mighty blows converts him
> Into trial shapes of clay which only God understands,
> While his tortured heart is crying and he lifts beseeching hands.[7]

When reversals come and we lift beseeching hands, let us recall with glory that although reversals are never circumstances we sought, we can view them like Paul viewed his: "I want you to know, brothers, that what has happened to me has really served to advance the gospel" (Phil. 1:12). It does not matter that we have never stood at the feet of God and "begged a whipping." Still, the whippings come. Make no mistake, however; it is never God who brings the lash. But since the pain has come, let us see what use he will make of it. If he uses our pains and our wounds to teach us, then "Gloria Patri!" Then we are blessed to know that there is sense to be made from the seemingly senseless seasons of our lives.

⥤◆⥢

Stephen F. Olford

⟜⟞◆⟜⟞

B orn in Northern Rhodesia (now Zambia), Stephen F. Olford is founder and president of Encounter Ministries and the Institute for Biblical Preaching in Memphis, Tennessee. He began his ministry as an army chaplain in South Wales during World War II. After a pastorate at well-known Duke Street Baptist Church in Richmond, Surrey, England, he became pastor of Calvary Baptist Church in New York City. For fifteen years he conducted a television ministry and for twenty-one years was heard on radio. He has received international recognition as one of the leading evangelical preachers of our day.

He received his Diploma in Theology from St. Luke's College, Mildmay, London, and his Th.D. degree from Luther Rice Seminary, Jacksonville, Florida. He holds four honorary degrees: the D.D. from both Wheaton College and Dallas Baptist University, the Litt.D. from Houghton College, and the H.H.D. from Richmond College, Toronto, Canada.

Olford has written numerous books and pamphlets, including *Heart-Cry for Revival, The Tabernacle: Camping with God, Preaching the Word of God,* and eight volumes in the *Stephen Olford Biblical Preaching Library.* His sermons and articles have appeared in more than fifty publications worldwide.

⟜⟞◆⟜⟞

When God called me to be an evangelist I determined, like the apostle Paul, to preach "Jesus Christ and Him crucified" (1 Cor. 2:2). This resolve has been based on a threefold consideration.

First, the death of Christ is central to history. As I point out in my sermon, it is the pivotal fact of time. It cleaves human history in two and is both universal and eternal in its redemptive relevance. It is the touchstone of all God's dealings in this day of grace, and will be the basis of all his dealings in the day of judgment.

Second, the death of Christ is central to theology. As P. T. Forsyth, the English Congregationalist, said, Christ is to us just what his cross is. We cannot understand him until we understand his cross.

Third, the death of Christ is central to reality. Life has little significance apart from the cross. This is why Paul says, "The message of the cross is foolishness to those who are perishing, but to us who are being saved [that means life and life more abundant!], it is the power of God" (1 Cor. 1:18); "He who did not spare His own Son, but delivered Him up for us all, how shall He not with Him also freely give us all things?" (Rom. 8:32).

Given these three aspects of the centrality of the cross, I regard the death of Christ of first importance. If I had only one sermon to preach, this is the message I would proclaim.

The Death of Christ

━━━▷◈◁━━━

Moreover, brethren, I declare to you the gospel which I preached to you, which also you received and in which you stand, by which also you are saved, if you hold fast that word which I preached to you—unless you believed in vain. For I delivered to you first of all that which I also received: that Christ died for our sins according to the Scriptures, and that He was buried, and that He rose again the third day according to the Scriptures, and that He was seen by Cephas, then by the twelve. After that He was seen by over five hundred brethren at once, of whom the greater part remain to the present, but some have fallen asleep. After that He was seen by James, then by all the apostles. Then last of all He was seen by me also, as by one born out of due time. For I am the least of the apostles, who am not worthy to be called an apostle, because I persecuted the church of God. But by the grace of God I am what I am, and His grace toward me was not in vain; but I labored more abundantly than they all, yet not I, but the grace of God which was with me. Therefore, whether it was I or they, so we preach and so you believed.

1 Corinthians 15:1–11 NKJV

In this opening paragraph of Paul's trenchant chapter on the resurrection we have four essential facts of the gospel: "Christ died . . . was buried . . . [was raised] . . . was seen." Included in these "gospel facts" is the statement that "Christ died for our sins." As David Prior observes,

There is no proclamation of the gospel which does not explain, in New Testament terms, the link between human sin and the death of Christ. *Indeed, there is no gospel at all unless the death of Christ can be seen to deal with sin once and for all.* The fact of the resurrection by itself says little about the heart of the gospel, unless it can be shown that "the sting of death is sin" and that the resurrection of Christ has therefore drawn that sting[1] (Rom. 4:25; Gal. 1:1–4, emphasis added).

205

So we see that the death of Christ is the pivotal fact of time. It cleaves human history in two and is both universal and eternal in its redemptive relevance. It is the touchstone of all God's dealings in this day of grace, and will be the basis of all his dealings in the day of judgment. It is little wonder, therefore, that the apostle considered of first importance the historical facts of Christ's death for our sins—his burial, his resurrection, and his appearances. This was the first creed of Christendom.

With that introduction in mind, I want to consider five salient aspects of the death of Christ from our text.

The Death of Christ Was Voluntary

"Christ died." Though we read that he was murdered, slain, crucified, and killed, yet, in the final analysis, "Christ died"; that is to say, his death was voluntary. Paul reminds us that "the Man Christ Jesus . . . *gave Himself* a ransom for all" (1 Tim. 2:5–6).

It Was Voluntary as to the Motive

With the cross before him, Christ could say, "Behold, I have come . . . to do Your will" (Heb. 10:7); "the Son of Man did not come to be served, but to serve, and to give His life a ransom for many" (Matt. 20:28); "for this purpose I came to this hour" (John 12:27). This last statement is well paraphrased by Dean Henry Alford: "I came to this hour for this very purpose. . . . The going into, and exhausting of this hour, this cup, is the very appointed way of my glorification."[2] The cross never took the Lord Jesus by surprise. Throughout his life and ministry it was ever before him.

It Was Voluntary as to the Method

The Lord Jesus escaped from being thrown over the precipice at Nazareth (Luke 4:29). He escaped death by stoning many times (John 8:59; 10:31). Throughout his earthly life he knew how he would die; he even told his disciples, "The chief priests and . . . the scribes . . . will condemn . . . and deliver [me] to the Gentiles to mock and to scourge and to crucify. And the third day [I] will rise again" (Matt.

20:18–19). Jesus had impressed the fact of his death on his apostles, but he had not specifically mentioned the mode. Intimations of such a death had been anticipated when he challenged his followers to take up the cross and follow him (Luke 9:23), and when he spoke of being "lifted up" like the serpent in the wilderness (John 3:14). But in Matthew 20:19, the Master was clear and concise: the Son of Man would be *crucified*. He knew the method of his death.

It Was Voluntary as to the Moment

When the moment of death came he bowed his head, and "gave up His spirit" (John 19:30). The bowing of Christ's head is not the helpless dropping of the head after death, but the deliberate, voluntary act of putting his head into a position of rest. The same verb is used in his declaration in Matthew 8:20, "The Son of Man has nowhere to lay His head." Our Lord reversed the natural order by positioning his head, crying "with a loud voice . . . , 'It is finished!'" and then voluntarily dismissing his spirit (Matt. 27:50; John 19:30).

Thus we see that this voluntary character of the death of Christ lifts the event right out of the realm of ordinary deaths—and even extraordinary deaths—into the place of uniqueness, infinite wonder, and redemptive significance. His death was voluntary. He anticipated this moment of death when he declared, "Therefore My Father loves Me, because I lay down My life that I may take it again. No one takes it from Me, but I lay it down of Myself. I have power to lay it down, and I have power to take it again. This command I have received from My Father" (John 10:17–18).

The Death of Christ Was Vicarious

"Christ died *for our sins*," not only because of, but on behalf of, our sins in order to take them away (Gal. 1:4; 1 Peter 2:24; 1 John 3:5). Christ did not merely die as a martyr, but as the bearer away of sin—"the just for the unjust, that He might bring us to God" (1 Peter 3:18).

> In one word, the great pillar of the Christian's hope is substitution. . . . In these days a direct attack is made upon the doctrine of the atonement. Men cannot bear substitution. They gnash their teeth at

the thought of the Lamb of God bearing the sin of man. But we, who know by experience the preciousness of this truth, will proclaim it in defiance of them confidently and unceasingly. We will neither dilute it nor change it nor fritter it away in any shape or fashion.[3]

So we see that Christ's vicarious death means a representative death; and our text tells us what was represented in that death.

God's Holiness Was Represented

"*Christ* died." He died to represent God's holy love and holy justice. For in that death Christ, in one crowning act, satisfied the holy claims of love and the holy claims of justice. All the righteous demands of a sin-hating and man-loving God were met. So Paul exclaims, "Christ Jesus, whom God set forth . . . to demonstrate His righteousness" (Rom. 3:24–25). And the psalmist echoes back, "Mercy and truth have met together; righteousness and peace have kissed each other" (Ps. 85:10). So we sing in the words of Elizabeth C. Clephane:

> O, safe and happy shelter!
> O, refuge tried and sweet!
> O, trysting-place where heaven's love
> And heaven's justice meet!

The Scottish theologian T. J. Crawford stresses this point:

It is altogether an error . . . to suppose that God acts at one time according to one of His attributes, and at another time according to another. He acts in conformity with all of them at all times. . . . As for the divine justice and the divine mercy, in particular, the end of [Christ's] work was not to bring them into harmony, as if they had been at variance with one another, but jointly to manifest and glorify them in the redemption of sinners. It is a case of combined action, and not counteraction, on the part of these attributes, that is exhibited on the cross.[4]

Sin's Heinousness Was Represented

"Christ died for our *sins.*" Christ died to expose, bear, and judge forever our heinous sins—"who Himself bore our sins in His own body on the tree" (1 Peter 2:24). If you want to see your polluted thought-life represented, look at the blood that trickled from his thorn-crowned brow. If you want to see your sins of action represented, fix your eyes on his bleeding, nail-pierced hands. If you want to see your shameful life of waywardness represented, behold the gory spikes that held his precious feet. If you want to see the utter corruption and desperate wickedness of your heart represented, watch the crimson flow that issued from his blessed side.

> Oh, wonder of all wonders,
> That through Thy death for me,
> My open sins, my secret sins,
> Can all forgiven be!
> Oh, make me understand it,
> Help me to take it in,
> What it meant to Thee, the Holy One,
> To bear away my sin.[5]

At a religious festival in Brazil, a missionary was going from booth to booth, examining the wares. He saw a sign above one booth: "Cheap Crosses." He thought, "That's what many Christians are looking for these days—cheap crosses." But the cross of Christ was not cheap: it cost him everything.[6]

Our Helplessness Was Represented

"Christ died for *our* sins." Christ died to reveal our utter helplessness as sinners, and thereby throw us entirely on God's grace and mercy for salvation. He demonstrated this helplessness by self-imposed physical weakness. We read that "He was crucified in weakness" (2 Cor. 13:4). This means that even though he finally died in a conscious and strong act of triumph, sacred love compelled his willing obedience unto death in order that he might save us. Thus Paul's word is true of us all: "When we were still without strength, in due time Christ died for the ungodly" (Rom. 5:6). The term "without strength" is very comprehensive. It is elsewhere translated "weak," "sick," and "impotent." It is used to describe the man who was lame from birth (Acts 4:9). Here it is employed in a moral sense

209

to denote our inability or feebleness with regard to any undertaking or duty. Indeed, Paul is exposing our total inability to make atonement for sin. We recall the lines of Philip P. Bliss:

> Guilty, vile and helpless, we;
> Spotless Lamb of God was He;
> "Full atonement" can it be?
> Hallelujah! what a Savior!

The Death of Christ Was Verified

"Christ died . . . and . . . *was buried*." It is significant that in the brief gospel statement of our text we have a specific reference to Christ's burial. Why, we may ask, is the burial of Christ mentioned here? Among other reasons, let me suggest two of utmost importance.

The Burial of Christ Verified That Jesus Was Dead

"Christ died . . . and . . . was buried." "If He was buried He must have been really dead."[7] The early church was in no doubt about the reality of Christ's death. Indeed, all four Gospels mention this fact. The burial of the dead body was the prelude to the empty tomb. This is why we can exclaim with the apostle, "O Death, where is your sting? O Hades, where is your victory?" We leave the sepulchre of our Lord, not in grief and sorrow, but with joyful expectation of what will shortly take place. Paul must have had this anticipation of victory in mind when he wrote, "I do not want you to be ignorant, brethren, concerning those who have fallen asleep, lest you sorrow as others who have no hope" (1 Thess. 4:13). For the Christian, the grave has been robbed of its cruelty and finality (Song of Sol. 8:6; Hos. 13:14).

The Burial of Christ Verified That Jesus Would Rise

"Christ died . . . and . . . was buried, and . . . rose again." Many scholars see in this reference to Christ's burial an allusion to the empty tomb and a confirmation of death and resurrection. The apostles preached the burial of Christ (see Acts 13:29; Rom. 6), because they believed that Jesus *really died* and that the empty tomb was evidence of the irrefutable fact of the resurrection. For you and me today, the empty tomb blasts the "swoon theory" and authenticates the one and only gospel of a crucified, risen, and reigning Lord (Gal. 1:6–9).

The Death of Christ Was Validated

"Christ died . . . *according to the Scriptures.*" The death of Christ was not just an untimely end. His death was rather the fulfillment of the Scriptures, according to "the determined counsel and foreknowledge of God" (Acts 2:23). Paul refers here, of course, to the Old Testament Scriptures, as did our risen Lord when speaking of his sufferings and the glory to follow (Luke 24:25–32). Addressing the two disciples on the road to Emmaus, Jesus began "at Moses and all the Prophets [and] expounded to them in *all* the Scriptures the things concerning Himself" (Luke 24:27). It is generally agreed that this covered the Law, the Psalms, and the Prophets.

The Law

The Law demanded Christ's death.

Long, long before the perfect Lamb of God Himself came, the Lord was preparing the world for Him by the multitudinous types in the Old Testament. Without blood there could be no atonement, and until the blood was presented the holy Law of God demanded justice and death upon the sinner. That is why, when God gave the two tables of the Law to Moses upon Mount Sinai, . . . He also gave to Moses, in the same Mount, the pattern of the tabernacle which was indeed built on blood. . . . God knew when He gave the Law that [Israel would] not keep it perfectly and must die, and so in mercy He gave the tabernacle and the altar and the blood so that a sinning people, condemned by the Law, might have life through the sheltering blood.[8]

God said to Moses, "For the life of the flesh is in the blood, and I have given it to you upon the altar to make atonement for your souls; for it is the blood that makes atonement for the soul" (Lev. 17:11). In the words of Gordon Wenham, atonement means "the blood ransoms at the price of life."[9] What a prophetic picture this is of our Sinbearer and Savior who offered himself for us!

211

D. L. Moody said, "If you are sheltered behind the blood of Jesus, you are as safe as if you were in heaven today."[10] Someone else has said that a little fly in Noah's ark was as safe as the elephant. It was not the strength of the elephant that made it safe, but it was the ark that saved the elephant as well as the fly. So it is the blood of Christ that saves us.

The Psalms

The psalms depicted Christ's death (Pss. 16; 35; 40–41; 69; 109; etc.). In particular, Psalm 22 has always been associated with the crucifixion of our Lord Jesus Christ. Few passages in the Old Testament so accurately illustrate divine suffering like this psalm. This is amazing when we remember that it was penned hundreds of years before the birth of Christ and that crucifixion was a Roman form of execution. This proof of biblical inspiration is irresistible! Jesus quoted the words of this psalm when he cried out on the cross, "My God, My God, why have You forsaken Me?" (Ps. 22:1; Matt. 27:46).

The Prophets

The Prophets declared Christ's death. They foretold the future, but even more, they proclaimed the will of God. They lived close to God and went everywhere pointing people to God.

The prophet Isaiah wrote: "He was wounded for our transgressions, He was bruised for our iniquities; the chastisement for our peace was upon Him, and by His stripes we are healed" (53:5; see entire chapter). Here again we have Old Testament literature vividly and comprehensively setting forth the substitutionary and penal character of our Lord's death and his subsequent triumphant resurrection.

"In His death twenty-five distinct prophecies recorded in the Old Testament were fulfilled within a few hours."[11] How this confirms our faith in the Word of God and our trust in the redemptive purposes of God!

The Death of Christ Was Vindicated

"Christ died . . . and . . . *rose again* the third day according to the Scriptures." The virtue and value of Christ's death were vindicated by his conspicuous and victorious resurrection. The apostle expounds on this in our immediate text and the rest of the chapter. We will, however, confine ourselves to a couple of relevant observations that vindicate the death of Christ.

The Death of Christ Was Vindicated by His Conspicuous Resurrection

"Christ died . . . and . . . rose again . . . and . . . was seen." His appearances as the risen Lord to his followers vindicated the virtue of his sinless life and the value of his substitutionary death. Even though some of the disciples were "foolish ones, and slow of heart to believe in all that the prophets had spoken," Christ had to suffer and "enter into His glory" (Luke 24:25–26). Thus his sinlessness on earth was vindicated "according to the Scriptures" (1 Cor. 15:3; see also Ps. 16:9–11). Peter confirmed this in his Pentecostal sermon (Acts 2:25–28). In like manner, our Lord's substitutionary death was vindicated. Jesus reminded his disciples of this fact after the resurrection. He said to them:

> "These are the words which I spoke to you while I was still with you, that all things must be fulfilled which were written in the Law of Moses and the Prophets and the Psalms concerning Me." And He opened their understanding, that they might comprehend the Scriptures. Then He said to them, "Thus it is written, and thus it was necessary for the Christ to suffer and to rise from the dead the third day, and that repentance and remission of sins should be preached in His name to all nations, beginning at Jerusalem. And you are witnesses of these things."
>
> Luke 24:44–48

The death, burial, and resurrection of our Lord were all part of that providential plan that the Old Testament writers had foreseen and foretold with deep spiritual insight (see Ps. 16:10; Isa. 53:9–10; Hos. 6:2). On the cross Jesus was exposed to the eyes of unbelievers, but after the resurrection he was seen by his own disciples who would be witnesses to his risen and redeeming life (Acts 1:22; 2:32; 3:15; 5:32). So the apostle Paul gives us here in our text a sampling of those appearances.

Peter saw him, and so did the disciples collectively. James (the half-brother of our Lord) became a believer after Jesus appeared to him. Over five hundred people saw him at one time, so it could not have been a hallucination or a deception. Last of all, he was seen by Paul in a life-transforming vision of resurrection power and blessing. From that moment he became the greatest preacher of "Jesus Christ and Him crucified" (1 Cor. 2:2).

The Death of Christ Was Vindicated by His Victorious Resurrection

"Christ died . . . and . . . rose again." This theme is argued brilliantly throughout the rest of this chapter and reveals that through death Christ conquered death.

Victory over the Power of Death. "O Hades, where is your victory?" The Bible states that "through death He [destroyed] him who had the power of death, that is, the devil" (Heb. 2:14); and again, "The Son of God was manifested, that He might destroy the works of the devil" (1 John 3:8). Like David of old who slew Goliath with the giant's own sword, so Christ on the cross defeated the devil with his own weapon of death.

> Death cannot keep his prey—
> Jesus my Savior!
> He tore the bars away—
> Jesus my Lord!
> Up from the grave He arose,
> With a mighty triumph o'er His foes;
> He arose a Victor from the dark domain,
> And He lives forever with His saints to reign.
> He arose! He arose!
> Hallelujah! Christ arose!

Victory over the Sting of Death. "O Death, where is your sting?" The apostle reminds us that "the sting of death is sin" (1 Cor. 15:56). On the cross our Lord extracted the very pain of death by taking the sting into himself, by tasting death for everyone (Heb. 2:9). The battle has been fought and the victory gained by the Crucified One.

214

A little girl ran in from the garden crying, "Mother! Mother! A wasp! A wasp!" "Come here," called the mother, "and I'll protect you." Holding her daughter, the mother said, "It's all right now. The wasp won't sting anymore." "Why not?" asked the little girl inquisitively. "Because I have taken the sting instead," explained the mother, pointing to her quickly swelling arm. Jesus has taken the sting of death for everyone.

Victory over the Fear of Death. "The sting of death is sin, and the strength of sin is the Law. But thanks be to God, who gives us the victory through our Lord Jesus Christ." At the cross our Lord triumphed over the fear of eternal doom, for whether we like to admit it or not, "it is appointed for men to die once, but after this the judgment" (Heb. 9:27). In that mysterious work of the cross and his victorious resurrection, the Savior delivered "those who through fear of death were all their lifetime subject to bondage" (Heb. 2:15).

Here, then, is the very heart of our gospel: the voluntary, vicarious, verified, validated, and vindicated death of Christ. This is the Christian gospel—"Jesus Christ and Him crucified" (1 Cor. 2:2). You and I have to respond to this message; we cannot be neutral. *We must either accept or reject this Christ of Calvary.*

Two remarkable pictures by Margaret Lindsay Williams were exhibited at London's Royal Academy in 1917–18. The first, "The Devil's Daughter," shows a ballet dancer turning away from the symbol of the cross, which represents eternal life through the death of Christ. She is a young lady who trips through life like a gay butterfly. In her arms she holds Death—a hideous skull with empty eye sockets and grinning teeth.

In the companion picture, "The Triumph," the ballet dancer is prostrate at the feet of One who is just visible in the background. Behind her are the soft lights, the stage, and the bright symbols of her past life. The girl has dropped the ugly head of Death and now caresses the feet of the One who stands before her. A tear falls from the dancer's face. The reason is not hard to find. Above the dancer's head, held by two nail-pierced hands, is a crown of life. The One she worships is the Man of Calvary. Her life has been yielded to him. Captured by the triumph of this picture, you can hear the girl saying:

215

Out there amongst the hills my Savior died,
Pierced by those cruel nails, was crucified.
Lord Jesus, Thou hast done all this for me;
Henceforward, I would live only for Thee.[12]

What is *your* answer to the Christ of Calvary? The death of Christ demands a verdict. To the religionist it is a stumbling block. To the rationalist it is a laughing stock. But to those who are called, Christ is the power and wisdom of God (1 Cor. 1:23–24). Will you bow right now in repentance and faith and pray these words ascribed to Bernard of Clairvaux?

What Thou, My Lord, hast suffered
Was all for sinners' gain;
Mine, mine was the transgression,
But Thine the deadly pain.
Lo, here I fall, my Savior;
'Tis I deserve Thy place;
Look on me with Thy favor,
Assist me with Thy grace.

What language shall I borrow
To thank Thee, dearest Friend,
For this, Thy dying sorrow,
Thy pity without end?
O make me Thine forever,
And should I fainting be,
Lord, let me never, never
Outlive my love to Thee.

John Piper

—=◆=—

John Piper has been senior pastor of Bethlehem Baptist Church, Minneapolis, Minnesota, since 1980. Previously, he was associate professor of biblical studies at Bethel College, in St. Paul, Minnesota. He received his B.D. degree from Fuller Theological Seminary, and his D.Theol. from the University of Munich, Germany.

Piper's published books include *Love Your Enemies: Jesus' Love Command in the Synoptic Gospels and Early Christian Paranesis*, *The Justification of God: An Exegetical and Theological Study of Romans 9:1–23*, *Desiring God: Meditations of a Christian Hedonist*, *The Pleasures of God: Meditations on God's Delight in Being God*, and *The Supremacy of God in Preaching*, which was awarded "Preaching Book of the Year" for 1992 by *Preaching Magazine*. He also contributed articles to *Baker Encyclopedia of the Bible*, and co-edited *Recovering Biblical Manhood and Womanhood: A Response to Evangelical Feminism*

—=◆=—

I have chosen this sermon because the most precious event in history is the death of God's Son, and the most pervasive evil of our times is the devaluing of God's glory. In the death of Christ our longing for salvation is satisfied and our self-exaltation is crucified. Our greatest need is met and our greatest delusion is shattered. The cross is first and foremost the exaltation of God's glory and the vindication of God's righteousness. Only then is it the ground of grace that saves hopeless sinners.

One of the greatest discoveries of my life has been the good news of the supremacy of God in the heart of God. It is good news because it guarantees that God will always uphold and display the ground of my gladness, the glory of God. My life is devoted to making known the message of God's supremacy. More than any other event in history the death of God's Son makes clear that God's zeal for his glory and God's love for his people are one passion. If I had one sermon to preach I would want to magnify God as much as possible and satisfy man as deeply as possible. The message of the cross is that these aims are not at odds, but are in fact one: God is most glorified in us when we are most satisfied in him.

Did Christ Die for Us or for God?

God put [Christ] forward as a sacrifice of atonement by his blood,
effective through faith. He did this to show his righteousness, because
in his divine forbearance he had passed over the sins previously committed; it was to prove at the present time that he himself is righteous
and that he justifies the one who has faith in Jesus.

Romans 3:25–26 NRSV

One of the reasons it is hard to communicate biblical reality to
modern, secular people is that the biblical mind-set and the secular mind-set move from radically different starting points.

What I mean by the secular mind-set is not necessarily a mind-
set that rules God out or denies in principle that the Bible is true.
It's a mind-set that begins with man as the basic given reality in
the universe. All of its thinking starts with the assumption that
man has basic rights and basic needs and basic expectations. Then
the secular mind moves out from this center and interprets the
world, with man and his rights and needs as the measure of all
things.

What the secular mind-set sees as problems are seen as problems
because of how things fit or don't fit with the center—man and his
rights and needs and expectations. What this mind-set sees as successes are seen as successes because they fit with man and his rights
and needs and expectations.

This is the mind-set that we were born with and that our secular
society reinforces virtually every hour of the day in our lives. The
apostle Paul calls this mind-set "the mind that is set on the flesh"
(Rom. 8:6–7), and says that it is the way the "natural person" thinks
(1 Cor. 2:14, literal translation). It is so much a part of us that we
hardly even know it's there. We just take it for granted—until it col-
lides with another mind-set, namely, the one in the Bible.

219

The biblical mind-set is not simply one that includes God somewhere in the universe and says that the Bible is true. The biblical mind-set begins with a radically different starting point, namely, God. God is the basic given reality in the universe. He was there before we were in existence—or before anything was in existence. He is the only absolute reality.

The biblical mind-set starts with the assumption that God is the center of reality. All thinking starts with the assumption that God has basic rights as the Creator of all things. He has goals that fit with his nature and perfect character. The biblical mind-set moves out from this center and interprets the world, with God and his rights and goals as the measure of all things.

What the biblical mind-set sees as basic problems in the universe are usually not the same problems that the secular mind-set sees. The reason for this is that what makes a problem is not first that something doesn't fit the rights and needs of man, but that it doesn't fit the rights and goals of God. If you start with man and his rights and wants, rather than starting with the Creator and his rights and goals, the problems you see in the universe will be very different.

Is the basic riddle of the universe how to preserve man's rights and solve his problems (for example, the right of self-determination and the problem of suffering)? Or is the basic riddle of the universe how an infinitely worthy God in complete freedom can display the full range of his perfections—what Paul calls the "riches of his glory" (Rom. 9:23)—his holiness, his power, his wisdom, his justice, his wrath, his goodness, his truth, and his grace?

Your answer to that question will profoundly affect the way you understand the central event of human history: the death of Jesus, the Son of God.

I have introduced our text (Rom. 3:25–26) with this long meditation on the significance of our starting points because the deepest problem that the death of Jesus was designed to solve is virtually incomprehensible to the secular mind-set. That is why this truth about the purpose of Christ's death is scarcely known, let alone cherished as part of everyday evangelical piety. Our Christian mind-set is so skewed by natural and secular man-centeredness that we can barely comprehend or love the God-centeredness of the cross of Christ.

The Innermost Meaning of the Cross

Our focus is very limited. We will go beneath the issue of justification and reconciliation and forgiveness to the bottom and foundation of it all—to what the New Testament scholar C. E. B. Cranfield calls "the innermost meaning of the cross."[1]

What you should listen for as we read this text is the problem in the universe that the biblical mind-set (God's mind-set) is trying to solve through the death of Christ. How does it differ from the problems that the secular mind-set says God has to solve?

> God put [Christ] forward as a sacrifice of atonement by his blood, effective through faith. He did this to show his righteousness, because in his divine forbearance he had passed over the sins previously committed.

Boil that down to the most basic problem the death of Christ is meant to solve. God put Christ forward (he sent him to die) in order to demonstrate his righteousness (or justice). The problem that needed solving was that God, for some reason, seemed to be unrighteous, and wanted to vindicate himself and clear his name. That is the basic issue. God's righteousness was at stake. His name or reputation or honor had to be vindicated. Before the cross could be for our sake, it had to be for God's sake.

But what created this problem? Why did God need to give a public vindication of his righteousness? The answer is in the last phrase of verse 25: "because in his divine forbearance he had passed over the sins previously committed."

Now what does that mean? It means that for centuries God had been doing what Psalm 103:10 says, "He does not deal with us according to our sins, nor repay us according to our iniquities." He has been passing over thousands of sins. He has been forgiving them and letting them go and not punishing them.

King David is a good example. In 2 Samuel 12 he is confronted by the prophet Nathan for committing adultery with Bathsheba and then having her husband killed. Nathan asks, "Why have you despised the word of the LORD?" (2 Sam. 12:9).

David feels the rebuke of Nathan, and in verse 13 he says, "I have sinned against the LORD." To this, Nathan responds, "The LORD has put away your sin; you shall not die." Just like that! Adultery and murder are "passed over." It is almost incredible. Our sense of justice screams out, "No! You can't just let it go like that. He deserves to die or be imprisoned for life!" But Nathan does not say that. He says, "Now the LORD has put away your sin; you shall not die."

Why Is Forgiveness a Problem?

That is what Paul means in Romans 3:25 by the passing over of sins previously committed. But why is that a problem? Does the secular mind-set feel that God's kindness to sinners is a problem? How many people outside the scope of biblical influence wrestle with the problem that a holy and righteous God makes the sun rise on the evil and the good and sends rain on the just and the unjust (Matt. 5:45)? How many wrestle with the apparent injustice that God is lenient with sinners? How many Christians wrestle with the fact that their own forgiveness is a threat to the righteousness of God?

The secular mind-set does not even assess the situation the way the biblical mind-set does. Why is that? It's because the secular mind-set thinks from a radically different starting point. It does not start with the Creator-rights of God—the right to uphold and display the infinite worth of his righteousness and glory. It starts with man and assumes that God will conform to our rights and wishes.

Notice what Paul says in verse 23: "all have sinned and fall short of the glory of God." What's at stake in sinning is the *glory of God*. When Nathan confronted David, he quoted God as saying, "Why have you despised *me?*" We could imagine David saying to God: "What do you mean, I despised you? I didn't despise you. I wasn't even thinking of you. I was just red hot after this woman and then scared to death that people were going to find out. You weren't even in the picture."

God would have replied: "I, the Creator of the universe, the Designer of marriage, the Fountain of life, the One who holds you in being, the One who made you king—that One, I the Lord, not even in the picture! You've got it all wrong, David. That's exactly what I mean. You despised me." All sin is a despising of God before it is a damage to man. All sin is a preference for the fleeting pleasures of the world over the everlasting joy of God's fellowship. David demeaned God's glory. He belittled God's worth. He dishonored God's name. That is the meaning of sin—failing to love God's glory above everything else. "All have sinned and fall short of *the glory of God.*"

The problem when God passes over sin, therefore, is that God seems to agree with those who despise his name and belittle his glory. He seems to be saying it is a matter of indifference that his glory is spurned. He seems to condone the low assessment of his worth.

Suppose a group of anarchists plot to assassinate the president of the United States and his whole cabinet, and almost succeed. Their bombs destroy part of the White House and kill some staff, but the president narrowly escapes. The anarchists are caught and the court finds them guilty. But the anarchists say they are sorry, so the court suspends their sentences and releases them. Now what would that communicate to the world about the value of the president's life and the importance of his governance? It would communicate that they are of little value.

That is what God's passing over of sin communicates: God's glory and his righteous governance are of minor value, or no value.

Apart from divine revelation the natural mind—the secular mind—does not see or feel this problem. What secular person loses any sleep over the apparent unrighteousness of God's kindness to sinners?

But according to Romans this is the most basic problem that God solved by the death of his Son. Let's read it again: "He did this [put his Son forward to die] to show his righteousness, because in his divine forbearance [or patience] he had passed over the sins previously committed; it was to prove at the present time that he himself is righteous" (vv. 25b–26a). God would be unrighteous if he passed over sins as though the value of his glory were nothing.

God saw his glory being despised by sinners (like David)— he saw his worth belittled and his name dishonored by our sins—and rather than vindicating the worth of his glory by slaying his people, he vindicated his glory by slaying his Son.

God could have settled accounts by punishing all sinners with hell. This would have demonstrated that he does not minimize our falling short of his glory—our belittling his honor. But God did not will to destroy us. "Indeed, God did not send the Son into the world to condemn the world, but in order that the world might be saved through him" (John 3:17).

223

This truth we know well. We know well that God is for us. We know that our salvation was his goal in sending Jesus. But do we know the foundation of it all? Do we know that there was a deeper goal in sending the Son? Do we know that God's love for us depends on a deeper love, namely, God's love for his glory? Do we know that God's passion to save sinners rests on a deeper passion, namely, God's passion to vindicate his righteousness? Do we realize that the accomplishment of our salvation does not center on us but on God's glory? The vindication of God's glory is the *ground* of our salvation (Rom. 3:25–26), and the exaltation of God's glory is the *goal* of our salvation. "Christ has become a servant to the circumcised . . . in order that the Gentiles might *glorify* God for his mercy" (Rom. 15:8–9).

Can Self-Exaltation Be an Act of Love?

Someone may ask, "How can it be loving for God to be so self-exalting in the work of the cross? If he is exalting his own glory and vindicating his own righteousness, how then is the cross really an act of love to us?"

I fear the question betrays the common secular mind-set that places man at the center. It assumes that for us to be loved, God must make us the center. He must highlight our value. If our worth is not accented, then we are not loved. If our value is not the ground of God's purpose in the cross, then we are not esteemed. The underlying assumption of such reasoning is that the exaltation of the worth and glory of God over man is not the very essence of what God's love for man is.

The biblical mind-set, however, affirms the very opposite. The cross is the pinnacle of God's love for sinners, not because it demonstrates the value of sinners, but because it vindicates the value of *God* for sinners to enjoy. God's love for man does not consist in making man central, but in making himself central for man. The cross does not direct man's attention to his own vindicated worth, but to God's vindicated righteousness.

This is love, because the only eternal happiness for man is happiness focused on the riches of God's glory. "In your presence there is fullness of joy; in your right hand are pleasures forevermore"

(Ps. 16:11). God's self-exaltation is loving, because it preserves for us and offers to us the only all-satisfying Object of desire in the universe—the all-glorious, all-righteous God.

The fundamental reason why the cross is folly to the world is that it means the end of human self-exaltation, and a radical commitment to God-exaltation. No, "commitment" is not quite the right word. To put it more exactly, the cross is a call to radical *exultation* in God-exaltation. The cross is the death of our demand to be loved by being made the center. It is also the birth of joy in God's being made the center.

Test yourself. What is your mind-set? Do you begin with God and his rights and goals? Or do you begin with yourself and your rights and wishes?

When you look at the death of Christ, what happens? Does your joy come from translating this awesome divine work into a boost for your self-esteem? Or are you drawn up out of yourself and filled with wonder and reverence and worship that here in the death of Jesus is the deepest, clearest declaration of God's infinite esteem for his glory and for his Son?

Here is the great objective foundation for the full assurance of our hope: the forgiveness of sins is grounded finally, not in our finite worth or work, but in the infinite worth of the righteousness of God—God's unswerving resolve to uphold and vindicate the glory of his name.

I appeal to you with all my heart: take your stand on this. Base your life on this. Ground your hope in this. You will be free from the futile mind-set of the world. And you will never fall. When God's exaltation of God in Christ is your joy, that joy can never fail.

━━━◆━━━

18

John H. Rodgers Jr.

John H. Rodgers Jr. is dean/president emeritus and professor of systematic theology at Trinity Episcopal School for Ministry, Ambridge, Pennsylvania. He also serves as director of Stanway Institute for World Mission and Evangelism in Ambridge. Earlier he served in parish ministry and was professor of systematic theology and associate dean of students at Virginia Theological Seminary.

A graduate of the United States Naval Academy, Rodgers earned his M.Div. degree at Virginia Theological Seminary, and his Th.D. at the University of Basel, Switzerland. He holds honorary D.D. degrees from Virginia Theological Seminary and from Nashotah House. He has been the North American Secretary of Evangelical Fellowship in the Anglican Communion (EFAC) since 1977. He is the author of *Theology of Peter Taylor Forsyth*.

I would preach this sermon if it were my last, first of all, because it addresses the central issues. If you have only one time to speak, you want to say the most important thing of all. As Paul put it, "This is of first importance." So I would want to speak of that which is of first importance.

Second, I believe this text offers a path into the central matters of the gospel that is easily understandable and memorable. It, therefore, allows people to continue to reflect on the content of the sermon after they have heard it.

The Fullness of Christ

He entered Jericho and was passing through it. A man was there named Zacchaeus; he was a chief tax collector and was rich. He was trying to see who Jesus was, but on account of the crowd he could not, because he was short in stature. So he ran ahead and climbed a sycamore tree to see him, because he was going to pass that way. When Jesus came to the place, he looked up and said to him, "Zacchaeus, hurry and come down; for I must stay at your house today." So he hurried down and was happy to welcome him. All who saw it began to grumble and said, "He has gone to be the guest of one who is a sinner." Zacchaeus stood there and said to the Lord, "Look, half of my possessions, Lord, I will give to the poor; and if I have defrauded anyone of anything, I will pay back four times as much." Then Jesus said to him, "Today salvation has come to this house, because he too is a son of Abraham. For the Son of Man came to seek out and to save the lost."

Luke 19:1–10 NRSV

We have all heard in one form or another that God the Father wants us to accept Jesus the Son as our personal Lord and Savior. The question arises, Why? What is it that Jesus brings into our life that makes this a crucial invitation? Why are we asked to believe that Jesus alone can meet our deepest needs, and help us to be the persons we are created to be and, in our best moments, want to be?

The New Testament refers to this as salvation—how Jesus is to be our Savior and to renew and remake our lives aright. The repeated claim of Scripture is that in Christ Jesus alone as our Savior and Lord can we become truly human beings. Only when profoundly affected by the influence of Christ can human societies be fair, just, compassionate, and good. If we are to take this claim seriously we need to know why it is true and how it applies to our lives.

229

The appropriateness of our text is that it leads us to the fullness of Christ and shows us how he meets the profoundest needs of our lives. Not everything that Christ brings into our lives is mentioned in this text, but three central aspects of his saving relationship to us are emphasized.

Forgiveness

The first aspect is forgiveness. God has made the world and human life with a certain moral shape. Life doesn't work well unless it is marked by goodness, righteousness, and love. When we treat one another in unloving, insensitive, and uncaring ways, when we organize our common life in ways that lack justice, compassion, and encouragement, we suffer the bitter consequences of frustration, anger, rebellion, war, hostile demonstrations, depression, and a sense of moral failure and guilt. One needs only to look at the front page of a newspaper or read a book on history to discover that the human race has never lived the good life, the righteous and loving life. The price has always been, and continues to be, costly, indeed.

We are all sinners. Consider Zacchaeus. We read that in Jericho there was a man named Zacchaeus, who was a chief tax collector and was rich. In many ways Zacchaeus typifies so much that is wrong with the human race and with our own hearts.

To begin with, he was a tax collector. For a Jew to be a tax collector was not like having a respectable job with the IRS. It meant that even though he was a Jew, he worked for the Roman government. The Romans had invaded the Holy Land and conquered God's chosen people. No self-respecting Jew would have collaborated with the Roman government and worked in its employ. To have done that would have been a betrayal of God and country.

To get a sense of how the people in Jericho must have felt about Zacchaeus, think back to World War II. Vidkun Quisling was a leader in Norway who betrayed his country to the Nazis and cooperated with them in their invasion of the land. So terrible was this man's treachery that his name became identical with a person who betrays his own country. So we now have the word "quisling" in the dictionary to refer to any person who undermines his own country from within—who is a fifth columnist and a collaborator. Zacchaeus was such a person. He had betrayed the holy people of God. He had betrayed the Word of God. He had betrayed everything sacred and true.

As a tax collector Zacchaeus was not only a collaborator with the Romans; he was also greedy. The temptation to greed was great for a tax collector in those days. Rome assigned a certain sum of money to be gathered from a region. The tax collector would then gather that amount plus more to cover his own costs and his salary. The temptation to squeeze harder and harder so that one might become more and more wealthy was great. To this temptation Zacchaeus had succumbed. He had become very wealthy. As a matter of fact, not only was he engaged in this occupation that in some ways amounted to a combination of Quisling and the Mafia, but he had risen to the top of the profession and had become a chief tax collector.

If you are wondering whether your sins are so terrible that they put you beyond the love and the grace and the forgiveness of God, think of Zacchaeus who had betrayed his people, his God, and his faith, and had sought to define the meaning of his life in money. The "surprise" of this event is that it was precisely to Zacchaeus that Jesus brought the forgiveness of God. Surely your sins and mine cannot be any more dramatic or any more profound than those of Zacchaeus.

Sometimes people say to me that they are not good enough to be Christians. The answer, of course, is that we are all bad enough to be Christians. We all need the forgiveness of God, which Christ brings and gives. This ministry of forgiveness finally led Jesus to the cross, where he bore our sins "in his own body," where the righteousness and justice of God, on the one hand, and the love and mercy of God, on the other, met together on our behalf.

God's forgiveness in Christ led the apostle Paul, who himself was a persecutor, even a murderer, of Christians, to say of himself after he became a Christian, "the life I now live in the flesh I live by faith in the Son of God, who loved me and who gave himself for me" (Gal. 2:20). The crucial thing to hear is that each of us is invited to echo the very same words—"the Son of God, who loved me and who gave himself for me." Forgiveness, deep and profound, sufficient and complete. Out of the fullness of Christ comes the fullness of God's forgiveness.

Fellowship

The second aspect of Christ's saving relationship to us is fellowship with God. A survey by well-noted pollster George Gallup's organization indicates that a massive search for belonging is going on in the United States—a belonging not on the basis of one's productivity or beauty, but on the basis that one is precious and treasured. Since all human community ultimately is lost in death, only an intimacy with God can meet the deepest need for belonging that lies in our hearts. The Christian faith teaches us that we are made for fellowship with God. This intimacy with God is what Jesus brings. His encounter with Zacchaeus makes this very clear.

Zacchaeus had climbed a tree. He had put his hope in wealth, but his wealth had let him down, or rather left him up a tree. It had not satisfied. He was ostracized in the city. His companions cared for him only because he was wealthy and successful. His success left him empty and searching. It was surely unusual for a successful, wealthy man to climb a tree in public so that he could see and hear a wandering preacher. Yet that is precisely what Zacchaeus did. He found himself spiritually and literally up a tree.

Now the "tree" is an interesting place, religiously speaking. For Zacchaeus it was a place where he could look at Jesus, but not be committed to Jesus; listen, but at a distance; observe, but not be part of the community that was related to Jesus. Zacchaeus could be an observer, but he was not a disciple of Jesus. Many in the church today are in this position. They are dragged to corporate worship out of habit, or by a spouse, or out of social convention, but they are only observers of Jesus. They are not closely related to Jesus nor to God through Jesus. There is a restlessness and loneliness in the hearts of such "observers." They feel that they are cosmic orphans in an impersonal universe, hoping all the while that a promotion, a better golf game, a faster car, or a larger swimming pool might do the trick for them.

The good news is that Jesus did not leave Zacchaeus up the tree, and he certainly doesn't wish to leave us up the tree either. He calls us out of our trees. Walking down the road, Jesus looked up and saw Zacchaeus in the tree. Undoubtedly he asked someone who that was. He received the answer, "Oh, that's the sinner, Zacchaeus. He's a collaborator. He works with the Romans. You'll want nothing to do with him." But Jesus was saying to himself, "Aha! That's my sort of man. He's the kind of person I have come to seek. The Son of Man came to seek and save the lost."

As he drew alongside Zacchaeus, Jesus did two things. First, he stopped and called him by name, "Zacchaeus!" How personal! How powerful! To be addressed by name is an invitation to fellowship. A song now sung in Christian circles tells us that if we listen closely, we will hear the Lord calling our names.

It is true. In and through Jesus, God was speaking to Zacchaeus, inviting him into fellowship with himself. Right now he is calling your name and mine—George, John, Helen, Blanche. If you listen closely, you will hear your names.

Then Jesus did a second, even more radical thing. After calling him by name, Jesus invited himself into Zacchaeus's home and life. He said, "Zacchaeus, hurry and come down [notice the urgency there]; for I must stay at your house today." God does not only want to have a relationship with us. He wants to live life with us, to be at the center of our life, so that even in our time alone—in our solitude—we are in his presence. We are made for this relationship. As Augustine prayed, "Our hearts are restless until they find their rest in Thee." Fellowship with God, and in that context, fellowship with the people of God, and supported by that, fellowship with one's neighbor, even the desire to find fellowship with one's enemy—this is what Christ brings. He is God drawn near!

How did Zacchaeus respond? He hurried down, ecstatic to welcome Jesus. Zacchaeus was quite overcome. Here he was, the man who had been ostracized by all the pious people in town. And suddenly now, Jesus—the very one in whom and through whom God came—was inviting himself into Zacchaeus's life.

People are still climbing trees and looking at Jesus from a safe distance. You can be baptized up a tree, confirmed up a tree, even ordained up a tree. But Jesus is still calling us out of our trees and onto our knees into the closest, richest fellowship with himself and with the living God. He is calling us home to a relationship with him and his people, which, in turn, leads to a new relationship with other people also. This is a gift out of the fullness of Christ that makes us whole.

I think of Revelation 3:20: "Listen! I am standing at the door, knocking; if you hear my voice and open the door, I will come in to you and eat with you, and you with me." These words were spoken by the risen Lord to a congregation that had climbed back up a tree. They are spoken to us also as individuals. Jesus calls each of us by name and invites us to open our hearts to him, so that he may be the primary partner at the center of our lives. I heard the Lord call my name. If you listen closely, you will hear him call your name.

Freedom

There is freedom: freedom *from* and freedom *for*. Freedom from falsehood, from idolatry, from selfishness, from immorality. Freedom for new life in Christ, for an openness and caring toward those around us. Freedom for the confidence that nothing will be able to separate us from the power and the love of God that are ours in Christ Jesus.

Freedom in Christ! What a transformation came upon Zacchaeus when Christ came into his life. "Zacchaeus stood there and said to the Lord, 'Look, half of my possessions, Lord, I will give to the poor; and if I have defrauded anyone of anything, I will pay back four times as much.'" What a change! Here's a man who once worshiped money and now is free to share his money. He has changed from being a worshiper of money to being a steward of money. How is that possible? He now has a different God. He now has the living God as his security, and as the One who shapes and directs his life. Money has become something to be used for the purposes of God and the well-being of those around him, not something to be worshiped.

Note, too, that Zacchaeus has a new freedom to care for others. He takes note of the poor. They have suddenly become human beings to him. He resolves to act responsibly toward them. He also shows a new honesty and concern for justice and fairness. If he has defrauded anyone, he wishes to make up for that.

Dear friends, if Jesus could change Zacchaeus, he can change us. He can change you and he can change me. Day by day, Paul tells us, all who are in Christ are being conformed to the likeness of Christ by the Spirit of God whom Jesus brings into the lives of his own. In the Spirit we find freedom to be for Christ and faithful to Christ openly before our co-workers, our family, our neighbors, and those around us. That is freedom, indeed!

Having been changed ourselves, by grace we can help change others, leading them to Christ who alone can transform them, too. Thus we act as yeast in society and society feels the effect. Can there really be major social improvement if everyone is still up the tree searching, still worshiping at the altar of money, still greedy and selfish? Social improvement ultimately flows from lives into which Christ has come and into which he has brought his transforming freedom.

Forgiveness, full and sufficient; fellowship, profound and intimate; freedom to become caring and serving, just and fair people. These are the riches that come out of the fullness of Christ. This is why the Father desires us all to open our hearts to him, to accept his forgiveness, to receive him as our personal friend and Lord, and to let him begin to set us free.

Jesus said to Zacchaeus and to those around him, "Today salvation has come to this house, because he too is a son of Abraham. For the Son of Man came to seek out and to save the lost." The crucified and risen Christ is still the Son of Man who comes to seek and to save the lost. Will you not receive him? Will you not accept the forgiveness, the fellowship, and the freedom of God in him, so that it may be said of you, "Today salvation has come to this house"?

—=>◆<=—

19

Warren W. Wiersbe

⟡

Warren W. Wiersbe, preacher, Bible conference speaker, and author, was general director of Back to the Bible and teacher on its daily radio broadcast from 1980 to 1989. He was previously senior pastor of the Moody Church, Chicago, Illinois, and speaker on "Songs in the Night," an international radio ministry of the Moody Church. He earned the Th.B. degree at Northern Baptist Seminary, and has received three honorary degrees, including a D.D. from Trinity Evangelical Divinity School.

Wiersbe has written more than one hundred books, including the popular "BE Series" of Bible studies, *Wiersbe's Expository Outlines, Real Worship,* and *Why Us? When Bad Things Happen to God's People,* and has compiled a dozen others. Recognized as a "pastor's pastor," he has published several volumes that focus on pastoral ministry, among them, *Listening to the Giants, Living with the Giants, Walking with the Giants, Confident Pastoral Leadership* (with Howard Sugden), and *The Wycliffe Handbook of Preachers and Preaching* (with Lloyd M. Perry).

⟡

I chose this sermon because the text is familiar, but the truth of the text is unfamiliar to most people. If I announced at the beginning that I was preaching from Psalm 23, most listeners would shift their minds into neutral, saying to themselves, "We've heard this before." There's a lot of animal behavior in our world today, and also in the church. We need more sheep, and the sheep need to act more like sheep.

The text also has an evangelistic thrust, and I think we must always preach the gospel. The relationship between Psalms 22 and 23 fascinates me. To think that our Lord became a worm for us!

⟡

Let's Talk about the Animals

—⟫◈⟪—

The LORD is my shepherd, I shall not want.
  He makes me lie down in green pastures;
he leads me beside still waters;
  he restores my soul.
He leads me in right paths
  for his name's sake.

Even though I walk through the darkest valley,
  I fear no evil;
for you are with me;
  your rod and your staff—
  they comfort me.

You prepare a table before me
  in the presence of my enemies;
you anoint my head with oil;
  my cup overflows.
Surely goodness and mercy shall follow me
  all the days of my life,
and I shall dwell in the house of the LORD
  my whole life long.

Psalm 23 NRSV

You and I, and people just like us, are the only creatures in all of God's creation who can decide what kind of creatures we want to be.

When a puppy is born, it will grow up to be a dog. When a kitten is born, it will grow up to be a cat. A duckling becomes a duck, and a calf becomes a cow. But you'd be unwise to wager on what kind of animal a little boy will become by the time he graduates from high school. That's a decision he has to make.

Now, if it bothers you that I'm comparing people with animals, just stop to consider that we do this frequently in our everyday conversation. What mother hasn't said to a child just home from a rendezvous with a mud puddle, "You're as dirty as a pig"? I've heard businessmen say, "Watch out for him—he's as slippery as an eel!" When a husband can't persuade his wife to let him go fishing with his friends, he says, "You're as stubborn as a mule!" And she may reply, "And you're as dumb as an ox!"

We should probably apologize to the animals for making these comparisons, but let's admit that sometimes we do evaluate our friends and neighbors as though they were behind bars at the zoo. I can see animal-like behavior in others, and others can see animal-like behavior in me.

When it comes to deciding what animal we want to be, what are the options from which we may choose?

David gives us two poor choices in Psalm 32:9: "Do not be like a horse or a mule, without understanding, whose temper must be curbed with bit and bridle, else it will not stay near you." Some people are like the horse, rushing impetuously into life, knocking down whatever stands in the way, always in a hurry to get to the next destination. And some people are just the opposite. Like the mule, they're stubborn—although they probably call it "conviction"—and they dig in their heels and refuse to move.

But God says, "Don't be like the horse or the mule. Otherwise, I'll have to put a bit and bridle on you to keep you out of trouble. I'd rather instruct you and teach you and guide you with my eye. That's the best way to learn my will."

If you don't want to be a horse or mule, how about becoming an ox or a stag? How do you do that? Well, focus on a graphic word picture that describes how a naive young man became an ox and ended up at the slaughter. Solomon describes the scene in Proverbs 7.

A young man from the country is visiting the city and feeling free because nobody knows who he is and nobody cares what he does. He wanders into the red-light district and a prostitute propositions him. "I have decked my couch with coverings," she says. "I have perfumed my bed with myrrh, aloes, and cinnamon. Come, let us take our fill of love until morning; let us delight ourselves with love" (vv. 16–18).

The young man listens and starts to weaken. "With much seductive speech she persuades him; with her smooth talk she compels him." Then it happens! "Right away he follows her, and goes like an ox to the slaughter, or bounds like a stag toward the trap" (vv. 21–22). Poor fellow! He came to the city to enjoy life and he ended up "going down to the chambers of death." We live in a society that enjoys "sexual freedom," but few people realize that "sexual freedom" turns people into animals.

Well, we can choose to become horses or mules or oxen or stags. Or we can become hogs or dogs. The apostle Peter writes about the hogs and dogs in the second chapter of his Second Epistle. In this chapter, Peter describes the false teachers who use religion as a means of manipulating gullible people and conning them out of their money. These teachers are false Christians, religious racketeers who are "like irrational animals, mere creatures of instinct, born to be caught and killed" (v. 12). These counterfeits pretend to follow the Lord; but if you wait long enough, the truth will come out and their true nature will be revealed. "It has happened to them according to the true proverb, 'The dog turns back to its own vomit,' and 'The sow is washed only to wallow in the mud'" (v. 22).

The image here is not a very pretty one, but it gets the point across. The dog threw up and felt better; the sow washed up and looked better. But the dog was still a dog and the sow was still a sow! Both the sow and the dog, however, eventually revealed their true nature by going back to their old ways.

Many people have attended church and had some kind of religious experience, but it didn't really change their hearts. Like the dog, they felt better; like the sow, they looked better; but nothing had essentially altered in their lives. Perhaps their "new look" lasted a month or two, maybe even a year. But then they went back into the old life again. "Too bad about Jim!" says one of his friends. "He lost his salvation!" No, my friend; *he never had it.* It was only a masquerade.

You and I are the only creatures in God's creation who can decide what kind of animals we want to be. We can become horses, mules, oxen, stags, sows, or dogs—*but God won't let any of these animals into his heaven.* No matter how popular these creatures may be on

241

earth, they will never enter God's heaven. The only animal God will welcome to heaven is a sheep.

Now we've arrived at the text of my message, a text so familiar that we sometimes miss what it is really saying. The text is Psalm 23, and it's all about the only animal God will accept: a sheep. Unless you can honestly say from your heart, "The Lord is my shepherd," you are not going to heaven.

If you have trusted Jesus Christ as your Savior and Lord, and you can honestly say, "The Lord is my shepherd," then you have two wonderful assurances. You can say with David, "I shall not want" (v. 1) and "I fear no evil" (v. 4). Because the Lord is your shepherd, you have *sufficiency* and *security, provision* and *protection.*

These are the assurances that the whole world is seeking! All the candidates who run for political office promise the voters sufficiency and security. They promise more jobs, higher wages, and lower taxes. They promise safer neighborhoods and protection from international enemies that threaten the peace of our land. Sufficiency and security are blessings that everybody wants to enjoy.

When Jesus Christ is your shepherd and you are one of his sheep, then you have *sufficiency.* He promises to meet your every need. To begin with, he will give you the necessities of life—green pastures and still waters. Don't spiritualize these things, because they are what sheep live on—green pastures and still waters. Without grass and water, sheep will die.

Our Shepherd promises to supply our every need, just when we need it. He says to us, "Do not worry about your life, what you will eat or what you will drink, or about your body, what you will wear. . . . your heavenly Father knows that you need all these things" (Matt. 6:25, 32). He supplies the necessities of life.

But our Good Shepherd is not only adequate for the necessities of life; he's also adequate in the emergencies of life. "He restores my soul" (v. 3). Sheep are really stupid animals and have a tendency to wander away and get lost. But the Shepherd knows each sheep by name and can tell when one is missing. The Shepherd seeks the lost sheep, finds it, and brings it back to the flock. "He restores my soul."

That word "restore" carries with it the idea of "reviving the faint." There are times when we are weary in body and spirit, and

242

that's when the Shepherd picks us up, carries us, and restores our strength. "Do not fear, for I am with you," says the Lord. "Do not be afraid, for I am your God; I will strengthen you, I will help you, I will uphold you with my victorious right hand" (Isa. 41:10).

When you know Jesus Christ as your Shepherd, you can be sure that he is adequate for the necessities of life, in the emergencies of life, and in the mysteries of life. "He leads me in right paths for his name's sake" (v. 3). All of us have decisions to make, and we don't always know exactly which path to choose. There are mysteries in life that our feeble minds just can't grasp. That's when we turn to the Shepherd and ask for his help. "If any of you is lacking in wisdom, ask God, who gives to all generously and ungrudgingly, and it will be given you" (James 1:5).

The Hebrew word translated "paths" in Psalm 23:3 means "well-worn paths, ruts." The paths of righteousness aren't new; they're the well-worn "ruts" that the saints of God have been trodding since Enoch started walking with God. Whenever I hear of a "new approach" to Christian living or a "new secret" of spiritual victory, I just look to my faithful Shepherd and ask him to guide me in the "ruts of righteousness" that others have found so satisfying.

When you follow Jesus Christ, the Good Shepherd, you have sufficiency; and you can say, "I shall not want." But you also have security and you can say, "I will not fear." That's one of the major themes of the last three verses of Psalm 23.

To begin with, when we look around, we don't have to be afraid. David pictures the shepherd leading the flock into a valley, a place where sheep don't feel very much at home. There might be an enemy hiding in the shadows, a lion, perhaps, or a snake; so the sheep do the smart thing and get very close to the shepherd. Did you notice that the pronoun changes in verse 4? It's no longer "he" but "you." The psalmist is no longer talking *about* the shepherd; he's talking *to* the shepherd. The shepherd is right there and the sheep find strength and comfort in his presence.

Life has its hills and valleys, and there are enemies that want to attack us. When it's dark, everything looks out of proportion; even the shadows frighten us. But they're only shadows, and the Good Shepherd guides us through the valley and into the fresh pastures that lie at the end of every valley. Whenever you enter a valley experience, just keep in mind that there's a banquet waiting for you when you come out on the other side.

We don't have to be afraid when we look around or when we look back. "Surely goodness and love shall follow me all the days of my life" (v. 6). Christians don't have to be afraid to look back, because nothing is following them that can do them any harm. What happens to us today may not look or feel like "goodness and love," but we can be sure that our Shepherd is making "all things work together for good" (Rom. 8:28). One day, when we reach heaven, we'll look back and view our lives from a different perspective. We'll see that all that happened to us happened because of God's goodness and love.

Finally, we don't have to be afraid when we look ahead. "I will dwell in the house of the LORD forever" (v. 6 NIV). "In my Father's house there are many dwelling places," said Jesus. "If it were not so, would I have told you that I go to prepare a place for you?" (John 14:2). No matter what paths the Shepherd may choose for us, the road always leads home to the Father's house. Heaven is a real place being prepared by a loving Savior for his beloved sheep. One day he will return to take his flock home.

To be able to say, "The Lord is my shepherd" means you have sufficiency and security, provision and protection. You can joyfully say, "I shall not want . . . I shall not fear."

But there is something so obvious, we usually overlook it. You can't walk into Psalm 23 and become one of his sheep *without first passing through Psalm 22*. In Psalm 22, the Good Shepherd dies for the sheep; and as he does, he is attacked by all sorts of animals.

> Many bulls surround me;
>   strong bulls of Bashan encircle me.
> Roaring lions tearing their prey
>   open their mouths wide against me.
>
> verses 12–13 NIV
>
> Dogs have surrounded me. . . .
> Deliver my life from the sword,
>   my precious life from the power of the dogs.
> Rescue me from the mouth of the lions;
>   save me from the horns of the wild oxen.
>
> verses 16, 20–21 NIV

It seems that Satan turned loose his entire zoo of evil beasts to attack our Shepherd when he offered himself for us on the cross! They mocked him, abused him, laughed at him, and even dared him to come down from the cross. His response was only a greater proof of his love. "I am a worm and not a man" (v. 6 NIV). Imagine the dogs and lions and bulls and oxen all attacking—*a worm!*

"All we like sheep have gone astray; we have all turned to our own way, and the LORD has laid on him the iniquity of us all" (Isa. 53:6). That's what the cross of Calvary is all about.

You have a decision to make. What animal will you choose to be? Will it be the horse or the mule? The ox or the stag? The sow or the dog?

Or will you choose to become one of his sheep?

The Shepherd's cross is in Psalm 22. On that cross he died for you. There he fought the animals for you so that you might be saved. Will you by faith come to that cross and trust him as your Savior?

Will you say, "The Lord is my shepherd," and gladly follow him? If you do, he promises you sufficiency and security all the days of your life—and you will dwell in the house of the Lord forever.

⇒◆⇐

Notes

Chapter 6

1. Cited in Marvin J. Hartmen, "Proclamation," *Vital Christianity,* November 5, 1967, 1.

Chapter 7

1. D. MacMillan, *The Lord Our Shepherd* (Bridgend, Glamorgan, Wales: Evangelical Press of Wales, 1983), 32–33.

2. Andrew A. Bonar, ed., *Letters of Samuel Rutherford* (1664; repr. Edinburgh: Banner of Truth Trust, 1984), 349.

3. John Flavel, *The Mystery of Providence* (1678; repr. Edinburgh: Banner of Truth Trust, 1968), 4:441.

4. John McNeill, *The Twenty-third Psalm,* 2d ed. (Glasgow: Pickering and Inglis, n.d.), 38. McNeill uses this material, but without bibliographical citation.

Chapter 11

1. William L. Lane, *The Gospel According to Mark* (Grand Rapids: Eerdmans, 1975), 432.

2. William Barclay, *The Gospel of Mark* (Philadelphia: Westminster, 1956), 309.

3. C. E. B. Cranfield, *The Gospel According to St. Mark* (Cambridge: Cambridge University Press, 1983), 379.

4. James McGraw, *Great Evangelical Preachers of Yesterday* (Nashville: Abingdon, 1961), 57.

5. Cited in William Barclay, *The Letters to the Corinthians* (Philadelphia: Westminster, 1956), 289.

6. Alexander Maclaren, *Expositions of Holy Scripture,* Vol. 8 (Grand Rapids: Baker, 1975), 150.

Chapter 12

1. Elisabeth Elliot, *Through Gates of Splendor* (New York: Harper and Row, 1957), 18.

Chapter 15

1. Madeleine L'Engle, *A Stone for a Pillow* (Wheaton: Harold Shaw, 1986), 188.

2. Cited in *Rocky Mountain United Methodist Reporter,* October 10, 1986.

3. Lee Iacocca with William Novak, *Iacocca: An Autobiography* (New York: Bantam Books, 1984), 230.

4. *Christian Clippings,* October 1986, Wesley Chapel, Fla., 20.

5. Cited in Judith Viorst, *Necessary Losses* (New York: Simon and Schuster, 1986), 264.

6. Max Cleland, *Strong at the Broken Places* (Lincoln: Chosen Books, 1980), 156.

7. Alex Davidson, *The Returns of Love* (Downers Grove: InterVarsity, 1970), 50.

Chapter 16

1. David Prior, *The Message of 1 Corinthians,* The Bible Speaks Today (Downers Grove: InterVarsity, 1985), 260.

2. Cited in R. V. G. Tasker, *The Gospel of John,* Tyndale New Testament Commentaries (Grand Rapids: Eerdmans, 1960), 149.

3. Charles H. Spurgeon, *Morning and Evening: Daily Readings* (Grand Rapids: Zondervan, 1956), 347.

4. Thomas J. Crawford, *The Doctrine of Holy Scripture Respecting the Atonement,* 4th ed. (Grand Rapids: Baker, 1954), 453–54.

5. Katherine A. M. Kelly, "Oh, Make Me Understand It," chorus #131, *Scripture Union Songs and Choruses No. 1* (London: Scripture Union Publishing Company, 1936). Used by permission of Scripture Union.

6. Adapted from Warren W. Wiersbe, *Be Joyful* (Wheaton: Victor Books, 1974), 56.

7. This observation of C. K. Barrett is cited in David Prior, *The Message of 1 Corinthians,* The Bible Speaks Today (Downers Grove: InterVarsity, 1985), 260.

8. M. R. DeHaan, *The Chemistry of the Blood* (Grand Rapids: Radio Bible Class, n.d.),15.

9. Gordon J. Wenham, *The Book of Leviticus,* The New International Commentary on the Old Testament (Grand Rapids: Eerdmans, 1979), 245.

10. Quoted in *The Herald of His Coming* (Newton, Kans., n.d.).

11. Francis Dixon, "The Place Called Calvary," a Good Friday meditation (Bristol, England: Evangelism Today, n.d.), 13.

12. N. Shaxson, "Calvary," chorus #2, *Scripture Union Songs and Choruses No. 2* (London: Scripture Union Publishing Company, 1938). Used by permission of Scripture Union.

Chapter 17

1. C. E. B. Cranfield, *The Epistle to the Romans,* International Critical Commentary (Edinburgh: T. & T. Clark, 1975), 1:213.

Other Books by
Richard Allen Bodey

Good News for All Seasons
26 Sermons for Special Days

Model sermons by leading evangelical preachers enliven the church calendar with a focus on special days.

Inside the Sermon
Thirteen Preachers Discuss
Their Method of Preparing Messages

J. I. Packer, Leighton Ford, Sinclair Ferguson, D. Stuart Briscoe, and other top preachers confide how they go about their task of preparation and delivery. A sample sermon from each is included.